Homi K . Bhabha

political campaigners, pressure groups, and to attempt to offer pragmatic as well as critically alert frameworks for thinking and acting, as well as delivering academic papers to national and international organisations and policy makers.

This book is an attempt to elucidate and to elaborate on the impact and continued relevance of Bhabha's thinking today. It seeks to outline and explore the significance of key critical terms in Bhabha's thought and to identify, through attention to particular political moments, and through a range of literary, critical and cultural readings, the ways in which this thinking has transformed the field of the humanities, with particular reference to his impact on the broad field of postcolonial studies. The chapters are organised around terms Bhabha introduces or develops in his critical discourse. Key terms discussed are ambivalence, hybridity, the Third Space, mimicry, time-lag and the unhomely. There has been such an explosion of use of these terms across disciplines in the humanities. This study attempts to trace the trajectories of these concepts as others deploy them, and to consider how they act as staging posts in Bhabha's own development of his thinking.

The introductory chapter addresses questions of origins and identity, through an account of the formation of Bhabha as an intellectual, introducing his very early critical writing, and examining several interviews where Bhabha speaks of his life in India and his Parsi heritage, but does not insist on the definitive power of biography. Rather, it pushes the assumptions about origins, identity and belonging to the point that the ontological assumptions underlying nation and community reveal themselves. The readings of Rohinton Mistry in this section consider literary accounts of Parsi identities and attempt to demonstrate how Bhabha refuses the call of uncomplicated belonging. Writing identity is always fraught and contested. Bhabha wryly notes in his preface to the Routledge Classics edition of *The Location of Culture*, 'I was not one of Midnight's Children. My belated birth some years after the midnight hour that marked India's tryst with freedom, absented me from that epochal narrative.'[2] Yet the impact of growing up in the Parsi minority in Bombay, Bhabha suggests, was significant, 'years later I asked myself what it would be like to live without the unresolved tensions between cultures and countries that have become the narrative of my life, and the defining characteristic of my work.'[3]

This study does not claim to be exhaustive. Rather, it has two primary objectives. First, it attempts to locate Bhabha's work in relation to several key critical voices that he has entered into dialogue with, or who, I argue, can be seen at play in his work. Secondly, it considers the significance of his work with that of emerging postcolonial theorists and critics, to stage a series of ongoing conversations that demonstrate how and why Bhabha's work is influential in emerging areas of postcolonial investigation and theorisation. To this end, the book addresses a range of key debates, and it attempts to situate Bhabha's work in relation to them.

It has been a welcome challenge to read alongside Bhabha, and a constant source of anxiety. A pleasure because Bhabha is so alive to the pleasures of the text, and to the creative possibilities of literary and cultural production, he exhorts us to listen to others, to read, to use, reuse and rework critical tools. An anxiety because all studies of this kind erect a kind of spectral presence of the critic they purport to introduce, which haunts the book with their silent reading, nodding and head shaking over the shoulder of the afflicted writer.

II

Minority-Majority

In his preface to the Routledge Classics edition of *The Location of Culture*, Bhabha reflects on the early academic journey from Bombay to Oxford, under the spell of 'an illusion' about the centre that left him 'intellectually fascinated but unmoved'.[4]

> What was missing from the traditionalist world of English literary study, as I encountered it, was a rich and paradoxical engagement with the pertinence of what lay in an *oblique* or alien relation to the forces of centering. Writers who were off-center.[5]

He comments that this led to his engagement with the marginal and the peripheral, not merely to glorify it or mistakenly celebrate it, but to consider how to unthink the 'nation-centred view of sovereign citizenship'.[6] The difficulty with this model, he argues, is that 'it can only comprehend the predicament of "minoritarian" belonging as a problem of ontology'.[7] Thinking differently, he argues, necessitates an understanding of the 'political practices and ethical choices' used by emergent groups and affiliations, whether of national minorities, of global migrant communities or diasporas.

In Palestinian poet Mahmoud Darwish's electrifying and terrifying prose-poem *Memory for Forgetfulness*, relating his experiences of the bombing of Beirut in 1982 by Israel and its allies, he finds that despite the bombs falling all around, the pressing question of literature, and how the writers being bombed should respond to the destruction of the city, people and infrastructure is unavoidable. Although the moment itself is too intense and traumatic to allow a space for writing, it enacts an immense trauma and is returned to three years later when Darwish produced the text of memory and forgetting in exile. The Palestinian writer, displaced, dispossessed, unhomed, doubtful about whom he writes for, must face the risk that he inhabits a dream, he represents an impossibility, he has, as Darwish wryly notes, come too 'early for a delayed appointment' a formulation of the time-lag that Bhabha would recognise only too clearly.[8] Yet, despite a terrifying lack of 'legitimacy', the writer must write,

> When we write, and call upon others to write, in the name of creative freedom, we are doing nothing more than bringing into focus the points of light and first efforts scattered by dissention over an idea founded on this simple assertion: we want to liberate ourselves, our countries, and our minds and live in the modern age with competence and pride. In writing, we give expression to our faith in the potency of writing. From this perspective, we don't feel we're a minority but announce that we are the minority-majority. And we announce further that we are children of this age, and not of the past or the future.[9]

The claim on the present, which refuses to accept that one is either consigned to the past or condemned to wait for an always-retreating horizon in the future, is made through the commitment to writing, but such a commitment also demands the help of the critic,

> At this juncture we cry out for help from criticism. We call upon it to regain its faith in its power and usefulness. We call upon it to enter the lists, now open for spoils. [...] And we call upon it to reject the sanctity claimed by a poetic text that allows no tool for its analysis except self-reference and, at the same time, reserves the exclusive right to load itself with all the ideology exterior to this claim that it can manage to disguise.[10]

Bhabha's commitment to theory, I would argue, answers such a cry and engages with the demands of the 'minority-majority' writer for a critic who will recognise the peculiar temporality, location and condition of the marginalised or peripheral, the terrorised and the outcast, whose writings are necessarily radically off-centre.

Acknowledgements

I thank the following for the different ways in which they offered intellectual stimulation and assistance in the writing of this book. Julian Wolfreys for generous and helpful editorial advice, John McLeod, Bart Moore-Gilbert, Mark Shackleton and James Proctor for valuable discussions of parts of the book delivered as papers. I also thank staff and students in the Department of English at University College, Worcester, especially Roger Ebbatson, and the Department of English at Manchester Metropolitan University, particularly Julie Mullaney and Angelica Michelis. Early encouragement from Huw Griffiths, Sarah Mills, Zoe Wicomb and staff at Strathclyde University was invaluable. This book was written with the support of a period of research leave from Manchester Metropolitan University.

Introduction
'The Missing Person':
Re-/Locating Homi K. Bhabha

You're your country's lost property / With no office to claim you back
You're polluting our sounds / You're so rude
'Get back to your language' they say.

Adil Jussawalla, Missing Person[1]

For a time, it became something of an orthodoxy to describe Homi Bhabha's writing style as difficult to the point of obscurity: opaque, teasing, evasive, disingenuous, illiterate, might be some of the less offensive adjectives that were used. His writing style achieved a brief mainstream notoriety when he was awarded second prize for 'bad writing' by the New Zealand journal *Philosophy and Literature*, in 1998.[2] It has variously been described as made up of neologisms, buzz words or offering troubling 'signature concepts', of 'hybridity', 'the third space' and the 'in-between'. Bart Moore-Gilbert offers perhaps the most apt term of 'clotted', to describe the frequently 'extremely dense texture of his style'.[3] However, his very early journalistic work, more recent informal articles in the journal *Artforum* and his radio broadcasting all suggest a measured, lucid and carefully (in conventional terms) argued polemical narrative approach is in no way anathema to Bhabha.

Where Bhabha is more consistent, however, is in his always challenging, and sometimes provoking, methodological and critical eclecticism. This is not, I would argue, an unconsidered eclecticism or the act of a postmodern dilettante: rather, it represents Bhabha's unceasing attempts to think in interdisciplinary and transnational ways. He has produced work that has delighted, surprised and disturbed in equal measure in his attempts to fuse the political, critical, theoretical and literary; to bring 'revolutionary' Fanon into imaginary dialogue with Said, to read Derrida as a migrant, and to find in Lacan a way to speak about race. Critics of Bhabha's most influential work, notably the essays collated in *The Location of Culture*, have accused him of

'bourgeois voluntarism, liberal pragmatism, academicist pluralism, and all
the other "isms" that are freely bandied about by those who take the most
severe exception to "Eurocentric" theoretic*ism* (Derrideanism, Lacanian-
ism, poststructuralism ...)' as he notes wryly in the essay 'The Commitment
to Theory'.[4] His response to this is to insist that the 'new' languages of theoretical critique must not simply be read as collusive with the geopolitical
divisions current in global politics. He asks 'Are the interests of "Western"
theory necessarily collusive with the hegemonic role of the West as a power
bloc?'[5] Bhabha has perhaps been unfairly represented in some camps as
an apologist for theory, as he has also consistently been in dialogue with
political campaigns around race, class and migration and in active part-
nership with black and minority interpretive and critical communities.
An attentive reading of 'The Commitment to Theory' reveals his insistence
on reaffirming the relation between politics and theory. He rejects a model
of political and theoretical commitment that opposes the 'theoretical' with
the 'activist' as a false opposition and attempts to rethink the places from
which both theory and politics might speak.

If his work deserves our careful attention it is because his 'interventions' (a term he has invested and re-situated with a vital critical impact)
in debates within and across literary theory and criticism, cultural studies
and postcolonial studies have enacted a series of transitions, both trans-
and intra-disciplinary, that have given rise to new vocabularies and political apprehensions. His most influential critical terms have migrated their
ways through debates around race, nation and colonialism, representation
and textuality and disciplinary border, such that cultural difference, mimicry, ambivalence, in-betweenness, the third space, cultural hybridity and
cosmopolitanism have become critical terms through which many such
debates now route themselves.

Early in his career, in an article for the *Times Literary Supplement* (*TLS*)
in February 1978 entitled 'Indo-Anglian Attitudes', Bhabha's prose showed
few signs of thickening or indeed curdling. However, his critical approach
to the subject of the tradition of English language poetry in India was, in ret-
rospect, full of signposts to key concepts developed in later essays, notably
cultural hybridity, in-betweenness and cultural translation. In this article,
he reviews several collections of Indian poetry in English.[6] He singles out
Adil Jussawalla's collection *Missing Person*, as offering a way of understanding and critically approaching the 'curious colonial phenomenon' of the
Indo-Anglian, a 'missing person' who 'has to be established in poetry for
the Indo-Anglian to achieve self-consciousness' (*TLS* p. 135). Jussawalla,

he suggests, owes something in equal measure to W. H. Auden and Frantz Fanon,

> From the former he has inherited the *paysage moralise* and the irony with which to tell a cautionary tale; from the latter, he apparatus for understanding the problems of an unproductive bourgeoisie, for and against whom he writes. Auden's irony and Fanon's theory are given a new relevance in Jussawalla's milieu, giving his missing person a multiple significance that is evoked in the montage of styles and languages, – filmic, conversational and symbolic – that Jussawalla uses.
>
> (*TLS* p. 135)

Bhabha's suggestive description of influence would appear to confirm that Indo-Anglian literature is best understood as trans-national and diasporic. It is marked by anxiety and written by 'missing' people. As such, it is an ambivalent hybrid cultural practice. This early piece of journalism is notable not only for the glimpses of a range of critical strategies being explored and tested, but for the rather interesting experience of witnessing Bhabha's emerging theories being thrust, if very gently, on an unsuspecting audience. Even the title demonstrates the irreverent borrowings and adaptations that have recognisably become part of Bhabha's rhetoric. However, it is the substance of his claims that provokes swift reposts from his opponents; of the trans-national influences on Indian poets writing in English and of the validity of the Indo-Anglian experience, 'as integrally Indian as any other.'(*TLS* p. 135)

> The poets of the 1960's and 1970's illustrate two tendencies. Nissim Ezekiel, Parthasarathy, Gieve Patel and Adil Jussawalla are committed to the explicit revision and deconstruction of the Orientalists' India. A. K. Ramanujan and Arun Kolatkar are free from this source of anxiety and are involved in a calmer revision and revaluation of indigenous traditions. Unlike the Orientalists, the first group have tried to come to terms with the darker side of Indo-Anglian reality. They have move away from exclusively English poetic precursors and their influences as enumerated by Jussawalla in his *New Writing in India*, are Voznesensky, Pablo Neruda, Borges, Camus, Sartre, Günter Grass.
>
> (*TLS* p. 135)

R. Parthasarathy's long letter of reply to the article, published in the *TLS* in March of the same year, illustrates precisely the complex relationships of Indian writing in English both to other languages and to traditions of the Indian subcontinent. Indian writing in English, as Bhabha himself notes, bears an intimate relationship with the establishment of English as the language of the Indian civil service and with Thomas Babington Macaulay's

infamous 'Minute' on Indian Education of 1835.[7] Indian writing in English
must bear the traces of what Gayatri Spivak calls the 'epistemic violence'
that has brought it into being as a phenomenon. In postcolonial India this is
coupled with what could arguably be viewed in some quarters as the 'scan-
dal' of transgressing beyond the borders of the nation and of exploring both
the specific history of Indian writing in English and the arbitrariness of the
rags and scraps that make up tradition. This, in turn, in Bhabha's work has
the effect of demonstrating the problematic construction of authentic Indianness, as well as aptly enacting what Bhabha will later come to term the
'heresy of hybridity'.[8] Parthasarathy comments,

> In the absence of an indigenous tradition I wonder how relevant is Harold
> Bloom's theory of poetic influence. The struggle between 'ephebe' and pre-
> cursor simply does not exist when there are no strong precursors to contend
> with. The framework of impressive references – Fanon's *The Wretched of the
> Earth*, Naipaul's *The Overcrowded Baracoon*, Prufrock, Meursault, Lowell's
> *Life Studies* – that Mr Bhabha has erected is pathetically inappropriate.
>
> (*TLS*)

He explicitly states that Bhabha has failed to understand Indo-Anglian
poetry, cannot relate to traditional India or feel at home in an Indian language because he is not a Hindu. He goes on to claim that 'A striking feature
of Indian verse in English today is its emergence from the mainstream of
English literature and its appearance as part of Indian Literature. It is rooted
in and stems from the Indian ethos'(*TLS*). He rejects a trans-national vision
of this poetry and seeks to confirm that the poets have embedded in their
poetry 'the Hindu world image which has endured through the ages with
remarkable continuity'(*TLS*, March 10, 1978).

Bhabha's insistence on the tradition of 'hybridity' as a significant area of
Indian experience is reasserted in his own letter of reply to Parthasarathy,
published in April of the same year. 'To deny the various often conflicting
influences that constitute [Indo-Anglian poetry] would be to blind oneself
to the conditions of its production and its creative tensions' (*TLS* p. 445).
Bhabha's rather minor exchange of views predates a more celebrated
intervention on the subject of Indo-Anglian writing by Salman Rushdie, by
twenty years. In his infamous introduction to *The Vintage Book of Indian
Writing: 1947–1997* Rushdie asserted that 'Indo-Anglian' literature represents perhaps the most valuable contribution India has yet made to the
world of books'.[9] Bhabha makes no such claim; his insistence that Indo-
Anglian writing can be both Indian and hybrid at the same time does not
support Rushdie's broader claims in his introduction that parochialism is a

serious problem for vernacular literatures in India. Clearly, such a position leaves itself open to charges of blatant elitism, given the problematic status of English in the Indian sub-continent that must inevitably be associated with the elite classes. However, in several more personal interviews that Bhabha has given in the past few years, he is quick to resist a characterisation of his own linguistic and cultural choices as reducible to elitism or Anglicisation.

Bhabha does not usually use anecdote or autobiographical references in his critical writings, yet despite this, as the toing and froing of letters in the *TLS* illustrates, in this early moment of Bhabha's critical career he is immediately identified as non-Hindu by others. It is only in more recent interviews that he has discussed his origins and cultural background as a Parsi, and on occasion allowed that the particularity of his background might resonate in his own critical project. Bhabha's family were descendants of Zoroastrian Persians who came to India from what is now Iran in the seventh century. In a frank and engaging interview with David Bennett and Terry Collits in 1991, Bhabha considers at length the relationship between his critical career and his particular Indian background. 'My position in India as part of a Parsi minority (that is, of Persian origins) already places me in an interesting kind of border position.'[10] He describes attending Parsi Nataks (popular plays) on New Year's day:

> On our New Year's Day instead of having great Indian mythological perform-
> ances that other Indian communities had we had these Bombay-Parsi farces
> that were set up by a distant relative of mine. We would have a celebratory
> meal and then go and sit down and laugh at ourselves.[11]

Although Bhabha does not foreground these cultural experiences in his work and does not include autobiographical or anecdotal examples in his own theoretical explanations, he does acknowledge the importance of this inheritance, while simultaneously recognising that it may be viewed as politically compromising,

> I think my taste for taking seriously certain kinds of border positions, mar-
> ginal positions, hybrid situations emerges from that. And yes I was much later
> very angry with my closest friend and my wife on occasions because they took
> a much more classically Marxist line on the Parsis, seeing them as an Angli-
> cised, bourgeois community.
>
> (p. 50)

Bhabha defends himself against this description, characterising Parsis as having a sense of 'a negotiated cultural identity', and speaking personally he confesses to 'an almost Kierkegaardian sense of original guilt' that one had as a Parsi. He comments,

> There were moments of immense adolescent angst and anxiety associated with not being authentically Indian, not having a real Indian language-the Gujurati that we spoke at home intermingled with English was a debased form of Gujurati. We didn't have many great nationalist leaders to call our own or to identify with. All of that created a lot of problems. But I think it gave me a sneaking sort of humorous sense of what it was to be seen as the belated one, who comes too late.
>
> (p. 50)

In an interview with Warren T. Mitchell, Bhabha outlines the curious anomalies as he sees them, the Parsis inhabit in India, to an extent viewed as non-authentic Indians, having their origins in Persian migrants. He also seems to acknowledge to some degree the partial validity of a 'Marxist' analysis of Parsi culture:

> Parsis were the middle persons between various Indian communities and the British. [...] They have also been a hybridized community: often their rituals pay formal respect to Hindu customs and rituals while articulating their own religious and ethnic identity.[12]

While following Bhabha's analysis, it might be anomalous to use the term 'Parsi novel' when discussing Parsi cultural traditions. The contemporary Indian-Canadian writer Rohinton Mistry, who also has a Parsi background, explores this in-between identity in different ways in two of his novels, *A Fine Balance* and *Family Matters*.[13] In both texts, locations and home spaces are fiercely contested, marked by internal and external boundaries and pressures that unsettle straightforward claims of belonging and continuity. In *A Fine Balance*, set in mid-1970s India under the State of Emergency imposed by Indira Ghandi, a young Parsi woman, Dina Dalal, finds herself a widow after only two years of marriage. She inhabits her deceased husband's flat bearing its engraved nameplate, Mr and Mrs Rustom K. Dalal, but with a rent book bearing the name of her deceased husband's dead father. She is under siege from Ibrahim the rent collector, whose instructions are increasingly to attempt to lever out tenants with agreements fixed under the rent act, so that higher rents can be imposed. From this already tenuous and unhomely location, she weaves a complex entrepreneurial relationship between the Dalit uncle and nephew who have trained as tailors to escape their caste position as Chamaars, who were traditionally leatherworkers, her paying lodger Maneck, who is the son of a friend, and

Mrs Gupta of 'Au Revoir Exports', for whom she produces dresses destined for Chantal Boutique, New York. This microcosm of sweatshop labour that supplies Americans with 'French' fashion is built on a series of borrowings and debts, rented sewing machines, illegitimate business activities, private lodging arrangements and hidden work, which, once labelled for Chantal Boutique's windows, has a further veil drawn across its origins.

Dina Dalal sits uncomfortably between a 'respectable' and 'unrespectable' identity: a widow who refuses to leave her apartment to live under the protection of her married brother, between a legitimate and illegitimate enterprise, using the advantages of property to participate in the global marketplace in a classic capitalist mode of production in which she herself offers no concrete skill but acts as the middle-woman between a clothing retailer and the tailors she employs illegally in her rented flat. Her precariousness is underlined by a narrow escape from eviction, which would not only make her and her lodger homeless, but also put an end to her business that is being secretly conducted from one of the rooms. At the same time, she benefits from her relatively high level of education and the middle-class professional background of her extended family that she falls back on at the end of the novel.

However, it is through her friendship with the tailors that she gains protection from the intimidating landlords. She is forced to accommodate the tailors once they are evicted from their shanty town or her own precarious economic relationships will collapse. Such a transgression involving crossing the borders of segregation and pollution that the Hindu caste system polices is an economic necessity. Although these are not sanctions that she must obey as a Parsi, the transgression re-centres power relations and her position in her home. Once they have moved into her flat permanently, all its inhabitants fall under the protection of the 'beggar master' who co-ordinates the seemingly chaotic movement of all the street dwellers in the city, but who also appears to have influence over the rent collector. The end of the novel sees her affirming her relationship with the tailors, now as covert friends not employees, after she has finally been evicted from the flat after the murder of the 'beggar master'. Although the tailors now live on the street and she has the relative comfort of sharing her brother's home, he bears witness to their terrible persecution and the physical violence they suffer. She now offers them the borrowed hospitality of her brother's flat, when the rest of the family are out. Mistry pointedly positions her at the axis of tensions between different economies and accommodations, both literal and cultural, that mark Dina's negotiations with diverse strands of postcolonial Indian society.

For Mistry, exploring Dina Dalal's in-between status through a new connection with Ishvar and Om, does seem to enable a critical account of the differentiations of caste, class and gender that permeate his depiction of India under the State of Emergency. However, Dina's predicament also underlines some of the problems of characterising Parsi culture as emphatically hybridised, any more than say Ishvar and Om are, having remade themselves in order to throw off the limits of caste. Nor is it clear that such a position inevitably offers a perspective that can transcend or critique existing cultural and political realities. For Tabish Khair in his study of contemporary Indian English novels, *Babu Fictions*, Dina inevitably belongs to what he terms the 'Babu' class, broadly speaking the middle or upper class, usually urbanised and westernised Indians, as opposed to what he terms the 'Coolie' or subaltern classes.[14] Although one might wish to take issue with his overlaying of this binary onto the complexities of Parsi cultural identity in Indian society, his critique of Mistry's writing might usefully address the problematic positioning of Parsi culture as in some sense on the margins. For Khair, the problem with *A Fine Balance* is that although Mistry clearly wishes to address the oppression of lower-caste Indians, his pivotal character Dina Dalal would have been too far removed from Ishvar and Omprakash, the low-caste tailors, to have enabled the dialogues that Mistry envisages.

> The extensive and complex discussions that (educated, westernised, upper caste) Dina and Maneck carry out with the low caste and geo-culturally removed Ishvar and Omprakash would have been impossible in real life. The two classes lack a common language through which they can communicate to the extent required by Mistry to further his narrative.[15]

In *Family Matters*, set in mid-1990s Bombay, the Vakeel family find themselves moving between the faded grandeur of 'Chateau Felicity' and the overcrowded 'Pleasant Villa' in their attempts to care for their grandfather Nariman. His son-in-law, Yezad, feels his tiny flat has been overtaken by the presence of Nariman incapacitated on his sofa. However, he is also haunted by his failed attempts to emigrate to Canada and is anxious about the status of minorities in India under the Bharatiya Janata Party (BJP; Indian People's Party) leadership. His attempts to benefit from increasingly fundamentalist politics in India involve him persuading his boss to enter politics as a moderate so that he in turn may be promoted in his place once he is elected. The disastrous results of this, resulting in the murder of his boss and his loss of a job, lead him to revisit his own Parsi faith in increasingly orthodox versions of belief and practice. Far from reinvigorating his family and its sense of identity, however, it provokes a crisis and split between his eldest son and himself.

This might be read effectively alongside Bhabha, who counters any attempt to understand a Parsi identity as purely experienced through issues around belief systems, birth or by the restrictions around conversion. His insistence on seeing any so-called ontological properties of Parsi identity as highly provisional, negotiated and always a result of historical and cultural negotiations is symptomatic of his own careful deconstruction of local, cultural or national traditions, myths and beliefs.

> What does it mean to be a Parsi? I don't think that question can be easily answered. And what is important in my background for some of the theoretical issues I'm involved in is that the question repeats its own terms: for Parsis as for any minority, the question of identity has been negotiated and performed in the context of cultural transition. The embourgeoisement of large sectors of the Parsi community should not be seen as minimising this complex and difficult process of identification. To be relatively affluent as a minority is not to be free of cultural anxiety.[16]

Although we might caution that self-report is notoriously unreliable, the description of a borderline identity and a hybrid cultural community is suggestive for the ways in which it foregrounds key aspects of Bhabha's theoretical concerns. It is further underlined by his description of his grandparents' and parents' homes and lives,

> 'In my grandparents' house, if I think about it, or my parents' house, even as it is today, they will have borrowings from Bauhaus, from 1950s and 1960s European style, 1920s chrome and art deco, art nouveau, a number of citations, and yet in the midst of all that, you will have the prayer table, showing signs of the strong ancestor worship within Parsee tradition.

He comments,

> Their lifestyle was you know, very 'post-modern'.[17]

For Bhabha, the concept of culture must be radically rethought by postcolonial criticism if it wishes to understand and revise the hegemonic and normalised structures of power in the contemporary world order. He comments in 'The Postcolonial and the Postmodern',

> Postcolonial perspectives emerge from the colonial testimony of Third World countries and the discourses of 'minorities' within the geopolitical divisions of East, West, North and South. [...] It is from those who have suffered the sentence of history - subjugation, domination, diaspora, displacement - that

> we learn our most enduring lessons for living and thinking. There is even a growing conviction that the affective experience of social marginality – as it emerges in non-canonical cultural forms – transforms our critical strategies. It forces us to confront the concept of culture outside objects d'art or beyond the canonization of the 'idea' of aesthetics, to engage with culture as an uneven, incomplete production of meaning and value, often composed of incommensurable demands and practices, produced in the act of social survival.[18]

This notion of culture as a strategy of survival, not as an ordered and uniform practice by homogenous and unified groups, does seem to bear a striking relationship to Bhabha's experiences of growing up as a Parsi in India. Cultural practices bore the marks of contingency, the necessary shifts of a minority population attempting to negotiate themselves through the cultures of dominant groups and colonial powers, bringing together and reworking disparate narratives in order to survive in the present cultural and political climate.

Bhabha goes on to insist that culture understood as a strategy of survival is both transnational and translational: it is marked by the 'specific histories' of cultures of displacement, exile, migration, such as slavery, international colonial expeditions, exploitative trade, Third World migration and the movement of political and economic refugees. For Bhabha therefore, attempting to represent the subjects of these profoundly diasporic and transnational/translational cultures involves a resituating, a relocating, of the notion of culture. 'The contingent and the liminal become the times and the spaces for the historical representation of the subjects of cultural difference in a postcolonial criticism.'[19]

This approach would, of course, problematise a discussion of something that could be called Parsi writing. Indeed, Rohinton Mistry's writing style and subject matter might appear much further removed from Bhabha's critical project than, say, Salman Rushdie's work with which Bhabha's work arguably extensively inter-relates, which is discussed in a separate chapter in this book. Some problems might attend a reading of Mistry as necessarily liminal and contingent. His own embourgeoisement seems unchallengeable, like Rushdie a Booker nominee and a cosmopolitan migrant. Indeed Bhabha's critical reception by several postcolonial critics working from a Materialist tradition strongly mirrors Khair's take on Mistry.

Aijaz Ahmad has notably criticised Bhabha's dismantling of notions of nation on similar grounds. He cites Bhabha's affiliations to poststructuralism as evidencing his increasing incorporation into an affluent and Westernised identity, which is further exemplified by what Ahmad sees as his 'exorbitant celebration' of Salman Rushdie.

> Bhabha of course, lives in those material conditions of postmodernity which presume the benefits of modernity as the very ground from which judgements on the past of this post- may be delivered. In other words, it takes a very modern, very affluent, very uprooted kind of intellectual to debunk [...] the idea of progress.[20]

However, Mistry's explorations of cultural compromise do seem amenable to Bhabha's view of culture as a strategy of survival. If *Family Matters* could be viewed as 'a Diasporic Parsi novel', does foregrounding Bhabha's Parsi identity make a difference to an engagement with his theoretical work? Does it at least partly offer a rejoinder to accusations of complicity with a Westernised postcolonial elite or confirm it? Bhabha's own discussion of the ethics of migrancy appears to turn upon him: asking what is a good or a bad Parsi raises a set of related questions about migrant and minority behaviours and affiliations. How does one describe one's own cultural or religious inheritance, and what level of ownership of it constitutes enough to claim it is hybrid against the desires or feelings of other Parsis, who might challenge such a description? One would have to acknowledge, as Bhabha does, that no community is homogenous, but is internally riven.

In *Family Matters*, Mistry explores a complex Parsi inheritance where a contemporary revival of 'tradition' finds itself crossed by the discovery of contesting material from the archives. Towards the end of the novel, Yezad has increasingly withdrawn from his close family into an Orthodox Parsi existence, which appears to baffle his wife and children. His son narrates the final section of the novel, puzzling over a moment that disturbs Yezad's circumscribed sense of his Parsi identity,

> Jal Uncle shows us a stack of holy pictures he found in one of the cupboards: Sai Baba, Virgin Mary, Crucifixion, Haji Malng, several Zarathustras, Our Lady of Fatima, Buddha.
> 'Where did these come from?' Asks Daddy.
> 'I remember seeing them as a child' says Jal Uncle. 'They used to hang all over the flat. You know how, in those days it was usual for most Parsis to keep tokens of every religion. Pappa took them down after Mamma and Lucy died.'
> Daddy examines the pictures, some in frames and some yellow and curling. There are dates on the framing boards of several, I notice, going as far back as 1869.[21]

Culture as compromise and provisionality is enacted as Yezad struggles with this evidence of a pluralistic and hybrid Parsi inheritance. The neo-Orthodox response to the discovery and the history that it reveals is also a form of negotiation, in this case with one's own inheritance.

> My father has at last decided about the holy pictures. He must have consulted his Orthodox League friends. He returned this afternoon from the meeting and said that all the non-Zarathusti images must go – in a Zarathusti home they interfere with the vibrations of Avesta prayers.
>
> He said they should be disposed of properly, in keeping with the Zarathustrian tradition of respect for all religions, which, he explained to me went way back to Cyrus the Great, the founder of the Achaemenina dynasty, who set the example when he conquered Babylon, liberated the Jews who were there in captivity, and even helped them rebuild their Temple, earning him the title of God's Anointed in the Hebrew Bible.[22]

The book ends with this uncomfortable realisation on Yezad's part that an imagined return to origins has resulted in an opening out onto other religious beliefs.

For Bhabha, Parsi culture might be understood as a highly readable model of cultural provisionality and hybridity; it is not a 'property' of Parsi culture that is then opposed to an unproblematic homogeneity of more dominant cultural groups. Here, then, the identification of Bhabha with a minority or marginalised position, as he himself comments, does not equate in any straightforward way with a celebration of such a position,

> The marginal or 'minority' is not the place of celebratory, or utopian, self-marginalisation. It is a much more substantial intervention into those justifications of modernity –progress, homogeneity, cultural organicism, the deep nation, the long past – that rationalize the authoritarian, 'normalizing' tendencies within cultures in the name of national interest.[23]

However, even in the process of insisting that a Parsi identity might be a proper attribution for Bhabha, in terms of property and propriety this cannot be an insistence on 'proper' ethnicity and identity that validates his theoretical interests. When Bhabha speaks of the hybridity of Parsi culture in interviews, there is always the risk of this in turn performing a slightly dizzying essentialising gesture. Is the discussion of Parsi in-betweenness occurring after the fact, as a re-reading of his formative experiences or could such theories only have emerged as a result of them? Certainly Bhabha's critical writing has not explicitly involved a discussion of his own ethnic and cultural affiliations along these lines. Rather, he has perhaps been called upon to assert an ethnic position in the context of postcolonial critical preoccupations with the location of the critic. This injunction to reveal and to situate oneself operates as a tension for Bhabha, that he continually problematises, where it is explicitly discussed in his critical work. 'The question of identification is never the affirmation of a pre-given identity, never a self-fulfilling prophecy – it is always the production of an image of identity and the transformation of the subject in assuming that image.'[24]

Bhabha's move from India to Britain and most recently to the United States may ironically have effaced the particular identification, with the in-between of a Parsi identity in Bombay. In these new locations, the generics, British-Asian and now Indian-American, might seem closer (unsatisfactory) identifiers. Indeed, in Rohinton Mistry's case, his migration from India to Canada has been cited, by Germaine Greer, as a reason not to take *A Fine Balance* seriously, 'a Canadian book about India, what could be worse?' Greer's rather surprising comments point to the ways in which there is embedded resistance to an imaginative rethinking of cross-border affiliations of cultural identification, which can be received as unsettling or inauthentic. Taking seriously Bhabha's apprehension of identity as only possible in the negation of any sense of originality, or completeness, this 'hyphenated identity' might equally respond to a critical vocabulary attentive to current debates about rootedness and displacement that Bhabha characterises as riven with anxiety. 'For too often,' he asserts, efforts to respond to cultural difference 'result in hyphenated attempts to include all multiple subject positions in an overburdened juggernaut that rides roughshod over the singularities and individuations of difference.'[25] Its significance would not only be to assert a new unproblematic stability, or a belated fitting in to a kind of diasporic mode of Indianness only possible outside India, however positive this might be.

Bhabha picks up the theme of his own hybrid identity again in a short essay 'On the Irremovable Strangeness of Being Different', in which he further elaborates on and qualifies concepts of cultural difference and translation that are critical in his work. Here, however, he is not turning to an account of an organic cultural inheritance; rather, it is to an apprehension of the postcolonial diasporic condition as necessarily hybrid. He discusses a model of cultural diversity proposed by Clifford Geertz in 'The Uses of Diversity' as relating to questions of 'cultural difference' and how it could be accommodated or understood as a demand for ethics. Geertz proposes that the traditional notion of culture as self-containedness must be challenged with the estranging, ethical responsibility of encountering diversity, which acknowledges 'us and everyone else as cast into the midst of a world of irremovable strangeness.'[26] However, Bhabha takes Geertz to task for his spatial model of cultures mapped into a landscape: 'Geertz's brilliant spatialization of the contingent, incomplete temporalities of ethical-political enunciation as a landscape of juxtaposed terrains of knowledge installs him in an Archimedian position from which he mediates, "The world is coming at each of its local points to look more like a Kuwaiti bazaar than like an English gentleman's club (to instance what, to my mind – perhaps because I have never been in either one of them – are the polar cases)".[27]

Bhabha refuses this polarisation, identifying how attention to postcolonial trajectories might demand a thinking of cultural relations in the midst of antagonism, or impossibly interwoven positions, such that the dislocated, the interstitial and in-between aspects of hybridity do not produce a sublation or synthesis of previously understood differences,

> As a postcolonial native who learned his morals in an Indian bazaar and picked up literature in what some (too hastily) consider an English gentleman's club (Oxford), I see the relation between bazaar and club as more agonistic and ambivalent [...] I take my lesson from *A Passage to India*, perhaps the greatest of all novels about the complications between oriental bazaars and English clubs.[28]

For Bhabha, this anxiety must be continually worked through, 'The anxiety of displacement that troubles national rootedness transforms ethnicity or cultural difference into an ethical relation that serves as a subtle corrective to valiant attempts to achieve representativeness and moral equivalence in the matter of minorities.'[29] Bhabha emphasises the ways in which cultural differences cannot simply be 'celebrated', but need to be understood as 'overlap without equivalence' (p. 36). He characterises himself yet again as a figure who traverses the hazardous passages that link the two spaces of bazaar and club, complicating our understanding of both in the process. The passage itself has to be accounted for – a third space, that calls attention to the incompleteness of the other two sites, just as the 'fear trees' in Forster's narrative separate the colonialists' civil station on the hill and the bazaar of Chandrapore down below, 'standing between oppositions and sowing confusion.'[30]

Might Bhabha's present re-location in the United States be seen as inaugurating yet further translations and affiliations? Bhabha worked closely with Black British cultural practitioners and artists while based in the United Kingdom, whose investigations of the limits of identity and engagement with questions of the body owed much to his work on Frantz Fanon. He began a fruitful intellectual relationship with the sculptor Anish Kapoor, and was crucially involved in the international responses by artists, activists and cultural critics to the 'Rushdie Affair'. He was always alert to the ways in which culture and cultural difference needed to be understood as under contestation and marked by anxiety. Now, in the United States, his intellectual and political affiliations and relationships have been informed by still further development of his understanding of the provisional nature of all cultures. These are always hybridised, not through a mixing of two previously organic wholes, but through the necessary ongoing remaking of cultures and practices, even where a national culture or homogeneity is being gestured towards.

Bhabha's work clearly also relates to and has partly inaugurated a critical vocabulary for a contemporary diasporic and hyphenated experience of identity. His engagement with the emergence of newness in cultural terms speaks to the concerns of contemporary Indian-American writer Jhumpa Lahiri. In Jhumpa Lahiri's Pulitzer Prize-winning collection of short stories, *The Interpreter of Maladies*, the chronicling of disparate lives of an Indian-American population spans two, sometimes three, generations, charting movements of people between India, Pakistan, Britain and the United States, whose affiliations to home and locations of their own identities are marked by ambivalence. Lahiri comments about her own experiences of growing up Indian and American: 'when I was growing up in Rhode Island in the 1970s I felt neither Indian nor American. Like many immigrant offspring I felt intense pressure to be two things, loyal to the old world and fluent in the new, approved of on either side of the hyphen. Looking back I can see that this was generally the case. But my perception as a young girl was that I fell short at both ends, shuttling between two dimensions that had nothing to do with one another.'[31] Lahiri seems to confirm here Bhabha's apprehension of 'overlap without equivalence', where a spatialised model such as Geertz's would come undone.

The movements of Lahiri's characters to the United States are frequently associated with academic imperatives, with different characters in the process of finishing theses, employed as college lecturers, or in university libraries, such that several of her stories might almost be combined to form a diasporic campus novel. Indianness is something to be both explored and examined, by those of the second generation with, in some cases, only a tentative first-hand experience, whereas Indian history is taught and made an object of knowledge by others, or visited in the capacity of a tourist in the title story 'Interpreter of Maladies'. For the first-generation migrant, India is both present in the food being eaten and absent in the memories that emerge and haunt the present while that food is being prepared. This is the case in the story 'Mrs. Sen's', where the memories of communal food preparation haunt Mrs. Sen's solitary afternoon ritual of chopping vegetables, transporting her elsewhere, enacting a symbolic feeding of memories and a mourning of what has been lost. Cultures are constantly being re-made and re-narrated in these short stories, which are attentive to an understanding of culture as always marked by hybridisation and provisionality.

In the striking story 'When Mr Pirzada Came to Dine', both of these generational rehearsals of loss and tentative belonging are intertwined as the young girl Lilia learns about the history of India and Pakistan through her parents' fraught watching of the news of the war between the two countries, while at school she makes dioramas of George Washington crossing the Delaware River. Their frequent guest is Mr Pirzada, whose company has been sought through the university campus directory, and who was telephoned by her parents who 'used to trail their fingers, at the start of each new semester, through the columns of the university directory; circling surnames familiar to their part of the world.'[32]

The scattering becomes a provisional gathering, but one in which the violent history of colonialism continually erupts, 'On the screen I saw tanks rolling through dusty streets, and fallen buildings, and forests of unfamiliar trees into which East Pakistani refugees had fled, seeking safety over the Indian border. I saw boats with fan-shaped sails floating on wide coffee-coloured rivers, a barricaded university, newspaper offices burnt to the ground.'[33] Lilia learns that Mr Pirzada is actually a Bengali from east Pakistan, that the date of Indian independence was also the year of partition. A nation simultaneously independent and displaced, 'One moment we were free and then we were sliced up', her father retorts. The diasporic present in America enables 'Indian' and 'Pakistani' to sit down together and eat in a shared cultural act that Lilia's father says might still be unthinkable for many at home. For his part, Mr Pirzada watches the violence unfolding on the television screen with 'an immovable expression on his face, composed but alert, as if someone were giving him directions to an unknown destination' (p. 31).

Structurings of a national imaginary are dislocated in a diasporic and minoritised affiliation to a nation that is elsewhere. However, at the same time Bhabha notes that for Jacques Derrida, 'the nation is rooted first of all in the memory or anxiety of a displaced – or displaceable population. It is not only time that is out of joint, but space, space in time, spacing.'[34] A statement that finds echoes in Edward Said's comment that 'All nationalisms in their early stages develop from a condition of estrangement.'[35] Lilia negotiates between the unravelling of the story of empire and its legacies, origins taking place both in her living room and on the other side of the world, and the traces of what Bhabha terms 'the memories of displacement that make national cultures possible', as she charts the journey of *The Mayflower* on the map at school and gets dressed up as a witch to go out trick-or-treating for Hallowe'en with her friend. The scenes of violence on screen in another postcolonial, distant, but also very close, location produce a scar on the face of the pumpkin that Mr. Pirzada has offered to carve, as he momentarily loses concentration, his knife slipping as he raises his eyes to the television screen. We might see this disfiguring of the sanitised ghoulish tradition of American Hallowe'en, opening up into its saccharine present the spectres of more archaic and foundational displacements, ones that refuse to be laid to rest in American history, and that continue to haunt the narrative of nation.

1   Migrant Visions

I   Writing exile

> Most people are principally aware of one culture, one setting, one home;
> exiles are aware of at least two, and this plurality of vision gives rise to an
> awareness of simultaneous dimensions, an awareness that to borrow a phrase
> from music, is contrapuntal. [. . .] Both the new and the old environments are
> vivid, actual occurring together contrapuntally.[1]

In Edward Said's comments in the final paragraphs of his essay 'Reflections
on Exile', he reiterates the 'plurality of vision' of the exile, one that he considers as echoing his theory of contrapuntal reading, a practice of reading texts
'against the grain' to reveal what has been suppressed or marginalised to
enable the text to be written. For Said, the exile has an unavoidable relation
to this double vision, finding its condition in the ambivalent nature of exile.
Exile is compelling because of its contradictory impulses of belonging and
strangeness, gain and loss. Even when stating that something is always lost
in the movement from home to elsewhere, 'the achievements of exile are
permanently undermined by the loss of something left behind forever', Said
finds he must address the paradox that 'if true exile is a condition of terminal
loss, why has it been transformed so easily into a potent even enriching motif
of modern culture?'[2] For Said, exile has a central ambivalence, it is 'beyond
the frontier between us and the outsider, the perilous territory of not belonging; yet a condition "legislated to deny dignity" has been "lent" some dignity'
through the work of the many exiled poets and writers both in the west and
across the postcolonial world, writers who increasingly demand our critical
and cultural attention wherever or however we locate ourselves.

   'How is it', he asks, 'that literature of exile has taken its place as a topos
of human experience, alongside literature of adventure, education or discovery?'[3] Behind this question lies Said's concern that the 'pleasures of
exile' can all too easily be celebrated in a 'literature of exile' and a critical
embracement of it. For Said, thinking about exile concerns 'putting aside

Joyce and Nabokov' and concentrating instead on 'the uncountable masses for whom UN agencies have been created'.⁴ Said's discussion is compelling as he resists any attempt to elevate the experience of exile to one of artistic privilege. Instead while he considers the work of Joyce, Nabokov, Conrad and Dante, he interweaves this reading with the work of Palestinian poet Mahmoud Darwish and anecdotes of his own exilic gatherings and friendships with across the world.

Said is also alert to the dangerous attractions of nationalism, of new forms of belonging that might make themselves felt in the experience of exile, writing with the Israel–Palestine conflict firmly in his vision he points to the risks of new ideologies of nation that can emerge from the exile's experience of loss and deprivation.

> Exiles are cut off from their roots, their land, their past. They generally do not have armies or states, although they are often in search of them. Exiles feel, therefore, an urgent need to reconstitute their broken lives, usually by choosing to see themselves as part of a triumphant ideology or a restored people. The crucial thing is that a state of exile free from this triumphant ideology – designed to reassemble an exile's broken history into a new whole – is virtually impossible in today's world.⁵

Bhabha's work continually evokes the moments of the 'gathering' of those 'exiles and émigrés and refugees' in the metropolitan centres of the West as well as elsewhere, forced across borders of failed or rogue states, and dispersed into refugee camps or permanent exile, waiting hopefully for opportunities to cross borders or return to lands they have been expelled from. He is perhaps most consistently understood as a theorist of migrancy and diaspora, but frequently also critiqued for a too easy celebration of the 'pleasures' of exile. Rather, his work on exile be seen to be trying to think into existence alternative ways of 'dwelling' in migrancy and exile, different kinds of belonging, gathering and regrouping in diasporic formations, that Said despairs of finding, in the comments cited above. He might usefully be seen as refocusing theories of migrancy and exile by attempting to rewrite orthodox perceptions of the exile's marginality to, and vulnerability in the face of, dominant world powers and seeming powerlessness in the face of decisions made at the international level, whether the United Nations, World Bank, NATO, International Monetary Fund, or multinational corporations like BP or Shell. At the opening of his essay 'Dissemination', Bhabha suggests an engagement with Said's rather troubled and troubling term 'uncountable masses'.

> Gathering on the edge of foreign cultures; gathering at the frontiers; gathering in the ghettos or cafes of city centres; gathering in the half-life, half-light of foreign tongues, or in the uncanny fluency of another's language; gathering the signs of approval and acceptance; degrees, discourses, disciplines; gathering the memories of underdevelopment, of other worlds lived retroactively; gathering the past in a ritual of revival; gathering the present.[6]

For Bhabha's purposes, these different gatherings are the disparate conditions of a variety of forms of migrancy, and the listing importantly involves putting some very different experiences side by side under the auspices of the 'postmodern' and 'postcolonial' condition. The exile, émigré and refugee are brought together in their 'lonely gatherings' through their perspective from the nation's margins, but this also effects their translation into and transformation of the Western nations.

There are clearly risks here of homogenising vastly different experiences in order to 'value' their perspectives. There is also the risk of extracting this 'surplus value' of a fresh perspective to reinvigorate and renew Western cultures and economies, where the migrant comes both to provide cheap labour and/or to provide an injection of novelty into jaded arts scenes. However, where Bhabha's theory works best is in the sense of the figure of the migrant, the exile or refugee never fully being contained in any of the pre-existing structures or narratives of belonging and strangeness, of familiar and unfamiliar, while also transforming and redefining how forms of belonging and culture are located.

Exile is haunted by its intimate connection with nation, just as the nation is haunted by its originating traumas of violence and displacement to the point that whether one term can be fully understood without the other. Exile must be predicated on a notion of home, belonging, ethnicity, for Said, when 'we come to nationalism' we also come to 'its essential association with exile'.[7]

> Nationalism is an assertion of belonging in and to a place, a people, a heritage. It affirms the home created by a community of language, culture and customs; and, by so doing, it fends off exile, fights to prevent its ravages. Indeed the interplay between nationalism and exile is like Hegel's dialectic of servant and master, opposites informing and constituting one another.[8]

Said is always concerned that the significance of the postcolonial exile, or refugee, is sometimes levelled uncomfortably. There may well be a risk in Bhabha's writing, such that for Bhabha, marginal positions might be equated too hastily, without attention to different experiences of being unhomed and vastly different kinds of propelling or motivating forces enacting themselves. Although it might be the case that the nation finds its history told 'from the perspective of the nation's margin and the migrant's exile' (*TLOC* p. 139), Said is cautious to differentiate between different exilic conditions even while witnessing their connections.

> Although it is true that anyone prevented from returning home is an exile, some distinctions can be made between exiles, refugees expatriates and émigrés. Exile originated in the age-old practice of banishment. Once banished the exile lives an anomalous and miserable life, with the stigma of being an outsider. Refugees, on the other hand are a creation of the Twentieth Century state. The word 'refugee' has become a political one.[9]

However, it would be over-hasty to claim that for Bhabha the exile, émigré, migrant or refugee is merely a convenient trope to celebrate a post-structuralist preoccupation with borders and limits, with narratives of nation. The translated experience of the refugee is both a personal experience of a dislocated subject and a social and political phenomenon that brings political issues urgently into focus. The vital point for Said is that 'exile is never the state of being satisfied, placid or secure. Exile is life led outside habitual order. It is nomadic, decentred, contrapuntal; but no sooner does one get accustomed to it than its unsettling force erupts anew.'[10]

II   Writing on the margins/reading beside Rushdie

In his influential essay 'DissemiNation', Bhabha offers a model of what he sees as the contradictory impulses that mark the narration of the nation. 'How to plot the narrative of the nation?', he asks.[11] Bhabha insists on a double narrative movement as crucial in attempts to narrate the nation, 'the nation's people must be thought in double time' (p. 297). Asserting the ambivalence of the nation as a narrative strategy, he offers a model of a split narrative that attempts to narrate its people both as historical objects of nationalist pedagogy, and as subjects of a process of signification in the present. This split narrative means that the people must be thought of in 'double-time': the former pedagogical, the latter performative. However, these doubles can never fully be merged or harmonised: they contradict or quite drastically disturb or menace one another, such that national celebrations such as the signing of historical treaties, or celebrations of 'founding' national events become sites of contest and political conflict, as differing narratives of their significance or meaning come into dispute with one another. The concept of 'the people' is crucial to this model of a double/split narrative movement, where they are both objects of discourse and historical sedimentation and subjects of signification and identification in the present.

Given that following Bhabha the narration of the nation can be characterised as always contradictory, always ambivalent, the predicament of migrants' writing of the nation would seem to be multiply marked. This attention to doubleness and double vision created through experience of more than one culture needs to be theorised while also interrogating any straightforward opposition between two supposedly holistic and complete cultures. It is the sense that the nation 'is no longer' (or never was) 'the sign of modernity under which cultural differences are homogenized in the "horizontal" view of society' that offers the possibility of the emergence of new constructions of identity and culture in the writing of nation.[12]

In Meera Syal's postcolonial *Bildungsroman*, *Anita and Me*, Meena, a young British Asian girl born to migrant parents, admits to the sense of living in a 'double space', with her front door functioning as a hinge between the two.

> Sometimes I wondered if the very act of shutting our front door transported us onto another planet, where non-related elders were called Aunties and Uncles and talked in rapid Punjabi, which their children understood but answered back in broad Black Country slang, where we ate food with our fingers and discussed family feuds happening five thousand miles away.[13]

Meena's double vision does not effect a transcendent position, from which to observe in a detached way the existence of two separate cultures. Rather, the hybrid postcolonial position comes as an inheritance, a result of extensive and uneven political and cultural relations. Such a position problematises rather than confirms the textual strategies of national narratives that seek to assert the completeness of the nation, and avoid the tricky confrontation with others at the nation's borders. This difficulty with national differentiation, as Geoffrey Bennington notes, 'does not come along to trouble the state after its perfect constitution, but precedes the fiction of such a constitution as its condition of possibility'.[14] For those who have crossed and re-crossed borders, writing the nation involves ambivalent senses of affiliation to more than one place, and a recognition of the limits of homogeneity in both. For Meena, shutting the door does not re-establish the fractured border between two spaces: it draws attention to the discontinuous histories and narratives occupying the same nation space. Partition stories survive the journey to Britain, and Meena's transgressing ear listens to both Hindu and Muslim who sit in the living room sharing horrific stories and crying together. Syal's characters have only partly evaded the border violence of national foundation that brutalised and separated them, and which crossed another in turn to redefine Britain in the process.

In Hanif Kureishi's writing on Britain and Pakistan there is no simple national allegiance. Emergent narratives of postcolonial 'nationness' offer predicaments rather than a simple recognition and acceptance of belonging. Kureishi writes of his first visit to Pakistan, witnessing the simultaneous presence of 'relics of the Raj, Oxford accents, libraries full of English books' *and* the contempt of its 'English-speaking international bourgeoisie' for Britain. He finds that his own identity exceeds national categories

> Strangely, anti-British remarks made me feel patriotic, though I only felt patriotic when I was away from England. But I couldn't allow myself to feel too Pakistani. I didn't want to give in to that falsity, that sentimentality.[15]

Crossing the border back into Britain involves a simultaneous double movement, a return, but also a rejection. 'I have never wanted to identify with England. When Enoch Powell spoke for England I turned away in final disgust. I would rather walk down the street naked than stand up for the national anthem' (p. 99). This sense of the impossibility, of the falsity of claiming an affiliation marks the necessity of finding a means of narrating the self that is not founded on a myth of origins and registers the contingency of national narratives.

For Salman Rushdie there is something particular about the condition of the Pakistani nation that speaks of the condition of migrancy. This contingency appears hyperbolic, such that the nation itself becomes a distillation of the migrant condition.

> When individuals come unstuck from their native land, they are called migrants. When nations do the same thing (Bangladesh), the act is called secession. What is the best thing about migrant peoples and seceded nations? I think it is their hopefulness. [. . .] And what's the worst thing? It is the emptiness of one's luggage. [. . .] We have come unstuck from more than land. We have floated upwards from history, from memory from Time. I may be such a person. Pakistan may be such a country.[16]

Rushdie has been taken to task for this notion of floating upwards from history, where this comment has been read as a denial of the role of history in the production of migrant and exilic conditions and the nations associated with them. However, arguably in *Shame* migrancy is a key trope through which the creation of Pakistan can be understood to operate. The act of naming is itself characterised as a form of migration,

> It is well known that the term 'Pakistan', an acronym, was originally thought
> up in England by a group of Muslim intellectuals. [. . .] So it was a word born
> in exile which went East, was borne-across or trans-lated, and imposed itself
> on history; a returning migrant.
>
> (p. 87)

Shame is perhaps Rushdie's most overlooked novel in his early trilogy map-
ping out the complex national narratives of India, Pakistan and the British
Asian diaspora, coming after the great reception of *Midnight's Children*
and before the furore over *The Satanic Verses*, the notable exception to
this lack of critical attention being Aijaz Ahmad's work.[17] It sits uncomfortably between these two huge texts to which so much critical attention has
been paid and through which questions of cultural difference have been
transformed in diverse ways, with some profoundly difficult and persistent
effects. *Midnight's Children*, as the 'Booker of Bookers', has been figured as
the text signalling the arrival of the postcolonial émigré writer in the British literary establishment, an event accompanied by many contradictions
and numerous criticisms of Rushdie's assumed abandonment of his native
country in favour of recognition from the privileged Western elite.[18] Alter-
natively for Bhabha, *The Satanic Verses* has increasingly come to represent
the crisis of white British liberal culture in the face of volatile and seemingly
unexpected expressions of cultural difference from different faith communities both within Britain and across the postcolonial world. Furthermore,
publication of *The Satanic Verses* had the power to change markedly the
way of life of its author, the text erupting onto and dominating the British
cultural and political scene at the time of its publication. This leaves Rushdie's immediately previous novel somewhat eclipsed.

Shame is simultaneously locked into the middle of these two moments
of *Midnight's Children* and *The Satanic Verses*, but arguably no longer exists
in any simple linear progression as an in-between moment; indeed, it
demonstrates the untimely nature of the in-between as Bhabha proposes
it. Although overshadowed by its predecessor, it is equally obscured by its
successor. This might even be said to apply to Ahmad's critique of *Shame*,
in *In Theory*, whose footnotes are testimony to the important retrospective
impact of the appearance of *The Satanic* Verses for his own commentary.[19]
It could also be said of Bhabha's work, where the value of *The Satanic Verses*
to his writing and thinking is clear, but *Shame*, despite offering multiple figures of translation and migration, is not extensively discussed.

If it has become impossible and pointless to speak of Rushdie without
reference to *The Satanic Verses* affair, then *Shame*, although chronologi-
cally before *The Satanic Verses*, must in a peculiar way also come after it

and cannot be removed from its relationship to *The Satanic Verses* in a critical discussion of its operations and narrative strategies. *Shame*'s untimely position further supports the case for a re-reading of the novel whose status might be figured as marginal in Rushdie's writing. Its status as such, I would suggest, is not simply due to the accident of fate that locates it between two other texts. It also reflects an increasing complexity and ambivalence in the relationship of the West and Britain with both the subject of Pakistan, of globalised political relationships that Pakistan has on the world stage, and with a revival of cultural production, performance and writing in the Pakistani and Bangladeshi diaspora in the UK and elsewhere.

In foregrounding the writing of the nation, he points to the problematic that as Geoffrey Bennington states 'at the origin of the nation, we find the story of the nation's origin'.[20] This writing also crucially involves the drawing of borders between Pakistan and India, writing on the land. This act of writing precipitates a great movement of peoples, who must decide to break with history and geography, either to settle in the new territory or to move out of it. Pakistan's borders with India were open from 1947–51, which suggests the added instability of a period of years where questions, decisions and movements were initiated.[21]

The violence of partition that turned people overnight into refugees is dramatised in the novel through the fate of Bilquis Kemal, later Bilquis Hyder. She experiences partition as an explosion, one that strips her naked and simultaneously strips her of her past. Also, critically, it locates her, enforcing a religious identity and a separation from the population of Delhi behind the walls of a fortress. This overturns the insistence of her father to 'rise above all this partition foolishness', by playing two differently religiously affiliated films in his Empire Picture House, on a double bill. This impossible project, and the empty cinema it produces, present a comic parody of a nation riven by cultural difference whose different and competing stories struggle to be told simultaneously. The tragedy for 'Mahound the Woman' is portrayed as the naïve politics of placing what are perceived to be 'different' or 'opposed' cultural products in a violent and destabilising proximity, risks producing an equally violent reassertion of spatial temporal and cultural difference. Placing himself as transcendent of different supposedly homogeneous groups, he attempts to demonstrate their provisionality, their internal fissures, their dependence on one another, their inability to represent themselves fully without recourse to the other. For Mahound the Woman, his artistic attempt to undo difference is tantamount to suicide, in a nation about to realise the full dividing and defining potential of the border.

In Delhi, Bilquis watches her past leave her as she gets herded into the fortress Al-Hambra for her own protection, as partition appears imminent.

> Naked and eyebrowless [. . .] wrapped in the delirium of the firewind she saw her youth flying past her, borne away on the wings of the explosion which were still beating in her ears. All migrants leave their pasts behind, although some try to pack it into bundles and boxes. [. . .] Bilquis's past left her even before she left that city; she stood in a gully, denuded by the suicide of her father and watched it go. In later years it would visit her sometimes, the way forgotten relatives come to call, but for a long time she was suspicious of history, she was the wife of a hero with a great future so naturally she pushed the past away.[22]

Having been stripped naked by history, the process by which she is re-clothed mirrors that of Pakistan's new and fragile state. Undressed by history, she is dressed by the future, in what appears as a realisation of what Bhabha terms the ambivalence of nation, when he quotes Ernest Gellner,

> Nationalism is not what it seems, and *above all not what it seems to itself.* The cultural shreds and patches used by nationalism are often arbitrary historical inventions; any old shreds would have served as well.[23]

Raza Hyder dresses her in clothes that her fellow women in the fortress suspect are looted, booty stolen from other women who may be dead or prisoners. Her new outfits are patchworks and ragbags taken from the other victims of the conflict. If 'the scraps, patches and rags of daily life must be repeatedly turned into signs of a coherent national culture', then it seems that Bilquis will have to remake herself whole with the disparate clothes she has acquired (p. 145). She does not consciously choose them, but she accepts that they will do. This undressing and re-dressing of Bilquis offers a vision where the individual immigrant must literally or symbolically participate in the remaking of culture.

That partition is dramatised on a woman's body is suggestive of the extent to which narratives of the nation are experienced as gendered, and is testimony to the ideological importance of women in the project of partition and the narratives that surrounded it. For Samir Dayal, *Shame* 'remains particularly interesting for its exploration of the border conditions that define both categories of gender and nation'. It is through this representation that Rushdie, 'gestures towards the political backdrop of border troubles'.[24] Research by Urvashi Butalia on the implications of partition for women in India and Pakistan has revealed the extent to which the historical moment of partition was experienced as a conflict over women's bodies. She recounts stories from different communities in which many women were in religious terms 'martyred' or committed suicide rather than falling into the hands of opposing communities with the possibility of being abducted, raped, forced to convert or forced into marriage. She notes at once the actual violence committed by different groups on women from different communities and the ways in which this violence is a highly symbolic and violent form of inscription and signification. She writes, 'There are accounts of innumerable rapes, of women being stripped naked and paraded down streets, of their breasts being cut off, of their bodies being carved with the religious symbols of the other community.'[25] Butalia's research reveals the extent to which women's bodies became elided with assertions of nation,

> Partition for both new communities involved actively abducting and converting women, 'figures vary widely, but it was said at the time that some 50,000 Muslim women had been abducted in India and about 33,000 Muslim women has been abducted in India'. The fate of these abducted women became cause for political concern as early as December 1947, when the 'recovery' of these women was a stated undertaking, on the part of both nations.[26]

In *Shame*, the rewriting of the nation is performed upon the single gendered body of Bilquis, the fictional narrative inhabiting a 'parallel universe' to the historical one. Bilquis is not forced to change faith, but is 'carried along' by a human tide, into the Muslim enclave in Delhi, and then ultimately to Pakistan. Questions of choosing to leave the past behind are qualified for Bilquis Hyder, as she stands briefly motionless while the past leaves of its own accord. The shattering, cracking and exploding of time has to lie at the core of the forging of a new identity and history, and appear to be necessarily accompanied by the pervasive fear of splitting that preoccupies the nation. It is also exemplified in the doubleness, and internal conflicts that many of the characters endure in their investigations of their own personal histories and locations.

The nation as narration involves two strategies, the establishment of borders and of origins. The writing over, of the new time of the nation onto the old, of new spaces onto the old in the case of Pakistan, could be seen as paradigmatic for the nation as narration, as Rushdie comments: 'I am not only writing about Pakistan'. The trope of the palimpsest, 'writing over' what has already been written, implies the absolute condition of national narratives. Here, Bhabha's suggestion of the double-time of the nation is suggested through the imposition of time on the timeless. The palimpsest is performed on both spatial and temporal logic.

> I must tell you what things were like in those early days after the partition: the city's old inhabitants, who had become accustomed to living in a land older

than time, and were therefore being slowly eroded by the implacably reve-
nant tides of the past had been given a bad shock by independence by being
told to think of themselves, as well as the country itself as new. Well, their
imaginations simply weren't up to the job, you can understand that; so it was
the ones who really were new, the distant cousins and half acquaintances and
total strangers who poured in from the east to settle in the Land of God, who
took over and got things going. The newness of those days felt pretty unstable;
it was a dislocated, rootless thing.[27]

However, this battle between what previously existed and what is newly
being written is not simply a conflict between the truth of the origin and
the imposition of stories. For as Bhabha points out, 'to study the nation
through its narrative address does not merely draw attention to its language and rhetoric; it also attempts to alter the conceptual object itself'.[28]
The writing anew of the nation reveals that the nation always was and
is narration. Taking seriously the narrator's claim that he is writing not
only about Pakistan is not merely to claim that 'in some way we are all
migrants'; rather, that other preciously held national narratives of atavistic belonging might be opened up to a comparable reading. In a sense,
then, *Shame* anticipates the kind of narration of Britain, and contestation
of the limits and purposes of narrative production that follow it in *The
Satanic Verses*. The conditions of this previous statement, though, have of
course to be that peculiar sense that *Shame* can be seen as coming after
The Satanic Verses.

The imperative that Rushdie articulates in *East, West*, 'choose, choose,'
also points to the phenomenon of *choosing* belonging. Omar Khayyam
Shakil, the peripheral hero of *Shame*, has to choose a father, as his own
has remained a mystery. In doing so he also chooses his inheritance. The
imperative to choose sets up an aporetic logic, where the desire for an
individual to choose which nation they belong to is expressed, in order
to consolidate the sense of nation and to confirm its atavistic aspirations.
However, the logic of choice threatens to destabilise the very notions of
belonging and inheritance that the narrative of nation depends upon. It
should be impossible to choose to belong to something that claims precedence over all choices. The conditions of the possibility of choosing to
belong are also the conditions of its impossibility. Hence the imperative to
choose is not to be confused with a celebration of endless choice. If choosing to join a nation has been depicted as the luxury of the postcolonial
émigré in the West, it is here in the metaphors of migrancy in *Shame* that
choice becomes an impossible demand, an imperative that must be but
cannot be adequately obeyed.

In *Shame* it is this logic that the new narrative of Pakistan cannot abide. The movement of peoples allows Barriamma to insult Bilquis Hyder as 'immigrant, mohajir,' or Raza Hyder posturing as a devout Muslim to be accused of having lived too many years among the un-godly, or of having a Hindu great-grandmother. The narrative of religious belonging at the heart of the nation fails to achieve a unification of peoples, and is constantly being usurped and undermined by the refusal to forget certain things. The substances of this conflict are culture, language and time: 'Midriff baring immigrant saris versus demure indigenous Sindhi shalwar-Kurtas, Urdu versus Punjabi, now versus then.'[29]

The act of choosing to belong, seemingly stabilising a relation, as Said's model of affiliation demonstrates, is also a profoundly destabilising decision. In *Shame*, it extends beyond the decision to move in or out of a country: it becomes implicated in the writing of history, choosing what will be included and what left out, choosing what should be forgotten and what remembered, choosing what it is that one professes allegiance to nationally and personally. If the possibility of choosing to belong, rather than having it thrust upon one by indisputable origins, is at the heart of Pakistan's dilemmas as a nation, it is also characterised by the narrator as a condition of the migrant. This process of choosing involves a re-writing, both of nation and of self, a performance of translation where narratives are continually being constructed and adapted.

Shame's narrator writes in a state of exile or migrancy, from outside the boundaries of Pakistan. Hence he is concerned with the status of his own exile, both in terms of how it inflects the narrative, and with his own personal experience of the creation of the new country, Pakistan. The complications of his own decisions about where to live are caused by the specific relationships between India, Pakistan and England. They do not embody a limitless choosing of identity, freed from historical imperatives. The question is clearly one of choosing-between, enforced choice, indeed almost of having no choice.

> I, too, know something of this immigrant business. I am an emigrant from one country (India) and a newcomer in two (England, where I live and Pakistan, to which my family moved against my will) [. . .] I have never been angrier than I was on the day my father told me he had sold my childhood home in Bombay.
>
> (p. 85)

Here, choice is more properly characterised as the dilemma of inheritance. This migrancy is neither ahistorical, being precipitated by British

'decolonisation' of India, nor does it involve an extensive array of cultures
to be freely consumed. If the migrant can float up from history, it is a history dependent on place, origin, linearity of narrative, not associated with
movement, flight, discontinuity. For the migrant, like Bilquis Hyder, time
cracks, space changes, the trappings of identity are removed and replaced.
She crosses, migrates, loses and remakes.

III   Cultural difference and translation

> All stability in a place being but a stabilization or a sedimentarization, it will
> have to have been necessary that the local difference, the spacing of a dis-
> placement gives the movement its start. All national rootedness, for example,
> is rooted first of all in the memory or the anxiety of a displaced – or displace-
> able – population. It is not only time that is 'out of joint' but space, space in
> time, spacing.[30]

> Vacillating boundaries – psychic, cultural, territorial. Where do you draw the
> line between languages? between cultures? between disciplines? between
> peoples?[31]

The problematic of the borders of the nation materialises in *Shame* when
Omar takes a trip to the frontier. Farah Zoroaster recounts,

> Incredible I swear, we just reached there in the Jeep and at once a cloud came
> down and sat on the ground right along the frontier, like it couldn't get across
> without a visa, and that Shakil was so scared he passed out, he got vertigo and
> fainted, even though he had both feet on the ground.[32]

Just as the nation is caught in the impossible logic of its conditions of possibility, an aporetic one, its peripheral hero dramatises the crisis of the
nation's borders, which must open out onto other nations and which act
as a hinge or frame on the nation space. Omar Khayyam, who is for *Shame*
a belated and peripheral version of *Midnight's Children*'s Saleem Sinai, is
overwhelmed by the frontier, mistaking it for 'his childhood nightmare of
the void at the end of the earth'. Khayyam's 'fear of the Edge' is suggestive
both of the unsettling impact of the border on narratives of nation, and of
an apprehension of his own status in a work of fiction concerned with the
boundaries of the text. (*Shame*, p. 50)
    This double preoccupation is also critically the concern of the narrator.
The narrator characterises his predicament through his depiction of himself as a kind of translator. His status as a translator is critically linked to the

specific circumstances of his migrant status. Such is the ambivalence of his situation and location that he is forced to raise this question himself, in a pre-emptive move against anticipated antagonism,

> Outsider! Trespasser! You have no right to this subject! [. . .] We reject your authority. We know you, with your foreign language wrapped around you like a flag: speaking about us in your forked tongue, what can you tell but lies?
>
> (p. 28)

Here, the difficulty of speaking for, or about, difference is exacerbated by the narrator's own anxiety about how his status as a translator might be contested. Yet this in itself is a translation, representing and rewriting the anticipated critical voice of 'insider' suspicious of the 'in-between' who in fact may be considered as an outsider. It appears that the translator/narrator is already involved in a dialogue with the subjects of his translation. Caught in his own translated state, he can only use his forked tongue to re-create that dialogue, in a partial and flawed form. It would seem therefore that the effectiveness of translation depends upon a rewriting which addresses the ways in which translation effects disturbance, remakes and redraws those cultures it engages with.

This can be read as being a critical dynamic in the text, exploring the interdependency of culture, language and geography. The narrator offers an explanation of the Urdu word 'sharam', translatable as shame, which observes a correlation between sentiment and place 'Sharam, that word . . . shame . . . embarrassment discomfiture, decency, modesty, shyness, the sense of having an ordained place in the world' (p. 39).

The word 'sharam' has itself crossed borders in its removal from one language and attempted to be meaningful in another. The translator is also involved in carving out a territory for the word, to the extent that it arrives as excess, multiple words. It is 'a short word, but one containing encyclopedias of nuance' (p. 39). The point for the narrator is that 'sharam' is not translatable as any one sentiment, but invokes a much more wide-ranging framework of values, ideals or morals, which enable a diversity of sentiments and states of being. The emphasis on the problems of translating an Urdu word that means more than can be said in a single English word raises questions about being 'translated' and 'borne across'. The narrator, having addressed all the ways in which Sharam cannot be adequately explained, then inverts this orthodox position: 'It is generally believed that something is always lost in translation; I cling to the notion that something can also be gained'(p. 29).

Although the translation changes the original, to characterise it only as loss is a privileging of authentic meaning endowed though authorial intent. The migrant voice that translates, simultaneously 'inside' and 'outside' lives, according to Iain Chambers, 'at the intersections of histories and memories experiencing both their preliminary dispersal and their subsequent translation into new more extensive arrangements along emerging routes'.[33] The possibilities for narratives of translation might then be to question the privileging of the desire for authenticity, for access to the originary meaning in narrative. Translatability becomes crucial as a critical concept, no longer associated only with the conversion of one language into another but used in relation to the need to translate between cultures. Bhabha suggests that, 'it is by living on the borderline of history and language, on the limits of race and gender we are in a position to translate the difference between them into a kind solidarity'.[34]

In Bhabha's model 'translation' appears as an apprehension of the need to consider different kinds of cultural exchange, from a diversity of subject positions aligned to but never simply representative of race, gender, sexuality and culture. Translation becomes such a critical concept for postcolonial theory because it offers a way of approaching cultural difference that does not fall into the trap of containing cultural difference through the 'creation of cultural diversity'. Without a concept of translation, the idea that cultural diversity is 'a good thing' and that it ought to be 'encouraged' amounts for Bhabha to little more than a kind of Western connoisseurship of other cultures, which, although it may encourage and accommodate cultural diversity, ultimately contains it. The translator cannot assume a third position of removal and distance, from which to objectify and judge the different strata of culture, or different cultures that are being translated. Comparison through the creation of a transcendent standpoint is no longer possible.

Although this proposition promises to subvert and revise the ways that master discourses, 'Other' than those that are colonised or dominated, it appears to suggest that the subject position of the translator, once liberated from the third transcendent position, is more easily freed from these presuppositions. Bhabha's model of cultural translation appears to consolidate such a position,

> The difference of cultures cannot be something that can be accommodated within a universalist framework. Different cultures, the difference between cultural practices, the difference in the constitution of cultures within different groups, very often sets up among and between themselves an incommensurability.[35]

Understanding this entails a re-evaluation of any concept of cultural diversity based around either some form of relativism, or transcendent universal category,

> The assumption that at some level all forms of cultural diversity may be understood on the basis of a particular universal concept, whether it be 'human being', 'class' or 'race' can be both very dangerous and very limiting in trying to understand the ways in which cultural practices construct their own systems of meaning and social organization.[36]

For Bhabha, the significant way in which all forms of culture are related to one another is not through the familiarity or similarity of contents, but 'because all cultures are symbol forming and subject-constituting interpellative practices' (p. 209). This theory of culture has a close affinity with post-structuralist theories of language and representation. Bhabha's model of cultural difference owes much to Jacques Derrida's use of différance, and his understanding of translation to Derrida's understanding of the iterability of the sign. Bhabha states,

> Meaning is constructed across the bar of difference and separation between the signifier and the signified. So it follows that no culture is full unto itself, no culture is plainly plenitudinous, not only because there are other cultures which contradict its authority, but also because its own symbol forming activity, its own interpellation in the process of representation, language and signification and meaning-making, always underscores the claim to an originary, holistic organic identity.[37]

Cultures therefore are subject to intrinsic forms of translation, always involved in a process of alienation in relation to themselves. Here, translation is used by Bhabha to suggest the activity of displacement within the linguistic sign. Bhabha goes further, though, to suggest that translation can also be understood to be a form of imitation, imitating an original in such a way that the priority of the original is not enforced, its very openness to translation meaning that it 'can never be said to have a totalized prior moment of being or meaning – an essence'.[38]

From these notions of cultural difference and cultural translation comes Bhabha's most renowned but equally misunderstood proposition of hybridity. In Bhabha's model, hybridity is understood as cultural, not biological or racial. Cultural hybridity is theorised as the result of the continual process of translation which is internal to any culture, which in turn stems from an apprehension of cultural difference. The translator acknowledges difference, and cannot avoid drawing attention to the otherness internal to any symbol-forming activity or signifying practice. However although hybridity might be said to be endemic in all cultural practice for Bhabha, giving post-structuralism 'a peculiarly postcolonial provenance' involves a theorisation of emergent cultural practices and identifications by migrant and minority communities in the West.

Bhabha's explicit references to Derrida in his early version of 'Interrogating Identity', locates questions of cultural difference and translation critically around questions of post-structuralist and postmodernist enquiries into the nature of identity.

> My insistence on locating the postcolonial subject within the play of the sub-altern instance of writing, is an attempt to develop Derrida's passing remark that the history of the 'decentred' subject and its dislocation of European metaphysics is concurrent with the emergence of the problematic of cultural difference within ethnology. He acknowledges the political nature of this moment but leaves it to us to specify it in the postcolonial text.[39]

Bhabha's description of his own position in relation to questions of identity might usefully be deployed to think about the role of the translator/narrator in *Shame*:

> Any attempt, on my part to frame the problem of identity leads inevitably to my being caught athwart the frame, at once inside and outside. And if the frame within the frame, mise en abime, is one of the central tropes of post-modern culture, then such double inscription also provides the mise en scene of the postcolonial writer – performing a certain problem of identification between nations and cultures, between foreign and floating signs.
>
> (p. 9)

The narrator of *Shame*, finding himself in this liminal borderline position, must be drawn into in the juggling of cultures, histories and languages. However, the role of the translator is far from unproblematic. If the narrator of *Shame* is considered as a translator, his investigation of the difficulty of finding a space to speak from comes through the problems of speaking from both inside and out of the territory he rewrites. His vision is self-consciously partial as he both narrates and reads the events, detached and yet connected. He inhabits a problematic space, realising Bhabha's 'in-between-ness' having been translated from one culture to another but not existing fully in either. A kind of doubleness or splitting of subjectivity then characterises his narrative. The problematic relationship between place and culture, the 'location' of culture, is immediately complicated by the difficulty of placing and identifying him.

The mechanics of what happens in translation of this kind attest to both a brutality and a reincarnation. Being 'borne-across' enacts an assault and a renewal. Original stories may be lost but they haunt other narratives, exerting their influence through a partial presence, a trace, which is ephemeral and ghostly. As Iain Chambers notes, to translate is always to transform:

> It always involves a necessary travesty of any metaphysics of authenticity or origins. We find ourselves employing a language that is always shadowed by loss, by elsewhere, a ghost: the unconscious, an 'other' text an 'other' voice.[40]

Such are the characteristics of a key translation in *Shame*, that of Sufiya Zinobia. Sufiya Zinobia's importance in Shame could be situated in terms of her translated hybrid state. She too is 'borne across' and bears the traces of three different stories. Her primary source is the story of a young Asian British woman murdered by her father for sleeping with a white boy and bringing shame on her family.

> She had brought such dishonour upon her family that only her blood could wash away the stain. The tragedy was intensified by the father's enormous and obvious love for his butchered child, and by the beleaguered reluctance of his friends and relatives to condemn his actions.

(p. 235)

Her story comes from a culture translated once to Britain and then a second time by the narrator to Pakistan, because the dead girl eludes him, becomes a ghost, who is written in translation, because, as the narrator puts it, 'I realized that to write about her, about shame, I would have to go back east, to let the idea breathe its favourite air.' The girl is 'deported, repatriated to a country she had never seen' (p. 116). Hers is a story partly founded in the British-Asian migrant experience, but one the narrator translates and redirects in order to ask questions about the 'origins' of her story and of his own.

Having been 'borne-across', she is deformed, changed, assaulted, interfered with by her family, becoming the physical embodiment of their shame. Sufiya Zinobia is born of an ambivalent cultural act – brutality that is marked by love. Sufiya Zinobia is therefore already a ghostly figure; her ghostly birth is precipitated by a death. The narrator claims she haunted him, while Sufiya Zinobia haunts Pakistan. Rather than be resurrected, she is retained as a ghost or trace in order to be reborn in translation.

By translating Sufiya Zinobia, the narrator engages with the kinds of question that this reading of cultural difference raises. Sufiya Zinobia emerges as all that has been repressed and is being repressed to unify and legitimate the homogenising narrative of the nation. She emerges from the migrant's vision to undermine the illusory continuity of culture and history. She is a ghost, a double person, afflicted with an internal splitting who calls attention to the inherent ambivalence in cultural authority. Omar Khayyam slowly recognises her monstrous properties in terms of her doubleness,

> He saw what casual eyes would have missed, which was that the edges of Sufiya Zinobia were beginning to become uncertain, as if there were two beings occupying that air-space, competing for it, two entities of identical shape but of tragically opposed natures.[41]

Sufiya Zinobia gives the lie to the illusion of wholeness, of fantasised unity, and shows how it can only ever be achieved as a narrative of repression and violence. As Raza Hyder becomes increasingly dogmatic and tyrannous, she undergoes a metamorphosis until she becomes both 'beauty and the beast'. Her increasing brutality and her transmogrification into a beast suggests that she translates the irrational violence done to her ghostly predecessors, enacting a cultural vengeance that surpasses an individual resentment or outrage, and becomes a retributive intervention of the repressed. She bears the burden of exposing the proliferation of shameful acts that have been lost and erased in Pakistan's history. They are translated into powerful physical affliction, disease, brain fever, blushing, finding a means to reveal themselves even as narratives of deceit and denial are being constructed. Sufiya's hybridity and various physical and visible afflictions appear as dangerously unstable traces of other narratives which threaten to deconstruct these cultural certainties before they ever fully realise their intended status.

Her monstrous qualities testify to the horror of hybridity that accompanies the new narratives of nation that Pakistan effects. Internal splitting is reviled, acceptable splitting is represented as a desirable externalising of difference which denies what Bhabha insists is the inherent ambivalence of national authority. Pakistan becomes a haunted nation, with the ghosts of Malauna Dawood and Iskander Harappa on president Raza Hyder's shoulders whispering of atrocities of the past and retributions to come, and Sufiya Zinobia is transformed into 'time's ghost, the future stalking the forests of the past' (p. 252). Sufiya Zinobia has come into being through the ghosts of the past; however, now she comes, in the strange logic of the spectre, that Derrida notes, from the future.[42] The monster that Sufiya Zinobia becomes is created, as Omar Khayyam notes, at the expense of her death; she is indeed a ghost, but one that inhabits a monster's body.

Omar's brother Babar, as poet, philosopher and separatist revolutionary, articulates how this issue functions in the creation of Pakistan. 'Separation', Babar wrote, 'is the belief that you are good enough to escape from the clutches of hell' (p. 130). He goes to live in the impossible mountains, and begins to turn into an angel. The rationale behind this is 'the belief in the golden angels gave the guerrillas an unshakeable certainty of the justice of their cause and made it easy for them to die for it' (p. 132). As his compatriots watch, he slowly begins to turn into an angel, separation effecting an avoidance of internal difference that is masked through a narrative concerned with expelling, pushing outside oneself all that threatens internal conflict.

Through the double vision of the migrant, *Shame* re-situates an internal ambivalence as absolutely unavoidable in narratives of nation and identity. Narratives of separation are undermined by the resurgence of the dialectic in geographical terms, between the East and West wings, in the competing versions of history, colonised and colonisers, and in the internal battles of Sufiya Zinobia, beauty and the beast all in one. This is not simply a splitting into two: it is marked by the existence of at least two presences within the same geographical or spatial co-ordinates, by the apprehension of cultural difference that allows for no transcendence and hence limitation of difference under the label of diversity.

Rani Harappa recollects how the urge for separation has become exaggerated into a manufactured dialectic: 'I remember those days, I remember Raza Hyder when he was not a devil with horns and a tail and Isky before he became a saint' (p. 108). The position of the migrant with a double vision makes for an awareness of internal contradictions. If the migrant vision is able to achieve anything, it is through a recognition of how the creation of 'devils' and 'angels' is implicated in the unifying narratives of nation.

IV The 'third space' and the heresy of hybridity: Re-reading *The Satanic Verses*

> Men make their own history but they do not make it just as they please; they do not make it under circumstances chosen by themselves – but from the past. And just when they seem engaged in revolutionizing themselves and things, in creating something that has never yet existed, precisely in such periods of revolutionary crisis they anxiously conjure up the spirits of the past to their service, in order to present the new scene of world history in this time honoured disguise and this borrowed language. [. . .]
>
> This paradox must be sharpened: the more the new erupts in the revolutionary crisis the more the period is in crisis, the more it is 'out of joint' then the more one has to convoke the old, 'borrow' from it. Inheritance from the 'spirits of the past' consists, as always in borrowing.[43]

> In the first part of my paper I will attempt the impossible: a reading of *The Satanic Verses* as if nothing had happened since late 1988.[44]

When Gayatri Spivak claims in her contribution to 'The Rushdie debate' in the journal *Public Culture* that she will attempt the impossible, by offering a reading of *The Satanic Verses* that is kept discreet from the knowledge of the political and cultural responses to the novel and its author in the late 1980s, she is well aware that it *is* impossible. The text can only be read as haunted, inhabited by the conflicting debates around its proper audience, its status as literature, its positioning by the media and others between a 'metropolitan' literate readership and demands for destruction and retribution from different groups and nations in the Muslim world and by different sections of the Asian-British population whose class positions and cultural backgrounds have often been, as Timothy Brennan notes, 'translated into religious ones alone'.[45]

One might take Spivak's comment a step further and note that after the events of September 11th in the USA, the subsequent invasions of Afghanistan and Iraq, and the announcement of the 'war on terror', it is impossible to read Rushdie's work without the knowledge of his subsequent journalism on this subject too. As Sabina and Simona Sawhney note in 'Reading Rushdie after Sept 11th 2001', Rushdie's pronouncements on 'global terrorism' and the invasion of Afghanistan have been at odds with the 'sections of the left that have drawn connections between the history of U.S. foreign policy and the attacks of September 11th'.[46] Rushdie's most recent writing, and perhaps more importantly reports of it and critical responses to it circulating in the media, have damaged his previously close relationship to leftist intellectuals who had been active in their defence of him.

The Satanic Verses explores both the Asian British migrant experience, in a narrative split between postcolonial London and India, and the status of origins and the authority of cultural and religious certainties, in its 'inversion' and pastiche of values and teachings of the Qur'an where the text is located in Mecca (Jahilia) and Madina. Aamir Mufti, in his thorough and insightful account of the 'Rushdie Affair', expresses a certain dissatisfaction with all of the above modes of positioning Rushdie's text and responses to it. He asserts that the 'Rushdie Affair' needs to be recognised as a complex cultural event within the Islamic world (something frequently overlooked in critical accounts of the text and responses to it), one that attempted to change the terms of discussion that were already taking place in a pan-Islamic context on a very broad range of issues about the role of Islam in the contemporary world. He comments, 'what has given the novel its transgressive force, is that instead of merely thematizing these familiar issues, it also forces a changing of the terms of discussion itself'.[47] The violent responses to the text, he suggests, are 'an accurate indication of the anger generated by its insistence on a sweeping rearrangement and rethinking of the terms of Muslim public culture'.[48] His point is to emphasise that the angry responses to the text were not a refusal of discussion and dissent seen as anathema to Islamic culture, but a response to an insistence that the terms of the debates themselves be radically altered. It is a fine distinction, but a useful one that lends his account of the 'politics of offense' in Rushdie some credibility.

Similarly for Bhabha, the terms of representation of the 'conflict' have polarised positions at the expense of reading differently,

> The conflict of cultures and community around The Satanic Verses has been mainly represented in spatial terms as binary geopolitical polarities – Islamic fundamentalists vs. Western literary modernists, the quarrel of the ancient (ascriptive) and modern (ironic) metropolitans. This obscures the anxiety of the irresolvable borderline culture of hybridity that articulates its problems if identification and its diasporic aesthetic in an uncanny, disjunctive temporality that is at once, the time of cultural displacement and the space of the untranslatable.[49]

Bhabha's work on Rushdie was brought into focus very sharply by the international 'event' of the '*Satanic Verses* affair'. Bhabha published a statement from the first meeting of the 'Black Voices in Defence of Salman Rushdie' group, in *The New Statesman* in March 1989, critiquing the terms upon which debates in the media about this book had become polarised, into 'an implacable antagonism' between 'the cultural imperatives of Western liberalism and a 'fundamentalist' interpretation of Islam, and insisting that another position needed to be put forward by those engaged in multiracial education, or working for migrant and refugee rights, alongside artists and cultural practitioners from diverse Black and Asian communities. 'Where do we turn?', he asks, 'we who see the limits of liberalism and fear the absolutist demands of fundamentalism?'[50]

Bhabha's statement of support for Rushdie's freedom of expression and condemnation of incitements to violence made in the name of Islam is also qualified by his insight into the 'implacable antagonisms' that have been created in public discourse around the text (p. 139). He goes on to comment,

> This is ironically the central problem in *The Satanic Verses*. It is Rushdie's painful and problematic encounter with the most intractable and intimate area of

his imaginative life. What the book uniquely reveals is a life lived precariously on the cultural and political margins of modern society. Where once we could believe in the comforts and continuities of Tradition, today we must face the responsibilities of cultural Translation. In the attempt to mediate between different cultures, languages and societies, there is always the threat of mis-translation, confusion and fear.

(p. 140)

As many critics have noted, the convergence of vocabularies and concepts in Rushdie's and Bhabha's writing offers an uncanny sense of their work each being paradigmatic of the others, or even inhabited by one another's words. Indeed, postcolonial critics reading *The Satanic Verses* seem to find themselves or others peopling Rushdie's scenes. As Rajeswari Sunder Rajan observes, Gayatri Spivak identifies herself as Swatilekha, 'a tall thin Bengali woman with cropped hair' (*The Satanic Verses*, p. 537), in her article *Reading the Satanic Verses*; while Sunder Rajan goes a step further and asks if Zeenat Vakil, an art critic, whose work has challenged myths of national authentic-ity and championed eclecticism and Bhabha himself might also usefully be paired.[51] Early in the novel, Zeeny, who (appropriately, if in any sense a fig-ure for Bhabha) is attributed with the quality of 'voicing the unspeakable', is given a tour of the Chamchawala art collection, of *Hamza-nama* cloths,

> The pictures also provided eloquent proof of Zeeny Vakil's thesis about the eclectic hybridized nature of the Indian artistic tradition. The Mughals had bought artists from every part of India to work on the paintings; individual identity was submerged to create a many-headed, many-brushed Overartist who literally *was* Indian painting.[52]

Leaving aside this gender-bending or transmutation which might appeal to Bhabha's most translational or interstitial tastes, key concepts of Bhabha's work have perhaps most evocatively been realised in this text.

The Satanic Verses opens with similar preoccupations to *Shame*'s ending, depicting two characters falling into opposing categories of good and evil, as they fall from an exploding plane into the space of the postcolonial British nation. The narrative of translation and mutation is transported back West to a postcolonial London. Yet, as Chamcha and Farishta fall, the narrator insists their names perform a diabolical union. 'Gibreelsaladin Farishtach-amcha. Condemned to this endless but also ending angelicdevilish fall.'[53]

> Chamcha and Farishta also appear to be falling to their deaths, their surpris-ing survival is also an *act of translation*, appearing as a kind of metaphorical afterlife, 'To be born again first you have to die' sings Gibreel in the opening line of the novel. It is through their transmutation and hybridization that both survive the fall that is impossible to survive.

Chamcha the actor and Farishta the film star are already both experienced translators of their own identities. Gibreel Farishta has undergone numerous 'secular re-incarnations', adopting the name of an angel, playing roles of many Gods of different denominations on the screen. Saladin Chamcha, an anglicised postcolonial graduate from an English university is a doubly translated man, who has abandoned India for Britain, until returning with a British theatre company. His crossing to India confers the 'diabolic humiliation' of having his loathed Indian traits involuntarily re-emerge to haunt him on the flight back to Britain (p. 34). Removed from his previous assimilation into Englishness, his carefully constructed voice and face, his status as 'British citizen, first class'. His return journey transforms him into the devil as he is translated into an illegal immigrant, falling through the hybrid cloud forms. His new status is dramatically on the margins, as he has to lodge with the Indian migrant community of London that he always loathed. He, like Sufiya Zinobia, is condemned to haunt those friends of his previous life, having to face the widespread acceptance of his death by relatives and friends.

It is this reviled position that becomes the focus for examining how the postcolonial migrant community that Chamcha cannot avoid can create narratives that are new, through the translation of different narratives of containment, racism, cultural tradition and difference into potentially enabling positions of hybridity. That Chamcha's position is characterised as that of the Devil, implies that his unbelonging, his lack of history and origins are coded as a specifically diabolic state in the dominant codings of the society he now inhabits. Reading this transformation with Bhabha in mind, translation is retrieved from a state of radical loss and disorientation, despite this risk of 'mistranslation'.

Chamcha's increasingly evident transformation into the devil prompts the Shandaar cafe owner, Sufiyan, to address possible philosophical positions Chamcha might adopt on the 'delicate subject of mutation'. His scholarly elaboration of Ovid and Lucretius in such a context appears to exemplify the predicament of an emergent migrant, postcolonial apprehension of identity. 'The problem consists in whether the crossing of cultural frontiers permits freedom from the essence of the self, or whether, like wax, migration only changes the surface of the soul, preserving identity under its protean forms.' He translates Lucretius; both literally from Latin, and effects translation, by shifting the terms of reference to make the translation applicable to Chamcha's physical experience of his possible loss of self.

For Bhabha, the importance of this paradigm is that this supposed opposition is deconstructed by the migrant experience, such that the migrant lives in-between the options of Ovid and Lucretius, finding neither fully adequate to their experience. Diasporic identity is ambivalent, 'caught between nativist atavism and postcolonial metropolitan assimilation'. It is not simply one thing or the other, nor both at the same time, but a kind of negotiation between both positions. It is this that Bhabha terms the 'third space', a kind of doubleness or splitting of the subject which is enacted in the writing or articulation of identity.

The scene in Club Hot Wax offers a popular British migrant response to the choice offered to Chamcha of Ovid or Lucretius. The crowd choose a waxwork of a reviled public figure to be melted down. The wax is gleefully melted, until the figure is a pool on the floor. This appears as a seizure of the very terms of the paradigm Sufiyan has offered Chamcha, a reversal of its established significance, a crucial migrant intervention into established systems of meaning, and in this case the metaphors that sustain or prove them.

This kind of reversal of terms and meanings has been claimed as both a particularly postcolonial strategy and a postcolonial predicament by Gayatri Spivak, and following her Bhabha is quick to co-opt catachresis as an enabling narrative strategy. Catachresis, in its critical sense, is borrowed from post-structuralism, which in turn borrows it from Freud. The significance of its meaning, the misuse of words or terms, the wresting of meaning from its original referents, is, according to Spivak, its realisation of an 'impossible necessity' in the articulation of contemporary post-coloniality. Such a reversal of meaning is a choice made of necessity, brought about by the condition of post-coloniality.

Catachresis, as Spivak understands it, becomes a key process enabling and typifying emergent migrant narratives,

> You take positions in terms not of the discovery of historical or philosophical grounds, but in terms of reversing, displacing and seizing the apparatus of value-coding. This is what it means to say 'the agenda of onto-cultural commitments is negotiable.' In that sense post-coloniality far from being marginal, can show the irreducible margin in the centre.[54]

Although this appears to be a convincing account of the kinds of contingent and creative methods necessary for an emerging narrative to create meaning, what is less clear is the specificity of such tactics to a postcolonial sensibility. Bhabha is obviously aware of this problem, as he warns against attempts to co-opt catachresis into a postmodern celebration of pastiche, play or self-consciousness. However, Spivak categorises catachrestic narratives as belonging to 'the deconstructive philosophical position' and goes on to call post-coloniality a case of this position. It appears that an effective appropriation of the term is ambivalent, even at the moment of critical postcolonial investment; hence it is with some qualifications that catachresis may be appropriated for postcolonial ends.

Catachresis also suggests a writing of the third space. The logic of the third space follows a post-structuralist understanding of the logic of the supplement, emphasising the contradictory meanings of supplement as both 'added to' and 'excess'. Approaching the question of postcolonial identity could in itself be considered catachrestic. For Bhabha, 'any attempt, on my part, to frame the problem of identity leads inevitably to my being caught outside the frame, at once inside and out'.[55] The narratorial style in *The Satanic Verses* is suggestive of such a negotiation of the limits of those 'frames', as it displays a concern with a wrenching of value-coding from dominant Western narratives and an attempt to write emerging voices. The text enacts an exploration of the narratorial position that constitutes a conscious attempt to explore some of the conditions acting upon an emerging British-Asian diasporic voice.

The text performs a pastiche of a speaking voice. A first person 'moratoria voice' in the text, who demands, somewhat disingenuously, 'Look' and 'Listen'. Who also simulates conversing with and speaking for an imagined reader.

> Under extreme environmental pressure characteristics were acquired? What characteristics which? Slow down; you think Creation happens in a rush? So then, neither does revelation . . . take a look at the pair of them. Notice anything unusual? Just two brown men, falling hard, nothing so new about that, you may think; climbed too high, got above themselves, flew too close to the sun, is that it? That's not it listen.[56]

In these moments the text mimics a performance, emphasising a narratorial presence that threatens to become increasingly tangible. This commitment to illusion has the effect of creating a dynamic narrator akin to a conjurer or magician, performing himself at the limits of the text, deceiving with sleights of hand or tongue. Indeed, the narrator appears to be threatening to spill out of the constraints of the text, pushing at its limits in order to find an adequate position from which to narrate both the story and himself. It is the narrator's ambivalence about his own identity that means he must be addressed as more than a postmodern self-consciousness and playful pastiche.

The narrator might therefore be usefully characterised as a 'heretic'. A migrant translator concerned with his own hybrid and transformed identity. He engages with such ambivalence, plays in the narrative with representations of his own identity, in order to examine how translation can explore the spaces between cultures. As such he demonstrates how powerful transcultural negotiations are performed in the context of a migrant experience and the formation of hybrid identities.

The heresy of being a translator, for the writer, is writing against, disrupting, dislocating sacred narratives of belonging, tradition, cultural identity; exploring the spaces where cultural purity and easy access to origins are lost, remade and transformed. The writer narrating new identities, who dares to remake, is the subject of the narrator's self consciously playful questioning;

> A man who sets out to make himself up is taking on the creator's role according to one way of seeing things; he's unnatural a blasphemer, an abomination of abominations. From another angle, you could see pathos in him, heroism in his struggle, in his unwillingness to risk: not all mutants survive.
>
> (p. 49)

The narrator of *The Satanic Verses* teases the reader, parodying the ambivalence of the God that Gibreel Farishta sees, by disrupting his own authorial position, in his hints at his own identity.

> You think they fell a long way? In the matter of tumbles I yield pride of place to no personage, whether mortal or im-. From the clouds to ashes, down the chimney you might say, from heaven to hellfire.
>
> (Rushdie, p. 133)

Through the reading of hybridity as heresy, it becomes possible to approach these ambivalent statements as an ironic performance of what could be emerging as new narratives of cultural translation that interrupt existing discourses. The migrant narrator writing himself both out of and into the position of the devil emphasises both how radical and how dangerous such narratives and narrators might be.

> I know the truth, obviously. I watched the whole thing. As to omnipresence and -potence, I'm making no claims at present, but I can manage this much I hope. Chamcha willed it and Farishta did what was willed. Which was the miracle worker?
> Of what type was the miracle worker?
> Of what type – angelic, satanic – was Farishta's song?
> Who am I?
> Let's put it this way: who has the best tunes?
>
> (Rushdie, p. 10)

Bhabha proposes that blasphemy is 'a transgressive act of cultural translation' and that 'hybridity is heresy'.[57] He writes:

> Blasphemy is not merely a misrepresentation of the sacred by the secular; it is a moment when the subject matter or the content of a cultural tradition is being overwhelmed, or alienated, in the act of cultural translation.
>
> (p. 225)

Sara Suleri in particular is approving of Bhabha's insistence on the figure of translation as a key critical paradigm for unpacking *The Satanic Verses*. She comments,

> Much of the extensive discourse on the Verses crisis would gain a new cultural finesse if its interlocutors could similarly apprehend the figurative status of translation in order to identify the mobility of postcolonial Islamic culture and its manifold capacity to be borne across.[58]

For Bhabha, the migrant narrator/cultural translator must therefore blaspheme, in order to re-write and re-make narratives that engage with the assumed transparency of culture, origins and identity. The notion of a transgressive act of cultural translation has resonances of a catachrestic narrative manoeuvre as Spivak defines it. The narrator engages gleefully in the process of entangling the sacred and secular writing each through the other and in qualifying the migrant positions of both Chamcha and Farishta. Here the idea of the wresting of meaning from its proper referents, the 'misuse of words and terms' in its most literal sense, pervades a text that is preoccupied with blurring the distinctions between sacred and secular. The 'satanic' verses themselves, as Gibreel relates them, could be viewed as a literal catachresis. That is if one allows a stretching of the term itself, as a perversion, a misuse of words, from Spivak's 'concept metaphor without an adequate referent that perverts its embedded context'.[59]

Gibreel's admittance, in the question of the verses, 'it was me both times, baba, me first and second also me' offers a postcolonial re-reading and re-writing of culture, enabled through the inhabiting of a third space, where the internal difference in writing is revealed, a deconstruction of oppositions, a reversal and displacement of meaning, and which finds itself inevitably heretical . Here then, if we follow Bhabha's arguments about the third space, hybridity (the third space) is heresy.

Gibreel's predicament of having words, sentences and an unknowable language pass through him, flowing without his agency or comprehension, appears no better than Chamcha's terrible utterances in the police van where his attempts to speak are translated into goat bleatings. His agency removed he becomes the object of a harsh racist discourse of the policemen that makes him unrecognisable to himself.

> Saladin had no way of telling if they were simply insulting him or if his vocal cords had truly been infected, as he feared, by this macabre demoniasis that had overcome him without the slightest warning.[60]

Without a 'seizure of the apparatus of value coding', the speaking subject will be rendered impotent, by an objectification that translates agency or intention away, re-coding it in terms unrecognisable to the speaker. This is the migrant state, as Bhabha notes, quoting John Berger's account of a Turkish worker in Germany. 'He learnt twenty new words of the new language. He learnt girl. What the word meant when he used it, was that he was a randy dog.'[61] The ironies of such an argument in relation to this text in particular can surely not be overlooked. Might not the demands for the banning of Rushdie's book itself by British-Asian Muslims in Bradford and elsewhere, find them ironically being translated and transformed in ways very similar to those that Bhabha describes here?

It is not that Rushdie is unaware of this as predicament for the migrant with little political or social capital; indeed, he continually dramatises this predicament in the text. Hence Chamcha's apprehension that his translation into a migrant has transformed him into a devil. The seizure of the apparatus of value coding suddenly appears as a miserable and demoralising affair. The reclamation of the devil as an act of cultural enablement appears futile and personally damaging to him.

> 'Chamcha', Mishal said excitedly, 'you're a hero. I mean, people can really identify with you. It's an image white society has rejected for so long that we can really make it our own. It's time you considered action.' 'Go away' cried Saladin in his bewilderment, 'This isn't what I wanted. This is not what I meant at all.'[62]

The uncanny repetition, Chamcha repeating a *repeated* line from Prufrock, effects a reading of Chamcha through a multiple spiralling of meanings. A catachresis that appropriates and perverts the embedded context of the line, situating the fact of Chamcha's 'reincarnation' as devil, read through the reference to the raising of Lazarus from the dead. Further, Eliot's line is disturbed in a translation of the recognisably modernist utterance, to become the rewriting of this reference, to evoke the condition of the migrant having to negotiate the construction of meanings from a position that cannot be avoided. The utterance is also an intervention, 'that is not what I meant at all', a statement referring to another, where intentionality has been thwarted, such that the line is a reclamation of intentionality even in the moment of frustration. The absurdity of the 'illegal immigrant' borrowing lines from the 'canonized great writer', (but also paradoxically an immigrant), to best describe his position, offers a comic and dramatic intervention. It is not a reply to, but an appropriation of, repetition of, the codes of the West that denies the priority of the original: the cultural heresy of postcolonial translation.

Britain is still living with the impact of Rushdie's exploration of the cultural heresy of hybridity. Although this 'heresy' has had drastic consequences for Rushdie, its significance clearly goes beyond the realm of the religious, of any particular offences Rushdie has been accused of. Although Rushdie's own position appears to have become less precarious, with the withdrawal of official financial incentives for the Fatwa by Iran, 'The Rushdie affair' points to the way in which Bhabha's model of cultural difference accurately approaches the incommensurability of competing demands both within the bounds of the nation and beyond them. It is also important not to figure the opposition to *The Satanic Verses* in terms of a conflict between ancient and modern in any simplistic historical dialectic. Bhabha comments in several interviews at the time that the protests against Rushdie were demands being made in the present, not from communities somehow trapped in the past, in ancient ways of life, but from people living and working in the 'modern nation' of Britain. Timothy Brennan's comments on class as an overlooked strand in the positions taken over the text are very useful here. As Pnina Werbner points out, the stereotype of Muslim readers as responding in purely religious terms to the novel needs to be challenged, and an understanding of aesthetic 'disgust and shock' needs addressing if an informed debate about this text is to take place.[63]

However, the attempt to account for and find a narrative strategy to address adequately the impact of migration on cultural and national identity remains central to any model of postcolonial Britain. Theories of cultural translation and the migrant's double vision, of time-lag and belatedness and of the haunting of national narratives by spectral narratives of colonialism, offer significant interrogations of the ways in which writing and living newness can be possible. In particular, if Bhabha's engagement with post-structuralist thinking, especially that of Derrida, is suggestive of the possibility of writing the nation anew, it is because it engages with the paradox of revolution: 'the more the new erupts [. . .] the more one has to convoke the old'.

In exposing the aporetic conditions of national identities, of choosing to belong, Rushdie has had an immense impact on revisions of both nation and identity in Britain. However, this suggests that the migrant's position is far from being an ahistorical embracing of all cultures and beliefs, rather the injunction choose, choose, provides a basis for the deconstruction of nation. In Spivak's words,

> I do not think the cosmopolitan *challenge* to national culture is perceived by Rushdie as only a challenge. It is an aporia for him, an impossible decision between two opposed decidables with two mutually canceling sets of consequences, a decision which gets made nonetheless.[64]

2 Unpacking Homi Bhabha's Library: Bhabha, Said and the Postcolonial Archive

Let us not begin at the beginning, or even at the archive.[1]

Unpacking My Library ... Again.[2]

Being mindful of the dangers of assuming one can start at the beginning and of presuming to define the limits of any text, or canon of texts, let us not begin at the beginning, but by 'unpacking' Homi Bhabha's library. Such a tentative beginning lies somewhere between citing a citation (Bhabha's title adapts Walter Benjamin's essay 'Unpacking my Library') and signalling an attempt to work through the sources, origins or inspirations for Bhabha's thinking.[3] Bhabha's work has been characterised by several highly influential interventionist essays and papers published in diverse places, some delivered to specific audiences ('The Commitment to Theory' at the *Questions of Third Cinema* Conference, in Edinburgh, 1986, 'Manifesto for the Re-Invention of Britain' at the British Council conference *Re-Inventing Britain* in 1998), as well as forwards and prefaces, editorials and art criticism. Bart Moore-Gilbert suggests that the re-publication of most of Bhabha's early essays in *The Location of Culture* has enabled a reconsideration of his contribution to contemporary critical debates.

> When they are considered as a developing body of work, rather than as a series of discrete articles published in journals that are widely dispersed in different disciplinary and geographical locations, it becomes much easier to appreciate the degree to which Bhabha challenges the vision of his predecessors in the postcolonial field and those of Fanon and Said in particular.[4]

Certainly the essays collected in this book do constitute a major part of Bhabha's output. And since its publication in 1994 it has enabled a consideration of these essays as representing definite and developed strands of thought, key preoccupations and the testing of certain theoretical propositions. Equally, though, the collection represents a diversity of thinking, investigation and subject, which also relates to the extensive writing that exists outside this text and which will be considered in this volume. There may be risks of homogenisation involved in attempting to address this collection of texts as an oeuvre.

Bhabha's postcolonial narrative strategies mirror many rhetorical aspects in the work of the critic he frequently expresses a debt to, Frantz Fanon. On occasion, Bhabha's comments on Fanon might easily be repeated and applied to his own work. This is a gesture performed by Robert Young when he notes that Bhabha writes of

> Fanon's search for a conceptual form appropriate to the social antagonism of the colonial relation' and of the 'colonial condition that drove Fanon from one conceptual scheme to another'. This description could equally well apply to Bhabha himself: in his essays we see him move from the model of fetishism to those of 'mimicry' hybridisation and 'paranoia'.[5]

It is intriguing to see the way in which Bhabha's style also 'attempts such audacious, often impossible, transformations of truth and value' that he claims for Fanon. Indeed, his apprehension of the ways in which Fanon's narrative can be seen to operate would seem to be precisely why his own work engages in shifting terminologies, word play, the exploitation of 'spaces' in ideological or conceptual schemas, a restless dissatisfaction with binaries, a constant moving back and forth between supposed singularities and opposites that seeks to unwork or unravel them.

One must also consider the strange order of repetition and translation, of iterability involved in the creation of any collection. In this case, some of Bhabha's original essays and the copies of them re-published in the collection have substantial differences. Locating a particular statement as it was originally delivered, reflecting on audiences, events, catalogues, produces a sense of these essays as potentially a body of developing linked ideas, but paradoxically also often very situated, such as Bhabha's essay on Anish Kapoor published in his exhibition catalogue for the Hayward Gallery.[6] It is questions of ordering, of location, that preoccupy Bhabha. Indeed, it seems quite fitting that Bhabha's work as represented in *The Location of Culture* appears both as an interconnected body of work and as discrete itinerant interventions in key critical and political and cultural debates.

I   Disordered texts

'Does the order of books determine the order of things?' This is the question, replete with its Foucauldian resonance, that Homi Bhabha asks in the opening paragraph of his essay 'Unpacking my Library ... Again'.[7] Bhabha

opens with Walter Benjamin's words, conjuring them into an echo, a translation, reading in a characteristically post-structuralist way, by at points
imitating or following the contours of another text. In this case it shares
its name and imbricates itself within that text, an activity that also leaves
a trace of itself in the text it reads, and which blurs the distinction between
original text, criticism and reading.

> I am unpacking my library again. Yes I am. The books are not yet on the
> shelves, not yet touched by the mild boredom of order ... Instead I must ask
> you to join me in the disorder of crates.[8]

Reflecting on his own then-recent move to Chicago and on the strange process of unpacking and shelving his books, he proposes that 'in subtle ways
that disorder challenges the shelved order of the study, and displaces the
Dewey decimal' (p. 199). He points to a certain kind of dislocation, a 'cosmopolitan' disorder, in which the contingency of unpacked, half-shelved
books, 'through their concatentation and contestation produce a shared
belief in the need for Benjamin's ethical and aesthetic imperative: the
renewal of life through dislocation, translation and re-situation' (p. 200).
Bhabha's description characteristically pairs or groups assonant terms,
contingency, concatentation and contestation, enabling them to jostle
together, while also calling attention to a self-reflexive awareness of the
metaphoricity of language.

This image of books that have been removed from their original shelves
(where one supposes some kind of order had been created, if not quite the
ordering of librarian's classification), boxed together in haphazard fashion
and then pulled out in piles or pairs is a useful figure for Bhabha's critical
and political interests. It works both as an actual practice and as a meto-
nymic figure for postcolonial interventions into Western epistemology. The
possibilities that re-ordering the books one has might in some way re-order
the knowledge held therein and create interesting new ways of reading those
books, perhaps even enable a new way of thinking, is one key strand of postcolonial practice, offering critical interventions into canonised and established ways of thinking and reading. Bhabha is taken by Benjamin's rather
tantalising suggestion that 'the acquisition of an old book is its rebirth'.[9] We
might stretch that terminology just enough to consider not only the physical
act of acquiring a book on the part of a collector, who perhaps values and
treasures the previously neglected text, but also considering the intellectual
acquisition, whether in an academic context or otherwise, of texts and the
thinking they engender within an academic context, a particular discipline,
or a revolutionary or insurgent movement. Bhabha adeptly illustrates such
a move himself, of course, by resurrecting Benjamin's words and asserting

a relation for postcolonial thinking with the work of a Jewish thinker and later refugee from Nazi Germany. The intellectual acquisition of Benjamin by Bhabha was also having the effect that Benjamin claimed for the collector of books, effecting the rebirth, and re-reading of an old text through its re-ordering, its accession into a new 'library', which we might take to mean not just the personal or institutional collection of books, but the sources or the archives of a discipline, a body of knowledge.

I want to suggest that this last description may be a particularly useful way of thinking about postcolonial theory and criticism which, it seems, has always been preoccupied with its status as a body of knowledge, with its perceived newness within academic departments, with its difference from, or relationship to, other critical approaches to literature, culture and politics. Bhabha's image of ordering and re-ordering books in a library seems particularly suited to certain strands of his postcolonial critical practice. This is not to say that postcolonialism only exists in the library: rather, it invokes the notion of the archive, the sense of archive as both Michel Foucault and Jacques Derrida have (differently) understood it, as central to the establishment of any form of knowledge, any discipline and hence the somewhat unruly 'discipline' (transitional and interdisciplinary) of postcolonial criticism.

Considering the way that the library is ostensibly at once a place for accessing information freely and retaining that information for all, but which also regulates and guards, protects and regulates access to that information, then it inhabits a kind of paradox. If we extend this to consider an archive, a place where all the sources, evidence, documents, etc. for any discipline, any society or civilisation might be stored, it is immediately apparent that this might be of interest to a postcolonial practice that involves *reading against* canonised and institutionalised versions of history. Following Bhabha's commentary then, clearly postcolonial criticism is characterised by a profound scepticism about the truth claims of 'archives' – understood as narratives that structure people's lives and interpellate them – in the West and in postcolonial nations. Critically for Bhabha, his echoing of Benjamin in this short essay is only a small part of a profound interaction with Benjamin's writings more broadly, notably the latter's *Theses on the Philosophy of History.*[10] For Bhabha, what is perhaps Benjamin's most quoted statement on history – 'There is no document of civilisation which is not at the same time a document of barbarism' – must be a central tenet of his own postcolonial critical models and interventions. It is evident in his understanding of colonial discourse and colonial power as ambivalent, both professing to civilise and attempting to contain and control.

If we take a brief detour into Derrida's understanding of the archive, it becomes clear that a preoccupation with archives, that is with the establishment of knowledge or 'truth' and power, is of central concern to postcolonialism, and of particular interest to Bhabha in critical parts of his work. Derrida suggests that,

> The meaning of the archive its only meaning comes from the Greek, arkeion: initially a house, a domicile, an address, the residence of the superior magistrates, the archons, those who commanded. [. . .] The archons are first of all the document's guardians. They do not only ensure the physical security of what is deposited and of the substrate. They are also accorded the hermeneutic right and competence. They have the power to interpret the archives. Entrusted to such archons, these documents in effect speak the law: they recall the law and call on or impose the law.[11]

In the case of Bhabha and to an extent Walter Benjamin, when referring to their own personal libraries, located in their own homes, of which they themselves are guardian, this might seems to exempt them from complicity with the rules of the archive as Derrida sees them. The rules align the archive with the state, with law and the protection of power that the archive seems to perform. However, the critical aspect of the *archon* is not just guardian but the one entrusted with the power to interpret. Bhabha evokes a 'guardianship' of meanings, histories and interpretations that have to be actively undone by a postcolonial intervention. This is another way of saying of course that the archive and the processes of archivisation are far from being neutral transparent cataloguers of actual events, or truths, but produce those events and decide what *constitutes* an event.

For postcolonial criticism this is an important assertion, one that Bhabha has explored in several important ways, notably in his work on colonial discourse analysis and in his proposal of the concept of time-lag or belatedness. Any complacent assumptions of a linear and progressive history are interrupted by the belated arrival and intervention of revisions, rewritings and challenges to the very foundations of key concepts of modernity. Bhabha restlessly returns to questions of modernity in his work through the concept of the time lag and belatedness in particular. In '"Race", time and the revision of modernity', Bhabha insists that postcolonial criticism has undergone a shift of emphasis, from 'elaborating an anti-imperialist or black nationalist tradition "in itself"', to attempting to 'interrupt the Western discourses of modernity through these displacing, interrogative perspectives they engender.'[12] Interruption is an important word here as it avoids a binary oppositional mode, – an 'anti-colonial' discourse – and asserts a model of displacing, unsettling and disrupting.

Bhabha might be understood, then, as a 'reader of archives', who in re-ordering them, intervening in their cataloguing process, inevitably re-orders the kinds of knowledge they are able to speak. In this sense he attempts not merely to guard them as an archon might, but rather to liberate them from what Derrida calls their domiciliation, their house arrest. This is a particularly suggestive image for Bhabha's work as he has (perhaps over-hastily) been associated with theories of migrancy, cultural translation and diaspora. This has been a key area in Bhabha's work that has attracted enthusiasm and dissent in equal quantities and will be further discussed in a later chapter.

Bhabha proposes a parallel between the private library and the rather larger body of knowledge, or archive of Western metaphysics, where the disciplines and knowledge prized in the history of Western knowledge and power may be re-read or re-written. His work frequently asks questions about how modernity might be understood and how modernity experienced otherwise or elsewhere might 'inhabit' or conversely 'unhome' existing models of the effects or principles of modernity.

He describes this practice again with recourse to Foucault, appealing to Foucault's 'rule of repeatable materiality', which is outlined in Part III of *The Archaeology of Knowledge*, 'The Statement and the Archive'. Foucault's text is an attempt to consider how knowledge is conceived in Western culture, and by what criteria it can be identified as such, how it is organised into disciplines or documented and verified. A brief discussion of his inquiry into the nature of a document in the discipline of history demonstrates the ways in which his work might be of use to Bhabha.

> The document then is no longer for history an inert material through which it tries to reconstitute what men have done or said, the events of which only a trace remains. [. . .] The document is not the fortunate tool of a history that is primarily and fundamentally memory; history is one way in which a society recognises and develops a mass of documentation with which it is inextricably linked.[13]

For Foucault,

> Despite the schemata of use and application that constitute a field of stabilization for the statement, any change in the statement's condition of use and reinvestment, any alteration in its field of experience or verification, or indeed

any difference in the problems to be solved, can lead to the emergence of a
new statement: the difference of the same.

(pp. 102–5)

This understanding of the ways in which documents might be read differently and will continue to be re-written lies at the heart of his notion of
time lag or belatedness. In Bhabha's model, the postcolonial intervenes
into Western narratives through 'the establishment of other historical sites,
other forms of enunciation'. More than this, its power lies in an almost tangible experience of 'slowing down', 'it is the function of the lag to slow down
the linear progressive time of modernity to reveal its "gesture", its tempi
'the pauses and stresses of the whole performance'. Bhabha returns here to
Benjamin in his final phrase, freely appropriating a discussion of Brecht
for his own ends, 'damning the stream of real life, by bringing the flow to a
standstill in a reflex of astonishment'.[14]

However, notwithstanding the critical role of postcolonial interventions
into master-narratives and the violent and violating histories of colonialism, postcolonial criticism as practised in academic institutions has several serious problematics to negotiate in terms of its own status and truth
claims, with which Bhabha is concerned. In an interview with David Bennet
and Terry Collits in 1992, Bhabha was asked a question frequently put in
different ways, about the status of postcolonial criticism:

> The term postcolonial criticism is a comparatively recent addition to the West-
> ern academic lexicon. Given that its perspectives are said to emerge from the
> subversive, 'subaltern' discourses of minorities and anti-colonial testimonies
> of Third-World countries could you comment on the institutional provenance
> of the term and the kinds of affiliations that it identifies, projects or – perhaps
> falsely – presumes?[15]

He comments,

> I think we should be very attentive to the fact that the Western liberal academy,
> by its very nature, requires new disciplines, new connections between the dis-
> ciplines; otherwise it is unable to represent the kind of liberal pedagogies that
> it is concerned with. But these new disciplines and new topics are not entirely
> generated at the institutional level. One has to grab the thorn of translation if
> one wants to change the terms in which the issues will be seen both within the
> culture industries and in the academies, if we can effect certain redefinitions
> there then that does actually press on policy institutions. [...] There is a form
> of communality that is to some extent specific to what I understand to be the
> most exciting, but also some of the most ambiguous conditions, discursive
> conditions, historical conditions – of postcolonial critique. This is the fact that

unlike say, Marxism, and its academic or theoretical manifestations or even
its political applications, postcoloniality doesn't have a master text.

(p. 60)

If we unpack this statement a little, it provides a useful point of entry into
thinking about the postcolonial critical field and Bhabha's position as one
of the major theorists to emerge in and transform it. He points to the perceived position of postcolonialism as a Western academic discipline that
looks to its origins in anti-colonialist discourses characterised by their
opposition to Western colonialism, power and ongoing hegemony. However, rather than seeing this as an acutely disabling paradox, he insists that
it is precisely from this very fraught and ambiguous position that postcolonialism can achieve some of its most useful insights.

The discipline may be to some extent caught by its incorporation into the
'Western liberal academy'. However, for Bhabha, any assumption that incorporation is complete and merely serves the interests of the Western establishment and its power and knowledge base, overlooks the ways in which
this 'interstitial' or interventionary position may transform, or in one of
Bhabha's key terms 'translate', the very terms by which culture or academic
knowledge may be understood. Although this risks giving the impression
that postcolonialism works best in theoretical terms, or textual, academic
terms, Bhabha also refuses any simple binary opposition between text and
politics, or establishment and subversive. Instead, he insists 'certain redefi-
nitions actually press on policy institutions'. This suggests that rather than
thinking in comfortable binaries, a postcolonial position might find itself
confounding the traditional oppositions between theory and politics, or
theoretical and activist. It also suggestively echoes Edward Said's interventions in the question of the 'politics of knowledge', in *Orientalism*, a text of
considerable importance for Bhabha's work, where Said comments,

> What I am interested in doing now is suggesting how the general liberal con-
> sensus that 'true' knowledge is fundamentally non-political (and conversely
> that overtly political knowledge is not true knowledge) obscures the highly
> if obscurely organised political circumstances obtaining when knowledge is
> produced.[16]

Bhabha's further assertion that postcolonialism does not have master text
also raises some interesting questions. What are the origins or conditions of
postcolonialism? How best can its operations be characterised if it is hard
to locate an origin for it, or to identify its limit or boundary in relation to
other disciplines or theoretical approaches? Postcolonial criticism and theory has spent a considerable amount of time thinking through its origins,

its source texts, its canon(s) and its status as a discipline. This is a pressing question at this moment for those thinking about, of and through, the postcolonial, which instead of receding with time has become ever more fraught and urgent. As Bart Moore-Gilbert, Gareth Stanton and Willy Maley note in *Postcolonial Criticism*,

> It is significant that much of postcolonial criticism is concerned with self definition, with circumscribing a space, academic, geographical, political – within which something called postcolonialism can occur. Every new movement or school sooner or later breaks down, through internal division or external pressure. In the case of postcolonialism, this process of dissolution has marked it from its inception. Most essays that begin by asking what postcolonialism is soon turn into diagnoses of what is wrong with it. It is difficult to think of a modern intellectual practice that has been subject to more self-criticism.[17]

One potential reason for this is the sense that the postcolonial *is* starting to become defined; a certain amount of sedimentation is taking place, which however unwelcome in certain quarters is also unavoidable. The 'skeleton' of a discipline is emerging, key texts and themes have established themselves, or perhaps been established. Paradoxically then, postcolonialism as a critical and political strategy may be being haunted by what it will become. The numerous readers and critical introductions also inevitably find themselves dwelling on this subject; that is to say, on the very difficult question of origins or beginnings of postcolonial criticism, and of the spaces and places it might have found in the academy and elsewhere. As Ania Loomba notes in *Colonialism/postcolonialism*:

> Many people are not clear what is new about these studies – it is true that the term postcolonialism has become so heterogeneous and diffuse that it is impossible to satisfactorily describe what its study might entail. This difficulty is partly due to the interdisciplinary nature of postcolonial studies, which may range from literary analysis to research in the archives of colonial government from the critique of medical texts to economic theory, and usually combine these and other areas.[18]

Certainly postcolonial criticism has undergone a rapid diversification and expansion in its subject matter, its attention to different histories, cultures, theoretical approaches, engagement with globalisation transnationalism, political movements for independence, autonomy and indigenous land claims. It might be possible to read this flood of new readers, introductions, critical journals, and so on (including this text) as signalling that postcolonial thinking is engaging with, or becoming overwhelmed by, issues of disciplinarity within the academy, the departments it might function in, the demands it makes on interdisciplinarity, the kinds of academics it fosters, and hence is in the process of establishing and being haunted by its archives. Simultaneously, postcolonialism has continually and is constantly exceeding the boundaries of its institutional incarnations: some of its earliest source texts were not written in academic institutions, it also makes claims for a radical political engagement with what it terms subaltern and minority discourses.

Thus Bhabha's characterisation of postcolonialism as at once to varying degrees embedded into the Western academy but also always exceeding its limits and transforming its concerns and frames of reference might be an appropriate way of characterising the troubling position of this discipline which wants to question the terms of disciplinarity as they currently operate.

Of course, in one sense every time any postcolonial writing takes place it must signal in some way its debt to thinking from elsewhere, to sources of whatever kind. In that sense, postcolonial work has always been involved in referencing and hence incorporating, or appropriating, that is 'archiving', a hugely diverse range of material. However, in certain incarnations it has particularly been characterised by its focus on a revisionary relation to 'other' archives, on the one hand, and by often quite bitter wrangling over the propriety of using different modes of thinking, not considered by certain critics to be properly postcolonial.

Post-structuralist thinking has been a particular focus of criticism from a range of postcolonial critics, based both in the West and in formerly colonised countries, such as Aijaz Ahmad and Benita Parry. Even the later writings of Edward Said have suggested that it is a Western mode of analysis and has no place in methodologies of those critiquing the dominance of Western ideologies and colonialism.

This will particularly concern us here, as Bhabha has been one of the major critics whose work is associated with this approach, along with Gayatri Spivak. As we have seen, this questioning of what is properly postcolonial has accompanied the rise of postcolonialism, both inside and outside academic debates. However, if the arguments seem to have taken on a new urgency, this may be because postcolonial thinking is perceived to have opened up new territories of investigation, to have made claims for new vocabularies, to have, in short, very firmly arrived in the institution, while retaining its very cogent critique of institutional practices in the West. As the dust settles, so does the intellectual fallout.

It is perhaps ironic that Said was at least initially viewed as bringing theory associated with post-structuralism into use in the realm of colonialism and issues of race, as this is precisely a criticism often levelled at Bhabha, as if his work had introduced an alien critical approach. Said's later crisis over this methodology and his return to professing a highly fraught and problematic humanism (while arguably his texts still perform post-structuralist readings) has led to a somewhat complacent perception that Bhabha has introduced extraneous theoretical models to postcolonial thinking proper. These characterisations have at least partly been founded in the identification of Bhabha's work with key concepts in Jacques Derrida's oeuvre. Bhabha's fruitful intellectual dwelling between post-structuralism, psycho-analytic theory (between Freud and Lacan) and postcolonial theory marks his eclectic vocabulary, his migrating metaphors and borrowings. Bhabha's important readings and critiques of Said's model of Orientalism owe much to this nexus.

In fact, Said relies heavily on the thinking of Michel Foucault to formulate his model of colonial discourse, and is explicitly exploring the suitability of post-structuralist models of discourse. In *The Archaeology of Knowledge*, Foucault identifies archives not as all the documents ever kept by a culture, but as a system of knowledge production, which actually defines what it is possible to say or know.[19] In doing so, he suggests a crucial post-structuralist tenet on the relation between the text and what is often referred to as 'the real'. Instead of opposing history and politics (as real things which are knowable and definable) to texts, literary or otherwise, post-structuralist criticism suggests this opposition is a false one. History and politics, even everyday life, are experienced through language and hence through the structures of textuality that presupposes. If we examine Said's description of his own project in *Orientalism*, he illustrates that a post-structuralist account of archiving is one of the founding premises of the text.

Said explicitly refers to Foucauldian thought in order to propose a methodology for the task ahead of him.

> I have found it useful here to employ Michel Foucault's notion of a discourse, as described by him, in *The Archaeology of Knowledge* and *Discipline and Punish*, to identify Orientalism. My contention here is that without examining Orientalism as a discourse one cannot possibly understand the enormously systematic discipline by which European culture was able to manage – and even – produce – the Orient politically, sociologically, militarily, ideologically, scientifically, and imaginatively during the post-Enlightenment period.
>
> (p. 42)

His assertion was that colonialism could not be fully analysed, understood or opposed without attention to the ways in which it had not only been a military and economic project, but had also operated crucially as a discourse of domination, one that produced 'knowledge' about the east or

Orient, by the West, which simultaneously attempted to (mis)interpret,
distort or silence indigenous cultural and political production. Said's proposal is that, from the late eighteenth century onwards, Orientalism operated as a way of 'dominating, structuring and having authority over the
Orient'.[20]

In *The* Archaeology *of Knowledge*, we also find Foucault's description of
archives; which, as we have already noted, are intimately linked with the disciplines and discourses they enable the West to produce. Archives are not

> The sum of all texts that a culture has kept upon its person as documents attest-
> ing to its own past; or as evidence of a continuing identity. [. . .] The archive
> is the first law of what can be said, the system that governs the appearance of
> statements as unique events. [. . .] The archive is not that which, despite its
> immediate escape, safeguards the event of the statement and preserves, for
> future memories its status as an escapee, [. . .] nor is it that which collects the
> dust of statements that have become inert once more, and which may make
> possible the miracle of their resurrection; it is that which defines the mode of
> occurrence of the statement-thing; it is the system of its functioning.
>
> (p. 129)

Orientalism is fascinated with this notion of archiving and with the violence of archivisation, as it impacts the colonial and postcolonial subject.
In Foucault's model, archives do not safeguard an event and preserve it for
posterity; archiving is not neutral, but a political process, which enables or
disables speech, statements, knowledge. In other words, the archive deter-
mines what events, disciplines or models of thought both did and can take
place.

Bhabha gestures towards the significance of this understanding in a postcolonial context in his long review of Henry Louis Gates Jr's *Black Literature
and Literary Theory*, in *Poetics Today*.[21]

> The initiatives of feminist criticism, black literature or the study of colonial
> discourse have not simply added different literary *content* to the annals of
> literature in English; they have, at best changed the very concept of *time*
> through which we construct the literary as a narrative of tradition, cultural
> cohesion and national, patriarchal or racial authority. The effect of this shift
> in time is nothing less than a re-orientation in our sense of the history of lit-
> erature itself.[22]

A contemporary example of this might be an experience that the Black
British critic Lola Young cites of Mary Seacole, a Black woman from
Jamaica, who worked as an informal doctor and entrepreneur ministering
to soldiers in the Crimean War. She published an account of her travels,

Wonderful Adventures of Mrs Seacole in Many Lands, (1857). However, until recently, she was little known compared with Florence Nightingale, despite her considerable fame as a cause célèbre in Britain during her own lifetime. The astounded pupils accused her of making it up to make them feel better.[23] Bhabha notes that Gate's account of the significance of creating a critical perspective and definition of 'a canon of literature that accounted for the African (or black) perspective', takes it as unquestionable that 'the canon of literature in English is a "genetic mulatto"'.[24] Yet Lola Young's experience as she recounts it is that the introduction of Seacole's text to the classroom is met with incredulity, such are the shifts in perception and conception of canonicity, history and narrative that it effects.

Bhabha comments that shifts in literary values do not take place 'simply through the revelation of authors or ideas or cultural traditions that were once "hidden from history" – masculinist or colonialist' but rather it is through the change in the 'semiotic "value" of the sign – its differential, non-mimetic articulation of a "reality" that is systemic rather than serial, *textual* rather than teleological – that the voices of otherness profoundly change the texture of Tradition'.[25]

Seacole's account of her early life in Jamaica, her hybrid Creole identity ('I am a Creole and have good Scotch blood coursing in my veins'), her travels to Panama, England and then the Crimea, demonstrates Bhabha's observations in its confounding of generic boundaries, as a travelogue, autobiography and at times war journal, its negotiations with conventions around female authorship, mobility and propriety, as she carefully stages her patriotic and empathetic motives for travel, her identity as 'Mother' Seacole tending to her 'sons' and her respectable relationship with the British Army evidenced through the inclusion in her text of numerous letters of commendation and thanks from soldiers and officers she has nursed or served in her 'British Hotel'. Sara Salih notes, in her introduction to the recent Penguin edition, 'the multiple and shifting nature of Seacole's cultural and "racial" affiliations is striking' such that the text must be read as a diasporic differential narrative interrupting canonical categories and orthodoxies about women's writing in the mid-nineteenth century. By bringing the material and violent histories of war, racism and slavery in 'other places' and 'other times' into radical collision with these orthodoxies, Seacole's text must also simultaneously attempt to insert itself into acceptable and respectable modes of presentation for consumption by a British reading audience.[26] Reading it and teaching it as Bhabha has suggested must effect a systemic shift in and re-orientation of an understanding of the history of literature, demand new vocabularies and profound shifts of focus.

II Disturbed archives

In his lengthy critique of *Orientalism*, Aijaz Ahmad is quick to identify Said's use of Foucault as a problem and to consider its implications for postcolonial thinking. He turns these proposals about archiving onto Said's own work, asking what archive Said's work comes out of and how this affects what it is possible for him to know or say. He is concerned about the question of the sources and origins for the framework of discussion in *Orientalism*, and the tension between acknowledged and unacknowledged precursors for Said's text. He notes that among the many sources cited by Said there are three key source texts, two of which are consciously referred to: the work of Michel Foucault, as we have already seen, Antonio Gramsci's *Prison Notebooks*, which Said also quotes from, and Eric Auerbach's *Mimesis*, which Ahmad suggests is not properly acknowledged. He goes as far as to suggest that Auerbach is the absent anti-hero of Said's text.

Turning first to Gramsci, Ahmad suggests that Said uses Gramsci as an inspirational voice, which initiates his own critical project. He comments,

> In the prison notebooks Gramsci says: 'The starting point in critical elaboration is the consciousness of what one really is, and is 'knowing thyself' as a product of the historical process to date, which has deposited in you an infinity of traces, without leaving an inventory.' The only available English translation inexplicably leaves Gramsci's comment at that, whereas in fact Gramsci's Italian text concludes by adding, 'therefore it is imperative at the outset to compile such an inventory'.[27]

Said goes on to say that his own investigation into Orientalism is marked by a personal involvement. 'In many ways my study of Orientalism has been an attempt to inventory the traces upon me, the Oriental subject, of the culture whose domination has been so powerful a factor in the life of all Orientals.'[28] Nevertheless, how easy is it to make an inventory of traces? Said suggests that postcolonial criticism must attempt to make an archive out of evidence left behind, or marks, traces on the individual, to piece together a political and critical account of colonial discourse and Orientalism. Ahmad takes issue with Said's choice of material to go into this inventory. He asks why this 'inventory' of traces should take the form of a counter-reading of the Western canonical textualities, mainly in the cognate areas of literature and philology, from Greek tragedy onwards?[29] Ahmad's point is that Said appeared to break with preceding critical models in humanities and social sciences, liberating his thinking processes, but in actuality he was deploying

the most traditional of reading and critical practices, from the discipline he
was trained in, comparative literature.

He comments,

> Orientalism was clearly not a book of Middle Eastern studies, or of any estab-
> lished academic discipline, but it did belong to the well known intellectual
> tradition of writers debunking the great monuments of their own academic
> disciplines or examining the complicity of intellectuals in dominant ideolo-
> gies and fabrications of illegitimate power.[30] Ahmad sees the outline of Said's
> own classical training as a scholar of comparative literature structuring Said's
> thinking and accuses him of trying to write a counter-history to Auerbach's
> 'magisterial *Mimesis*'.

Although Said admittedly has huge difficulties squaring his use of Foucault
with his commitment to humanist thinking as exemplified by Auerbach,
Ahmad seems to miss here the formation of one of Said's most critical
strategies of reading: counterpoint. In *Culture and Imperialism*, Said notes
that the effect of reading dominant narratives in literature or history is
that the marginalised or silenced voices of the colonised need to be read
back in to the picture. The effect of such counterpoint, however, is that the
once-marginalised narrative does not simply get added on to the existing
dominant one to create a fuller or better picture. Rather, the contrapuntal
reading calls into question the assumptions and values of the dominant,
hegemonic narrative.

Bhabha's own work on what he terms postcolonial 'interventions' into
narratives of modernity would appear to have much in common with Said's
model of counterpoint. The unending revisions and disruptions of a notion
of a smoothly evolving Western history performed by the 'time-lag' Bhabha
identifies have something in common with the musical model that Said
uses.

Ahmad's dissatisfaction with Said's starting point reflects, I think, a much
wider anxiety about beginnings and origins. Bhabha's comment on this
subject in a different context seems particularly helpful here,

> supposing I suggest to you that the real anxiety posted by post-structuralism
> is that its temporality is such that it always makes you pose the question of
> where you are beginning. Its not the problem of ends; it always re-poses as it
> were, from the end the question of where one is starting from, where one is
> demanding one's authority from.[31]

Bhabha's insight is enabling in that he is referencing a body of work, which
retains an anxious relation to post-structuralism. This is exemplified by

Ahmad's response to Said, querying Said's point of entry into his own inventory and wrestling with Said's position as a kind of 'originator' for postcolonial work in the academy. Said does not explicitly state that any beginning must be provisional, but he enacts that provisionality. Although Bhabha too has taken issue with many of Said's theorisations of Orientalism and the relationship between colonial and neo-colonial power and culture, in contrast to Ahmad and other materialist postcolonial criticism, he has taken Said not as too post-structuralist but as not post-structuralist enough.

Said, following Gramsci, makes the point of departure himself, a provisional place of initial investigation, but this can also produce a range of problems, for the very provisionality of the point of departure tends to emphasise the 'accident' of birth, and of identity. Identity is not a safe place from which one speaks securely but is actually unravelled through this inventory making, as a position that is legislated and coerced to speak in certain ways. This is evident from Gramsci's notion of the trace and the inventory. His words are, 'history has deposited in you an infinity of traces'.[32]

One might respond to this as Derrida comments, with the question, 'Where does the outside commence? This is the question of the archive. There are undoubtedly no others' (Archive Fever, p. 8). The archive is not memory; on the contrary, the archive takes place at the place of originary and structural breakdown of memory. 'There is no archive without a place of consignation, without a technique of repetition, and without a certain exteriority. No archive without outside.' Where does this outside commence for Said? Is it strictly possible to write an inventory of those traces as Gramsci suggests? For according to this model, at the heart of the monument, of archiving itself, is forgetfulness.

> Right on that which permits and conditions archivization, we will never find anything other than that which exposes it to destruction and in truth menaces with destruction, introducing, a priori, forgetfulness, and the archiviolithic, into the heart of the monument.
>
> (*AF*, pp. 11-2)

For Bhabha also, a trace or a mark speaks of a moment in history that is not recuperable, that cannot necessarily be restored. This is the postcolonial relationship to what is repressed, forgotten, overlooked, kept secret, in the archive. Archiving is not a keeping alive or bringing back to life, rather post-structuralist language might wish to characterise it as a haunting or trace.

For postcolonial criticism, the anxiety engendered by such post-structuralist formulations centres around questions of the political and the ways in which counter narratives, whether Said's counterpoint, or a notion of hidden history and Bhabha's formulation of the belatedness of the colonial subject, are central to postcolonial critiques of Western canons and disciplines.

Document one: School report

Said's most sustained 'inventory of traces' is in the volume *Out of Place*, his autobiography. It is an unforgettable and intimate narrative frequently evoking the claustrophobic atmosphere of a confessional with its uncomfortable portrayal of his childhood. Alongside his narrative he reproduces several documents and photographs that follow his childhood experiences, which are intended to elaborate his detailed recall of growing up in exile from Palestine in a hybridised colonial Cairo. In 'Cairo Recalled', Said comments on the 'messiness' of his reality, describing himself as living in badly fitting boxes. His father had left Jerusalem to go to the USA as a young man, and during World War I fought in France, returning as an American citizen to Palestine to run a family business that then expanded to Egypt. This intertwining of personal fortunes with international events produced a personal archive for Said of seemingly irreconcilable differences. 'So there I was a Palestinian, Anglican, American boy, English Arabic, and French speaking at school, Arabic and English speaking at home, living in the almost suffocating, deeply impressive intimacy of a family all of whose relatives were in Palestine or Lebanon, subject to the discipline of a colonial school system and an imported mythology owing nothing to that Arab world among whose colonial elites for at least a century it had flourished'.[33]

Included is his school report at the age of fifteen from Victoria College, Cairo, a school that he comments was intended to be the Eton of the Middle East. 'Except for the teachers of Arabic and French the faculty was entirely English (not a single English student was enrolled)' (p. 182). The report follows the standard format of listing subjects with accompanying comments and grades from each teacher, and in the listing and marking of subjects the belated arrival of the colonised is rehearsed.

English,	A
History	B
Egypt History	
Geography	C+
French	D+
Arabic	
Mathematics	C−

These categorisations are tantalising in both what they reveal and what
is absent. 'Egypt. History' and 'Arabic' remain unmarked, sitting uncomfortably alongside the traditional English public school subjects. Said
comments, 'We were tested as if we were English boys, trailing behind an
ill defined and always out of reach goal from class to class, year to year'
(p. 183). He uncannily affirms with the words 'trailing behind' the condition of belatedness that Bhabha proposes is so characteristic of the colonised condition. With English as the language of the school, and anyone
caught speaking Arabic punished (outside the carefully circumscribed Arabic class), Said comments, 'Arabic became our haven, a criminalised language'. Said acknowledges that by the time he reached Victoria College, he
had become 'hopelessly paradoxical' to himself, frequently described as a
nuisance or troublemaker, 'edging from crisis to crisis, from catastrophe to
catastrophe'.[34] The effect of what Bhabha notes is the iterability of the document in the archive though, is precisely that in the re-situating of the school
report, in the context of the autobiography of the colonised pupil, it is no
longer only an official document certifying Said's intellectual competence
or lack of it. Instead, its role is as a document of colonial control and nor-
malisation of a range of subjects imposed by a British colonial curriculum,
the very foundations of which can be challenged, indeed are challenged, by
the gaps and categorisations that it chooses to defend.

Document two: Photograph of Mrs Farraj

> No-one writing about Palestine – and indeed, no one going to Palestine – starts
> from scratch: We have all been there before, whether by reading about it,
> experiencing its millennial presence and power, or actually living there for
> periods of time. It is a terribly crowded place, almost too crowded for what it is
> asked to bear by way of history or interpretation of history.
>
> Edward Said, *After the Last Sky*, (p. 4)

In their moving tribute to Said after his death in 2003, *Edward Said: Continuing the Conversation*, both Homi Bhabha and Warren J. T. Mitchell turn
to the collected photographs and writings *After the Last Sky: Palestinian
Lives* in order to speak of Said's commitment to and engagement with 'the
patterns of life and art' of the Palestinian experience, 'broken narratives,
fragmentary compositions, and self-consciously staged testimonials'.[35] In
1983 Edward Said was serving as a consultant to the United Nations International Conference on the Question of Palestine. Said suggested commis-
sioning a photographer to make portraits of Palestinians to be hung in the
entrance hall at the main conference in Geneva. The resulting photographs,

taken by French photographer Jean Mohr, had an ambivalent reception. While the exhibition took place, Mohr and Said were forbidden to write any explanations of the photographs underneath them. Said bitterly recounts their response, 'You can hang them up, we were told, but no writing can be displayed with them. No legends, no explanations' (p. 3). For Said the paradox is painfully ironic: whereas Palestine has been represented, written over, to the point of illegibility at times, it cannot be represented, the United Nations (or some of its member states) refusing in principle to allow writing about the Palestinian people.

'Wherever we Palestinians are, we are not in our Palestine, which no longer exists' (p. 4), Said comments. The colonised subject comes too late to the meeting discussing the terms on which he might (not) be allowed in. Three years later, Said and Mohr jointly published the photographs accompanied by an eloquent and moving text, under the title, *After The Last Sky*, borrowing these words from the Palestinian poet Mahmoud Darwish. They were attempting to account for, to claim and to re-narrate Palestinian people, staging the belated arrival of the Palestinian long after the Geneva conference had packed up its bags and taken down its silent exhibition. The complex layers of estrangement counter the apparent accessibility of the photographs, and exile, emphasizing the distancing and decoding that make up Said's experience of viewing. The photograph is not access to the event, but a departure from it, a kind of exile in itself.

> Exile is a series of portraits without names, without contexts. Images that are largely unexplained, nameless, mute. I look at them without precise anecdotal knowledge, but their realistic exactness nevertheless makes a deeper impression than mere information. I cannot reach the actual people who were photographed, except through a European photographer who saw them for me.
>
> (*After The Last Sky*, p. 12)

For Bhabha, the descriptions of interiors of Palestinian homes is particularly resonant, owing to Said's depiction of 'the Palestinian's fundamental sense of loss and displacement [that] repeats and refigures itself in rituals of excess: too many places at a table, too many pictures; too many objects; too much food.'[36] Yet there is an uncanny moment of recognition and connection in this book, an unexpected and (again) belated recognition of a personal link that Said has with one of the subjects Mohr has photographed, Mrs Farraj. Said shows the photographs he has selected for the book to his sister, who recognises her. 'As soon as I recognised Mrs Farraj, the suggested intimacy of the photograph's surface gave way to an explicitness with few secrets. She was a real person – Palestinian – with a real history at the interior of ours' (p. 84). The politically and personally motivated mission to Palestine, the previous refusal of accompanying texts for the Geneva conference exhibition for which these photographs were originally taken, do not in themselves create the untimely recognition. '[A]ll the connections came only to light, so to speak, sometime after I had seen the photograph, after we had decided to use it, after I has placed it in sequence' (*ATLS,* p. 84).

Said has looked many times at the face of Mrs Farraj, in the photograph, a woman he knew, without recognising her, even in the act of sorting photos and creating an alternative archive of Palestinian daily lives and domestic interiors. Somehow the movement from Mrs Farraj's domestic interior into the realm of the archive, the public display or record, has actually severed the private link between the archiver and the subject of his endeavour. Or, in an equally unsettling movement, the displacement of the viewer, Said, from inhabiting Palestinian culture, from the inside, to an exiled tangential experience of Palestinians that has made the familiar and personal strange. It is perhaps that moment when, according to Bhabha, 'the recesses of the domestic space become sites for history's most intricate invasions. In that displacement, the borders between home and world become part of each other, forcing upon us a vision that is as divided as it is disorienting' (*TLOC,* p. 9).

Might there not, in Said's comments on writing on, visiting and representing Palestine, – that we have all been there before – be detected an echo or a trace of another great exiled writer's remarks on visiting remarkable and overwritten cultural, political and archaeological sites that bear the weight of history? In Sigmund Freud's essay 'The Disturbance of Memory on the Acropolis', he offers an account of a trip he made with his brother to the Acropolis in Athens, as a younger man, dwelling on the intense feeling of déjà vu, a 'derealisation' and 'depersonalisation' that he experienced on finally seeing the temple he had read of and learned about in school. He has 'already seen' the great monument hundreds of times in reproduction, but the visit produces a kind of splitting of identity, an acute self-awareness encapsulated in the remark, 'So all this really does exist, just as we learned at school'.[37] The moment that Freud describes the moment of briefly feeling he is seeing something that is not real, but also that exceeds the experiences itself. It is somehow not the first time at all, despite all evidence to the contrary.

Said's comments offer a politically charged rewriting of this uncanny moment for Freud, who comes face to face, as Ranjana Khanna notes, with 'one of the founding monuments of Western Civilisation'.[38] Not because one was privileged to travel further and more widely than his own father, as in Freud's case, but, as in Said's, impeded from accessing Palestine and restricted in both movement and in representing it. The unsettling quality of the archive is that it troubles boundaries between the public and the private, which actually have an impact on what can be recognised as personal, private and belonging to the self, and what is perceived as impersonal and public or official.

Bhabha sees this uncanny moment, where what was strange becomes familiar, or what was familiar becomes strange, as having a critical role in the histories of the colonised. Following Freud's long deliberations on the mode of the uncanny in his essay of the same name,[39] Bhabha picks up a particular resonance in Freud's essay, which he sees as opening up a postcolonial application of Freud's discussion. He renames the conventional English translation of uncanny through a 'catachrestic' re-translation, of the German, *Unheimlich*, one of whose meanings, in a literal translation, can be unhomely.

Although Freud's essay has become indispensable to some strands of contemporary literary criticism and theory such that its arguments are well known, Bhabha's re-reading has been very productive. *Heimlich* is initially understood as 'belonging to the house, not strange, familiar, tame, intimate, friendly'. However, as Freud's investigations progress, it becomes clear that the 'homely' notion of *heimlich* contains within it a lurking threat. One of the definitions Freud cites from Grimm's dictionary (1887) contains the following,

> [3] (b) Heimlich is also used of a place free from ghostly influences. . . . familiar, friendly, intimate.
>
> (p. 875)

> Familiar, amicable, unreserved.

> 4. *From the idea of 'homelike', 'belonging to the house', the further idea is developed of something withdrawn from the eyes of strangers. Something concealed, secret; and this idea is expanded in many ways.*
>
> (p. 246)

Further on in the citation is the following,

> 9. The notion of something hidden and dangerous which is expressed in the last paragraph. Is still further developed, so that 'heimlich' comes to have the meaning usually ascribed to 'unheimlich'. Thus: 'At times I feel like a man who walks in the night and believes in ghosts; every corner is heimlich and full of terrors for him.(Klinger, Theater, 3, 298)'
>
> (p. 347)

Freud comments, 'Thus heimlich is a word the meaning of which develops in the direction of ambivalence, until it finally coincides with its opposite, unheimlich'(p. 347). For Bhabha, the attractions of the uncanny as Freud discusses it are that notions of being unhomed, or the unhomely, resonate suggestively with the disturbed relation to home and belonging that Bhabha sees as characterising migrant, exiled or refugee experiences. He states, 'the unhomely is a paradigmatic colonial and postcolonial condition' (*TLOC*, p. 9). To feel at home and strange or estranged at the same time, or to feel not at home even when one is 'at home', might be a painfully familiar condition for the colonised or postcolonial subject, a condition not limited to the migrant or exile alone.

Bhabha's range of literary examples of the unhomely, in his introductory essay to *The Location of Culture*, are, as he acknowledges, somewhat erratic: Henry James's *Portrait of a Lady*, Toni Morrison's *Beloved*, Nadine Gordimer's *My Son's Story* and Rabindranath Tagore's *The Home and the World*. Perhaps one of the strongest criticisms of Bhabha's work is of his tendency to flatten out historical and cultural differences and locations. He does, however, acknowledge that 'the historical specificities and cultural diversities that inform each of these texts would make a global argument purely gestural' (TLOC, p. 9). Nonetheless for Bhabha there remains a sense that the unhomely or *heimliche–unheimlich*, does resonate suggestively in diverse colonial and postcolonial conditions. He comments 'To be unhomed is not to be homeless, nor can the "unhomely" be easily accommodated in that familiar division of social life into private and public spheres. The unhomely moment creeps up on you, stealthily as your own shadow and suddenly you find yourself taking the measure of your dwelling in a state of incredulous terror' (*TLOC*, p. 9).

Perhaps his analysis resonates most suggestively with Said's archiving experience in his apprehension of the ways in which the unhomely can be seen to dramatise the profoundly unstable boundary between public and private realms. 'The recesses of the domestic space become sites for history's most intricate invasions. In that displacement, the borders between home and world become confused; and, uncannily, the private and the public become part of each other, forcing upon us a vision that is as divided as it is disorienting' (*TLOC*, p. 9).

3 Fanon, Bhabha and the 'Return of the Oppressed'

> To mention Homi Bhabha's writing on Fanon is […] to reference a fault line running through the centre of postcolonial studies.[1]

> To read Fanon is to experience the sense of division that prefigures – and fissures – the emergence of a truly radical thought that never dawns without casting an uncertain dark.[2]

It may well be the case, as Neil Lazarus suggests, that Bhabha's writing on Fanon has inaugurated a series of crises in postcolonial theoretical circles that extend considerably beyond discussions of Fanon himself. Fanon's work has enjoyed such an unprecedented rebirth, in postcolonial studies, race studies and cultural studies, a resurrection or appropriation depending upon one's critical perspective. Yet this division or fault line in different readings is partly marked by pre-existing divisions in the field in contemporary postcolonial criticism. It forms part of larger discussions around the provenance of post-structuralist approaches in so-called postcolonial work.

Contention from other critical fields, notably Marxist- and materialist-influenced writing, such as that of Neil Lazarus, Aijaz Ahmad and Benita Parry, presents this shift as a creative re-visioning at best, at worst a betrayal and an abuse of the real revolutionary Fanon, who is then seen as having been stripped of his political potential. The *New Formations* special issue on Fanon in 2002 revisited the changing modes of discussions and questioned how far Fanon had been 'appropriated' beyond the legitimate reach of his critical and political horizons. Central to their interests was the publication of David Macey's detailed and carefully researched biography of Fanon, *Frantz Fanon: A Life*, which for some of the contributors to the edition of *New Formations* demonstrated both Macey's dissatisfaction with Fanon's treatment by Bhabha and confirmed for Lazarus that 'Bhabha's Fanon' was 'wildly anachronistic and ideologically appropriative'.[3] Gautam Premnath's

essay in this collection offers a condensed account of what was perceived
to be at stake,

> There was a time, not so long ago, when Frantz Fanon seemed to figure in aca-
> demic discussion primarily as the author of a striking little document called 'the
> fact of blackness' – or at best of the work from which it was taken, *BSWM* [*Black
> Skin White Marks*]. Taking their cue from Homi Bhabha's influential writings a
> generation of theorists turned to this early work of Fanon to explore the politics
> of marginality and elaborate psychoanalytic theories of race. Kobena Mercer
> announced this elevation of *BSWM* over Fanon's other texts was 'a response to
> the failures of revolutionary nationalism'. With the stroke of an academic's pen
> the curtain seemed to have dropped not just on the epoch of national libera-
> tion, but also on all the intellectual energies and achievements it had fostered.
> Those of us beginning a serious intellectual engagement with Fanon in the early
> and mid 1990s seemed to be presented with a deeply unsatisfactory choice:
> either to sin on to this particular project of 're-membering Fanon' or to be seen
> as maintaining an obstinate attachment to a previously prevailing image of him
> as a revolutionary lion and tragic hero. The appearance of David Macey's judi-
> cious, comprehensive and theoretically informed biography will now make it
> more difficult to persist in the loosely dehistoricising discussion of Fanon that
> tended to be the norm in the recent past.[4]

Certainly Bhabha does not hold back his criticism of materialist readings
in this introductory essay (although the reprinted version in the collection
The Location of Culture edits this section out). He takes English socialism to
task for what he calls 'its empty gestures towards Fanon's work as simply a
rallying call to "ethnocentric little Englandism and large trade union inter-
nationalism" (p. vii). His insistence that Fanon cannot simply be absorbed
into dominant liberatory narratives of the left is centred on an apprehension
of a redundancy of the vocabulary of struggle and solidarity. He comments,
'When that labourist line of vision is challenged by the "autonomous struggles" of the politics of race or gender or threatened by problems of human
psychology or cultural representation it can only make the empty gesture of
solidarity'(p. vii).

However, there is also arguably a radical instability in both Fanon's shifting historical contexts, the competing and complex strands of his identity
and different locations, as well as in his writings that contribute to this
sense of shifting territories and possibilities in his work. This is something
that Bhabha acknowledges in his introduction to the 1986 imprint of the
English translation of *BSWM*,

> this palpable pressure of division and displacement that pushes Fanon's writ-
> ing to the edge of things; the cutting edge that reveals no ultimate radiance but,

in his words 'exposes an utterly naked declivity where an authentic upheaval can be born'.

(Bhabha, *BSWM* ix)

Indeed, the rush of intellectual activity around Fanon, from the late 1980s onwards, needs to be seen as partly inaugurated by what Stuart Hall calls Bhabha's 'symptomatic' mode of re-reading. Fanon's earliest text is 'translated' in ways that are far from uncontroversial, yet which certainly fulfil the remit of Fanon's actual last words in the text, that Bhabha recites/resites as the opening epigram for his forward to *BSWM*, 'Oh my body, make of me always a man who questions!'[5]

From Bhabha's own work on this text and the subsequent very fruitful field it has enabled, it is clear that this is one of the central questions, around the experience of 'the black body'. In his much discussed chapter, which Macey, among others, argues is misleadingly translated as 'The Fact of Blackness', Fanon outlines theories of the ideological construction of racial categories and narratives, the relation of race to gender and to sexuality.[6] He also resists the 'fact' of his title and considers the paradoxical simultaneous physicality and immateriality of black bodies defined under colonial discourse, the violence enacted against them that operates both physically and through unequal power relations, narrative and the look or 'the gaze' as well as other forms of surveillance and control. This urgent and impassioned analysis is undertaken, as Diana Fuss and David Macey among others have pointed out, using the critical vocabulary available to a black Martinican French subject who had met Jean-Paul Sartre and who was heavily influenced by his writings and his use of Hegel, and was a reader of Merleau-Ponty's work on phenomenology, now residing in France undertaking training in psychiatry.

Macey goes further still, arguing in a short article that Fanon could not have written *BSWM* if he were not Martinican, and consequently positioned in a very particular way in relation to French colonial politics, a point that I continue later on in the chapter. Stuart Hall comments,

> There are some critics who believe that the status of Fanon as a black hero and icon is damaged even by the suggestion that he might have learned anything – or worse – actually been in dialogue with the themes of European philosophy. This kind of essentialism is worse than useless if we are to think seriously about Fanon. It reveals how little such critics understand Fanon's deep implication in French culture and philosophy as a result of his French colonial upbringing, formation and education in Martinique. [...] These critics forget that Fanon like many other bright young colonial intellectuals went to study in France became locked in a deep internal argument

with the various currents of thought which he found there and went to North Africa as a salaried member of the French colonial psychiatric service. They do not understand that in Martinique for many intellectuals to be anti-colonial and opposed to the old white indigenous plantocracy was to be for French Republican ideology, with its rallying cry of liberty equality a fraternity.[7]

The tone and style of Fanon's writing is as remarkable as the positions he puts forward: it is arresting, self-dramatising, a bricolage of vocabularies and modes of address from rather dry psychiatric assertions to extended personal anecdotes and footnotes that take an entire page, as well as reversals of logic, counter-intuitive remarks that set an new train of thought in process. For Nigel Gibson, the combination of philosophy, politics, literature, psychoanalysis, film and popular culture combined with 'what seems like an authorial and autobiographical "I"' can 'create a certain uneasiness in the reader'.[8] Such is the suggestive quality of his writing, giving rise to graphic images, to disturbing reversals of the logical or seemingly material, that it is hardly surprising that his work should attract a reading like Bhabha's.

Henry Louis Gates Jr, in his very significant survey, 'Critical Fanonism' echoes some of Bhabha's assertions, and highlights the sense of ongoing contestation around his critical and political legacies,

> Fanon's current fascination for us has something to do with the convergence of the problematic of colonialism with that of subject-formation. As a psychoanalyst of culture, as a champion of the wretched of the earth, he is an almost irresistible figure for a criticism that sees itself as both oppositional and postmodern. And yet there is something Rashomon-like about his contemporary guises. It may be a matter of judgement whether his writings are rife with contradiction or richly dialectical, polyvocal, and multivalent; they are at any event highly porous, that is, wide open to interpretation, and the readings they elicit are, as a result, of unfailing symptomatic interest: Frantz Fanon, not to put too fine a point on it, is a Rorschach blot with legs [9]

I   First and last words

The critical developments around Fanon's work in recent decades follow Bhabha's interventions in those discussions through his introductory essay reprinted and extended in the essays 'Interrogating Identity' and 'The Other Question'. It is impossible to avoid concluding that the rise of questions of identity and discourse in postcolonial studies, in conjunction with writing on race, diaspora and identity, owes a great deal to Fanon's work and a revisiting of his writings that has to some extent, in Bhabha's case at least, re-ordered the significance of his writing for the perceived needs of the present. Bhabha critically offers an introduction to the 1986 reprint of the English version of *BSWM*. His discussion of questions of identity, otherness, ambivalence and stereotyping, as well as broad discussion on the relationship between politics and theory, rely on his readings of Fanon, especially but not exclusively the first book *Black Skin White Masks*. His reading must be viewed as having dramatically influenced a wider shifting of attention to these arenas, especially identity, in critical fields within the humanities in the 1980s and early 1990s.[10]

Gates offers a timely account of some of these shifts and the effects that a 'revival' of interest in Fanon's work has produced.[11] He comments on the ways on which, at the end of the 1980s, Fanon had been mobilised by those engaged in Renaissance studies, British romanticism and New Historicism. He suggests that the ascendancy of the colonial paradigm in contemporary criticism has been accompanied by a reinstatement of Fanon as a 'global theorist', moving him outside the remit of 'Third World or subaltern studies'.[12] Such a proposal is at least partly confirmed in Bhabha's view, where he comments on the vital significance of *Black Skin White Masks* to contemporary cultural theory as having its foundation in a turn to questions of identity. For Bhabha,

> In shifting the focus of cultural racism from the politics of nationalism to the politics of narcissism, Fanon opens up a margin of interrogation that causes a subversive slippage of identity and authority. Nowhere is this slippage more visible than in his work itself where a range of texts and traditions – from the classical repertoire to the quotidian, conversational culture of racism – vie to utter the last word which remains unspoken.
>
> (p. xxv)

When Bhabha wrote his introduction to the new imprint of C. L. Markmann's English translation of *Peau Noire* Masques *Blancs*, – *Black Skin, White Masks* – published by Pluto Press in 1986, he called forth, or perhaps conjured, some of Fanon's theoretical ghosts or neglected textual 'incarnations' to speak again. The 'last words' that 'remained unspoken' in Bhabha's view are, rather strangely, attributed to his earliest publication, written while still in France, before his posting as a psychiatrist to North Africa. Yet for Bhabha it signals an opening up of a critical dialogue with Fanon's earliest text – still yet to reveal its secrets, whose knowledges are still unspoken – that accommodates something of the quality of Bhabha's fruitful and influential revivification of Fanon's work for so-called postcolonial criticism, as well as perhaps demonstrating an untimely timeliness, that enables François Vergès more than ten years after Bhabha's essay was published to comment that 'a Specter is haunting our postcolonial world, the spectre of Frantz Fanon'.[13]

Stuart Hall has also commented at length on this re-engagement with Fanon. He identifies several key strands of cultural and political significance that are brought together in Fanon's early writing that make it so amenable to the kind of work Bhabha does with it. He comments,

> The view, boldly dictated by Fanon in his introduction to *BSWM* – that 'only a psychoanalytic interpretation of the black problems can lay bare the anomalies of affect that are responsible for the structure of the complex, that is racism ad colonialism' – is what constitutes the novelty of this text. The problem is that Fanon's 1952 text anticipates poststructuralism in a startling way, even if the addition of the phrase; effective disalienation of the black man entails an immediate recognition of social and economic realities inflects his anachronistically prescient observation in an unexpected direction. He always insists, the 'corporeal schema' is cultural and discursive not genetic or physiological. Bhabha's work points to the ways in which Fanon's model of the operations and intersections between power and knowledge under colonialism cannot be understood without reference to question of identity and identification. A condition applicable whether for white or black, under a colonial system, but operating in dramatically different ways.[14]

Hall comments that in recounting this contest over which texts of Fanon's should be regarded as most significant, and how they should be read, Louis Gates, who is basically sympathetic to a post-structuralist or deconstructive re-reading that Bhabha inaugurates, nevertheless 'takes some delight' in exposing how varied, even internally contradictory, the recent readings of Fanon as a 'global theorist' have been. Notwithstanding this, Hall comments without approval, that in an essay entitled 'The Appropriation of Fanon' Cedric Robinson argues that to privilege *Black Skin White Masks* over *The Wretched of The Earth* is a motivated political strategy which perversely reads Fanon backwards, from his 'immersion in the revolutionary consciousness of the Algerian peasantry' to the 'petit-bourgeois stink' of the former text.[15] The fault lines of discussions and dispute around Fanon may be more complex and interwoven than a series of binaries such as early/late, bourgeois/revolutionary, text/world might allow.

This model of Fanon's critical, political and intellectual development from 'alienated' to 'authentic', or from complicit with the colonial state as one of its employees to radically opposed to it, had perhaps been the most dominant interpretative model for approaching Fanon's oeuvre. A reappraisal of the significance of *BSWM* might be a rather unsettling and untimely 'return of the repressed', as Stuart Hall has it, following Freud, which very much fits with the untimely and aporetic time of the postcolonial. Hall rejects the proposal that there is a kind of 'graduation' in Fanon's work from childish petit-bourgeois things to a greater maturity, it 'does not explain why *The Wretched of the Earth* ends, in a chapter on 'Colonial War and Mental disorders', with a series of psychiatric case studies presented in a language that clearly echoes the idea first sketched in *Black Skin White Masks*'.[16]

Diana Fuss also refuses the oppositional mode of interpretation, in her very useful attempt to think through the role of identification in relation to colonial history.

> The critical debate over the relation between Fanon's psychoanalytic training and his political education – posed in the oppositional terms of a dramatic break or seamless continuity obscures the critical fault lines upon which Fanon's own work is based, for Fanon himself was interested precisely in the linkages and fissures, the contradictions and complications, the translations and transformations of the theory-politics relation.[17]

To comprehend the significance of this new body of work on Fanon and its relevance to postcolonial studies and diasporic, and black visual and filmic culture, we need to retrace some of the previous modes of addressing Fanon and the subsequent critical shifts of vision that the new work undertook. In his essay 'The After-Life of Frantz Fanon: Why Fanon? Why Now? Why *Black Skin, White Masks*?', Hall addresses many of the pressing questions around the turn/return to Fanon, as his title might suggest. He asks,

> Why of the many figures whose emblematic presence could have triggered off such a profusion of discursive and figural production does the incitation turn out to be Frantz Fanon? Though at one time his name would have been widely known and recognised – usually as a signifier of a certain brand of incendiary Third World-ism – he is now virtually unknown even among those young, practising, black writers and artists whose work appears, unwittingly, to betray a trace of his presence. Of course, events do not obey any singular, unfolding teleology of causality or time. But I cannot help feeling that the recall of Fanon now in this moment here in this way has something of the overdetermined 'return of the repressed' about it – a timeliness constituted from many directions at once as well as a certain un-timeliness.[18]

Untimely the postcolonial may be, belated, melancholic, in its refusal to forget and restless in its seeking for new modes of justice and remembering. Bhabha comments, 'it is not for the finitude of philosophical thinking nor for the finality of a political direction that we turn to Fanon', but rather because his thinking is restless, transgressive and transitional, never 'possessed by one political moment or movement'.[19] It is in this spirit that I hope to consider the significance of Fanon is in Bhabha's thinking and to offer some critical readings that are attentive to the contested bodies of Fanon and his writing.

II   Stereotyping, ambivalence and mimicry

> There is a quest for the negro, the negro is in demand, one cannot get along without him, he is needed, but only if he is made palatable in a certain way. Unfortunately the negro knocks down the system and breaks the treaties.
>
> (Frantz Fanon, *BSWM* p. 114)

> niggers-are-all-the-same, I tell you
> they-have-every-vice-every-conceivable-vice
> [...]
> Or else quite simply how they love us!
>
> Aimé Césaire, Return *to My Native Land*

There is, as Stuart Hall notes, a central figure at the heart of *Black Skin White Masks*, the male Antillean, whose relation to self can never be disentangled from the oppressive scenarios of the colonial relation, a sense of self described by Fanon as shattered, as an 'amputation, excision, haemorrhage', as fragmented, experienced as 'crushing objecthood', as battered down by the endlessly repeating stereotypes.[20] In doing so, he outlines his understanding of the ways in which racism is not a bodily schema, enacted on pre-existing and obvious biological difference, but is a discursive regime that creates the differences it claims to find. Hall observes that Fanon is aware that 'Not only must the Blackman be black; he must be black in relation to the white man. As Bhabha correctly observes, this is "not a neat division" but a doubling, dissembling image of being in at least two places at once'.

The exercise of power through the dialectic of the look, 'sealed into that crushing objecthood', he/she becomes self as Othered as Bhabha puts it, 'not Self and Other' but the 'Otherness of the Self inscribed in the perverse palimpsest of colonial identity'.[21] Hall notes that,

> The Antillean, [...] is obliged, in the scenarios of the colonial relation, to have a relationship to self, to give a performance of self, which is scripted by the coloniser, producing in him the internally divided condition of 'absolute depersonalisation'. The mechanisms of this substitution are very precisely described.

> The bodily or corporeal schema, which Fanon says is 'a definitive structuring
> of self and the world, necessary to any sense of self because it creates a real
> dialectic between my body and the world, is fragmented and shattered'. [...]
> In its place, Fanon suggests there a rises the 'historico-racial schema' which
> weaves him 'out of a thousand details, anecdotes, stories – battered down by
> tom-toms, cannibalism, intellectual deficiency, fetishism, racial defects, slave
> ships and above all: *Sho' good eatin'* (*'Y'a bon Banania*).[22]

However, he is not merely shattered by a range of images that rely on primi-
tiveness and aggression. The enacting of stereotypes draws on a peculiarly
bifurcated set of images that Bhabha identifies as a schema, as the necessary
structuring of stereotyping, 'they have every conceivable vice', 'or else how
they love us' Césaire comments, in his hugely influential long poem, or as
Fanon says himself, 'battered down by tom toms, cannibalism [...] and above
all else "Sho' good eatin"' (*'Y'a Bon Banania!'*). Bhabha asks what desires and
fears are at play in this strangely split production of stereotypes. He turns to
Said's account of 'Orientalism' and the production of stereotypes about the
East in colonial discourse. He explores Said's use of the term 'vacciation' [*sic*]
around the production of stereotypes that Said in his analysis claims is left
undeveloped. For Said,

> What gives the immense number of encounters [between East and West];
> some unity however is the vacillation I was speaking about earlier. Something
> patently foreign and distant acquires, for one reason or another, a status more
> rather than less familiar. [...] A category emerges that allows one to see new
> things, things seen for the first time as versions of a previously known thing,
> the orient at large therefore vacillates between the West contempt for what is
> familiar and its shivers of delight in – or – fear of – novelty.[23]

Bhabha rewrites Said's figure of 'vacillation' as one of his key critical terms,
ambivalence. Ambivalence works for Bhabha because it registers internal difference and deferral – a kind of undecidability, a term well used in
deconstruction, as well as opening onto questions of desire and affect. He
proposes that the stereotype might be understood through Freud's model
of the fetish, paralleling the fetish with the stereotype as it 'gives access to
an identity which is predicated as much on mastery and pleasure as it is on
anxiety and defence, for it is a form of multiple and contradictory belief in
its recognition of difference and mastery of it'.[24]

This is perhaps Bhabha's most deft interpretive stroke, where he pushes
Said's reading beyond what it is able to say, and follows Fanon's re-centring
of the analysis of colonial power and discourse onto questions of identity
formation and identification as inextricable from the operations of power

under colonial regimes. He asks, 'does the Freudian fable of fetishism (and disavowal) circulate within the discourse of colonial power requiring the articulation of modes of differentiation –sexual racial, as well as different modes of theoretical discourse – psychoanalytic and historical?'[25] 'Foucault insists that the relation of knowledge and power is always a strategic response to an urgent need at a given historical moment. In this spirit I argue for the reading of the stereotype in terms of fetishism. [...] There is both a structural and functional justification for reading the racial stereotype of colonial discourse in terms of fetishism. My re-reading of Said established the structural link Fetishism is the disavowal of difference. [...] The functional link between the fixation of the fetish and the stereotype (or the stereotype as fetish) is even more relevant. For fetishism is always a play or vacillation between archaic affirmations of wholeness/similarity and the anxiety associated with lack or difference. The fetish or stereotype gives access to an identity which is predicated as much on mastery and contradictory belief as it is on anxiety and defence. It is a form of multiple and contradictory belief in its recognition of difference and disavowal of it.'[26]

Bhabha proposes the justifications for his reading as both structural and functional. Structurally, fetishism operates as the disavowal of difference, 'For fetishism is always a "play" or vacillation between the affirmation of wholeness/similarity and the anxiety associated with lack or difference.'[27] As a form of splitting and multiple belief, the stereotype requires for its successful signification a continual and repetitive chain of other stereotypes, 'the same old stories must be told again and again and afresh, and are differently gratifying and terrifying each time'.[28] Bhabha asserts that it is the major discursive strategy of colonial discourse a form of knowledge that 'vacillates between what is always "in place" already known, and something that must be anxiously repeated'.[29] This analysis shifts the emphasis from seeing a stereotype as a fixed and simplistic misrepresentation to be opposed, to what Bhabha calls 'an understanding of the processes of subjectification made possible (and plausible) through stereotypical discourse'. One would therefore look at stereotypes as a critical indicator of the 'regime of truth' operating at any particular time under colonial discourse. Instead of seeing the stereotype as serving to support the continuation of power, the recognition of ambivalence is a vital shift for Bhabha. This ambivalence would be a case of Derrida's understanding of deconstructive model of the text, where the fixity of the stereotype would be constantly working against itself from within, undoing its meanings, unable to keep them stable, and anxiously repeating them in every new situation, but never gaining the desired closure.

Bhabha comments, with his characteristic ear for the resonances in psychoanalytic parlance (substituting the psychoanalytic concept of repression with the colonial act of oppression and thereby conferring a link between the two) that it would be impossible 'without the attribution of *ambivalence* to relations of power/knowledge, to calculate the traumatic impact of the *return of the oppressed* – those terrifying stereotypes of savagery, cannibalism, lust and anarchy which are the signal points of identification and alienation, scenes of fear and desire in colonial texts'.[30]

Bhabha's insistence on a traumatic splitting of impulses of fear and desire in the production of the stereotype demonstrates possibilities for reading it differently. 'This conflict of pleasure/unpleasure, mastery/defence, knowledge/disavowal, absence/presence, has a fundamental significance for colonial discourse. For the scene of fetishism is also the scene of the reactivation and repetition of primal fantasy – the subjects desire for pure origin.'[31] Therefore the stereotype is not a simplification because it is 'a false representation of a given reality', it is a simplification because it is 'an arrested, fixated form of representation, in denying the play of difference'. He points to the way that 'wherever he goes Fanon despairs, the Negro remains a Negro. /We always already know that blacks are licentious, Asiatics duplicitous'.[32]

Bhabha explores the ways in which the racial fetish is not like the sexual fetish, a secret. Skin is the key signifier, recognised as 'common knowledge'. The sexual fetish is closely linked to the good object, it facilitates sexual relations, whereas the colonial deployment of racial stereotypes can also be seen as producing 'that particular fixated form of the colonial subject that facilitates colonial relations and the exercising of colonial power'. He comments, 'if it is claimed that the colonized are most often objects of hate then we can reply with Freud, 'Affection and hostility in the treatment of the fetish, are mixed in unequal proportions in different cases', what this statement recognises is the wide range of stereotype from loyal servant to Satan'.[33]

Bhabha describes his concept as 'stereotype-as-suture', the stereotype works hard to fix knowledge but is constantly undoing itself, and revealing the ambivalence of its operations. 'The role of fetishistic identification, in the construction of discriminatory knowledges that depend on the "presence of difference" is to provide a process of splitting and multiple/contradictory belief at the point of enunciation and subjectification.'[34] He illustrates this complex structure again by turning to Fanon's corporeal crisis narrated in *Black Skin White Masks*, 'Assailed by the stereotype 'the corporeal schema crumbled, its place taken by a racial epidermal schema ... It was no longer a question of being aware of my body in the third person, but in a triple person. I was not given one, but two, three places.' For Freud, fetishism is articulation of multiple belief, allowing for the simultaneous belief in contradictory things, one official, one secret, one archaic, one progressive, one that allows the myth of origins, the other that articulates difference and division.'[35]

III   Stereotype as impossible object: *'Y'a Bon Banania'*, Fanon and the *Tirailleures Senegalais*

> The stereotype is an 'impossible' object [. . .] Stereotyping is not the setting up of a false image which becomes the scapegoat of discriminatory practices. It is a much more ambivalent text of projection and introjection, metaphoric and metonymic strategies, displacement, overdetermination, guilt, aggressivity; the masking and splitting of 'official' and phantasmatic knowledges to construct the positionalities and oppositionalities of racist discourse.[36]

> Racism is not a biological but a discursive regime, The so-called bodily insignia – black skin, thick lips, curly hair, penises as big as cathedrals and the rest – which appear to function as foundational, are not only constituted through and through in fantasy, but are really signifying elements in the discourse of racism. Fanon certainly knew that, in the system of radicalised exclusion and abjection sustained by the look from the place of the other the bodily schema is constituted, not given, and culturally and historically shaped.[37]

The role of psychoanalytic theory in Bhabha's account of Fanon is controversial. In particular, it is Bhabha's alleged 'discovery' of Fanon as Lacanian 'avant la lettre', as Stuart Hall puts it.[38] Certainly Fanon reads Lacan in specific ways in relation to his attempts to understand colonised identities. As Hall suggests, he performs a substantial appropriation of Lacan, in his long footnote on the mirror phase. 'First 'the other' is raced. It is not difficult to agree that he writes here as if 'the real Other' is indeed a fixed phenomenological point, secondly the split subject which the mirror phase engenders is relocated by Fanon in the specificities of the colonial relation.'

Hall suggests, 'this divergence is critical, it reminds us how strikingly unraced Lacan's discourse is on the other it clearly marks Fanon's distance from the logic of Lacan's position.'[39] Fanon's reading resists a universalising impulse in Lacan, but nonetheless considers very seriously how his model could still provide insight into the mental condition of the colonised. However, a Lacanian model of identity relies on identity as 'never an a priori nor a finished product it is only ever the problematic process of access to an image of totality'.[40] That is to say, Fanon sees the potential in Lacan to account for productions of identity under colonial conditions but refuses to see these as general mechanisms for all identities. 'For Lacan identity operates at the level of the imaginary. [...] But for Fanon the blockage which detotalises the Hegelian recognition of the One by the Other in the exchange of racialised looks arises from the historically specific specular structure of racism, not from the general mechanism of self-identification.'[41] The political implications of this deviation are highly significant. Hall notes that for Bhabha 'living with ambivalence is the political consequence of a Lacanian theoretical position whereas Fanon's theoretical position that this radicalisation of the "mirror stage" is a "pathological condition, forced on the black subject by colonialism has the political question of how to end this alienation inscribed in it. Fanon cannot, politically, live with the ambivalence since it is killing him" '.[42]

Hall observes Fanon's engagement with psychoanalysis also reaches a critical impasse when faced with assumptions of the universal applicability of the Oedipus complex. 'It is in the context of the passage in which Fanon both acknowledges and disavows that there is any homosexuality in Martinique that he makes the astonishing remark about the "absence of the Oedipus complex in the Antilles."'[43] This again highlights the sense of Fanon struggling to apply a non-racialised schema of identifications in the colonial context. For Hall,

> The Caribbean is the least promising scenario in which to try to prove the absence of the Oedipal drama. With its son-fixated mothers and mother-fixated sons, its complex paternities common to all slave societies of 'real' black fathers and symbolic white ones, along with its deeply troubled assertively heterosexual and often homophobic black masculinities, the Caribbean lives out the loss of social power by substituting an aggressively phallo-centred black manhood.[44]

He suggests that the absence of women and the mother in Fanon's text might suggest that Fanon has substituted 'the triadic structure of the Oedipal scenario with the binary coupling of the master/slave trope' (p. 30).

Fanon's complex relationship with psychoanalytic models is unresolved in *Black Skin White Masks*. His rejection of the Oedipus complex in the French West Indies is suggestive of his desire to find mental illness resulting from colonial violence, and to retrieve a healthy original society underneath the layers of colonial deformation. It is contact with the white world that initiates psychological damage for the black child in Fanon's writing. Macey comments that 'In his attempt not to lose sight of the real, Fanon may well be misrecognising an aspect of psychoanalysis, but he is also insisting that psychoanalysis itself may be projecting European cultural values'.[45]

Françoise Vergès's carefully argued account of the role of psychoanalytic theories in Fanon's writing goes considerably further, and considers the vexed question of gender in relation to this text. In 'Creole Skin, Black Mask: Fanon and Disavowal', she argues that Fanon's relationship to Martinique and to the Martinican 'family' was critically ambivalent and that he 're-created his family, re-invented his filiation, and situated his symbolic ancestry in Algeria'.[46] For Vergès, Fanon invests in the filiation of the 'fathers and brothers' of the revolution and disavows his Creole filiations, as 'sites of anxiety and ambivalence'.[47] She notes that he wrote of the Algerians as *nos péres* in his journalism for the nationalist newspaper *El Moudjahid*. She also argues that his protective account of the sacred space of Martinican family and culture masks a profound denial of history. 'He reconstructs Antillean reality as both protected from alienation and subjected to alienation. He is confronted with the difficulty of working through a story that begins with deportation, violence, and the rape of the mother, and of locating this negativity in a symbolic world.'[48] Her reading is interesting, not least in the ways in which it interrogates constructions of gender Fanon's models of psychic violence or trauma in *Black Skin White Masks*. Certainly Fanon's work in *BSWM* on gender and race provides a highly ambivalent characterisation of black women's identifications and desires that evades the issues Vergès raises.

IV   Primal scenes

Bhabha claims that there are two primal scenes in *Black Skin White Masks*, two 'myths of origin of the marking of the subject within the racist practices and discourses of a colonial culture'.[49]One where a white girl 'fixes Fanon in a word and a look' with the line 'Look, a Negro ... Mama, see the Negro! I'm frightened'; the other when the black child encounters racial and cultural stereotypes in children's fictions where white and black are offered as points of identification, such dramas are enacted every day in colonial societies. Both of these conform to Fanon's stated model of the psychic violence of the white look or the return of the gaze and misrecognition of self. Following Vergès and Macey, I want to suggest a third scene that complicates the model Fanon suggests but one that recurs in the text of *Black Skin White Mask*, and use this to consider how Bhabha's understanding of stereotypes, introjection and identification might assist a reading of this.

It is partly explored in Vergès's work on race, disavowal and colonial identity, and in Macey's account of Fanon's time in the army during World War
II, another critical marking of the subject that inhabits Fanon's writing as
well as his lived experiences. Vergès comments,

> When he was thirteen he had been fascinated by tales of World War I Mar-
> tinican veterans who described the 'cruelty' of the Senegalese soldiers. But
> one detail about these soldiers captured his imagination: their uniform and
> particularly their red chechia (fezzes) and belts. So when Senegalese soldiers
> were in town, Fanon looked for the soldiers through the streets of Fort de
> France and was 'in rapture' along with the rest of his family when his father
> brought home these items.[50]

Significantly, Macey recounts the same memory from Fanon's childhood
that Vergès discusses, with a notable difference, 'When a Senegalese unit
stopped in Martinique in transit from French Guiana *his father brought
two of them home*. The family was delighted with them. The Fanon family
behaved in much the same way as the Marrette family; they were hospi-
table to their colonial boys, recognised them as *nègres* and misrecognised
themselves.'[51] The fascinating difference in interpretation of this line from
BSWM might be instructive, where Vergès sees the signs of the fetish, the fez
and belt, and Fanon's fascination with the sexualised and terrifying black
African men, Macey reads the men themselves not their uniforms. What/
who was it that Fanon's father brought back to the family house, people or
objects? The logic of the stereotype as fetish works here all too clearly.

By the time that Fanon recalls this experience and complains of the
oppressiveness of '*Y'a bon Banania*', he has already fought for France in
World War II with the Free French and had his unit merged with a Senegalese one, bringing to the fore the racial hierarchies at play between
Senegalese, Antillean and Arab in North Africa. However, the image of the
Tirailleur Senegalais used for the *Banania* advertisements conforms strikingly to Bhabha's model of repulsion and desire, denial and fetishisation,
'that otherness which is at once an object of desire and derision.'[52]

Macey traces the development of the *Banania* image,

> During the First World War, the image of the *Tirailleur Senegalais* became still
> more ambiguous when it was used to sell Banania, a breakfast drink made
> from banana flour, cocoa and sugar. All over France posters showed a grin-
> ning soldier dressed in his exotic uniform, and spooning Banania into his
> mouth. The image of fear merges with one of cosy domesticity.[53]

Fanon does not offer an in-depth reading of the *Banania* image, found on
posters and on the Banania packaging, but he does offer a footnote on the

'grin' and constructions of 'smiling negroes' in chapter two of *BSWM*, 'The woman of colour and the white man'. He cites Bernard Wolfe,

> 'It pleases us to portray the Negro showing us all his teeth in a smile made for us. And his smile as we see it – as we make it – always means a gift. ...' Gifts without end, on every screen, on every food-product label. [...] Service with a smile every time. ... "The blacks", writes anthropologist Geoffrey Gorer in *The American Spirit: a study of national character*, "are kept in their obsequious attitude by the extreme penalties of fear and force and this is common knowledge to both the whites and the blacks. Nevertheless, the whites demand that 'the blacks be always smiling, attentive and friendly in all their relationships with them".[54]

David Macey and François Vergès are two critics that notice the translation of 'Sho good eatin' from the French '*Y'a Bon Banania*', stripping the line of its French context and replacing it with a stereotypical representation of African-American vernacular associated with food advertising, making something else of it. Certainly there are trans-cultural parallels, between the two phrases, the creation of '*Y'a Bon Banania*', relied on a similar use of a Black colonial vernacular French, the derogatorily termed '*petit nègre*'. Both phrases reference a black speech act, commodified in the service of consumption, where the potentially explosive history of the speaker's identity is sanitised under a benevolent invitation to consume. However, there are some significant differences inevitably between the representation of an African-American's vernacular in the USA and the significance of the *Tirailleur Senegalais* in the French colonial imaginary, as well as in Fanon's own personal history.

It is worth pursuing Fanon's original example of this, the 'above all else', the last word in racist formulations that he particularly resists, for the specificity of this reading offers an interesting elaboration of Bhabha's model of the profoundly ambivalent structures of desire that operate in the logic of the stereotype. David Macey has argued forcefully and persuasively, both in his remarkable biography of Fanon and elsewhere, for a reassessment of the specificities of the French context in any readings of Fanon, ones that have been obscured through the application of his work to American contexts from the 1960s onwards; and this line in translation by Markmann certainly demonstrates this problem for readers of the English translation of *Black Skin White Masks*. Revisiting French contexts for Fanon's work adds a materiality to interpretations that is valuable but also emphasises his immersion in metropolitan French culture and the writing that prefigures French post-structuralism.

David Macey considers the 'translation', both textual and contextual, of *Black Skin White Masks*, 'impossible to work with', for several reasons, but most significantly because it removes the resonance of the term '*nègre*' and it removes Fanon from his Martinican context.[55] 'There is considerable textual evidence to indicate that *Peau Noire* could not have been written by anyone but a Martinican. It is deeply rooted in the Martinican experience, in the experience of people who were French citizens and not colonial subjects, and who occupied a curious position within the racial hierarchy. One of the island's more peculiar exports was the French-educated black civil servant and citizen who administered black subjects in the African colonies and who was in a sense neither black nor white. Fanon found himself in that anomalous position as a young soldier at the end of World War II: he was neither indigene nor toubab, neither "native" nor "white man". Fanon's black man is Martinican, in other words a West Indian who does not think of himself as black: he thinks of himself as West Indian. Subjectively, intellectually the West Indian behaves as a White. But he is a *nègre*. He will notice once he is in Europe, and when they talk about *nègres*, he will know they are talking about him as well as about the Senegalese'.[56]

Again, the *Senegalais* exists as a crucial marker of racial difference and one of terrifying loss of identity when the Martinican is fatefully confused with the African. However, race is imbrecated with sexuality and desire quite explicitly in the constructions of the Tirailleurs, both in their construction in the colonial imaginary and arguably in the material history of their formation as colonial troops to be used on other colonial peoples instead of white French soldiers, such that the model of Bhabha's stereotype/fetish holds significance. Macey comments,

> The colonial regiments recruited in Africa were surrounded by a particular aura. On the one hand they were highly regarded as fighting men; on the other they had a nasty reputation for rape and pillage – and were apparently encouraged in those practices by their white officers. When they were stationed in the French-occupied Rhineland after the First World War, their unenviable reputation spread to England. The Daily Herald of al papers ran headlines like 'Black Peril on the Rhine', 'Sexual horrors Let Loose by France', 'Black menace of 40,000 Troops' and 'Appeal to the Woman of Europe'.[57]

It was certainly this reputation that fascinated Fanon as a child and one that continued long into his adult life. It erupts in several places in *BWSM*. The first mention of the Senegalese troops occurs in chapter one, where Fanon's experiences during World War II in a troop of Senegalese infantry are used to illustrate a problematic status of Antillean officers identifying problematically with white officers: 'the Senegalese were ordered to attack three times, and each time they were forced back. Then one of them wanted to know why the toubabs did not go into action. At such times, one no longer knows whether one's a toubab or a native.'[58]

Passing and instability mark the relationships between modes of black colonial identities in this context. In Bhabha's vocabulary this is most clearly understood as the logic of mimicry. Mimicry might indeed be seen as a response to stereotyping and to the impossible demands of colonial discourse. The Martinican trembles on the threshold of 'native' and 'toubab', and passes back and forth between the positions, uncertainly. However, such an in-between identity does not necessarily only connote privilege, in that the Martinican might sometimes be mistaken for the toubab: it marks the radical instability of these categories, unpicks the narratives that hold them in place. A racialised hierarchy is made nonsense of, allowing a stretching of categories, a masking and unmasking of racist colonial discourse, while it may save the life of the Martinican who is seen as less expendable than the Senegalese soldier.

A little further on in the same chapter Fanon comments, 'A Senegalese learns Creole in order to pass as an Antilles native: I call this alienation / The Antilles Negroes who know him never weary of making jokes about him: I call this lack of judgement'.[59] Mimicry might initially appear to provide a source of humour, 'in order to be effective, mimicry must continually produce its slippage, its excess, its difference'.[60] Although the Antillean might laugh at what he perceives as poor impersonations of his own identity, and refuse to recognise them, this slippage critically points to the ambivalence at the heart of colonial demands for 'a reformed recognisable Other'.[61] Bhabha suggests that Fanon's title *Black Skin White Mask* supports his model of fetish/ stereotype, as indeed these examples of mimicry do, where 'the disavowal of difference turns the colonial subject into a misfit – a grotesque mimicry or doubling that threatens to split the soul and whole undifferentiated skin of the ego'.[62]

Perhaps the most extensive reference to the Senegalese is in chapter four, 'The So-called Dependency Complex of Colonised Peoples', where Fanon explicitly rejects Octavio Manonni's theories of a 'dependency complex' in relation to the colonised people of Madagascar. Fanon's 'radicalisation' of psychoanalytic models refuses to accept a naturalisation of traumas relating to race, and insists on understanding the regimes of power and knowledge that produce particular psychic conditions. Mannoni 'illustrates' his model of innate need to be colonised and fear of blackness explicitly through his readings of the dreams of his patients that relate to terrifying images of black men and Senegalese soldiers.

Fanon comments on the use of Senegalese in Madagascar 'We know from other sources that one of the torturers in the Tananarive police headquarters was a Senegalese. Therefore, since we know all this, since we know what the archetype of the Senegalese can represent for the Malagasy, the discoveries of Freud are of no use to us here. What must be done is to restore this dream to its proper time, and this period is the time during which eighty thousand natives were killed.' Here Fanon explicitly quotes a materialist reading of Pierre Naville, that 'the content of a human being's dreams depends also in the last analysis on the general conditions of the culture in which he lives', to insist that Mannoni's reading through Freud for father figures and 'primal ancestors' is to be blinded to the actual conditions under a colonial regime that terrorises its subjects. Fanon curiously refuses to see sexualised and racialised images as imbrecated in this case, 'The Rifle of the Senegalese soldier is not a penis but a genuine rifle, model Lebel 1916.'[63] He cites in a vast three-page footnote the testimony of a witness Rakatovao at a trial in Tananarive, on the extensive torture that he suffered at the hands of a Senegalese soldier. This extensive use of the footnote is part of a sustained writing strategy on Fanon's part, conscious or not, that is constantly crossing from the official 'body' of the text to the elements, narratives or bodies that are hived off, displaced or put at the margins. Accounts of the Senegalese and readings of their historical and ideological positions appear to initially fall outside the body of the text, but at this moment the displaced figure of the black torturer serving the French colonial regime erupts and arrests the official narrative.

Does this insistence on the 'reality' of the torturer problematise the question of the stereotype? The material reality of the use of the Tirailleur on other colonised populations is undeniable. Can the two modes of reading be reconciled or at least held in productive relation? Bhabha's argument that colonial discourse produces a fixity of imagery, which is nevertheless always troubled and subverted by ambivalence and disavowal, makes necessary a new thinking through relations between material and imaginary, and the role of representation in producing that experience of reality, the 'lived experience of the black man'. For Hall, 'our dilemma is how to think together the overwhelming power of the binary which persists despite everything and in all racially inflected systems of power and representation and simultaneously the ambivalences, the openings, the slippages which the suturing of racial discourse can never totally close up'.[64]

Fanon appears to view the *Tirailleur Senegalais* as somehow outside the regime of representation and at the same time as haunting the unconscious of the colonised Malagasy, and performs this textually. At the other extreme of the desire and fascination that he recounts from his childhood is a refusal, a resistance and a repulsion from the knowledge of how the fetish cannot be unpicked from the materiality of experience. Although he illustrates contemptuously the ways in which the stereotype has been 'naturalised' and the colonised pathologised as a result, in Mannoni's account, the passage suggests, I think, an inadvertent example of Bhabha's model where the stereotype troubles Fanon and he tries to disentangle the Senegalese from its regime. Not the penis, not the fetish, but the gun and the man. It is arguably with the Senegalese that he tries hardest to put together the black body that has been ripped apart under the colonial gaze. This is perhaps an example of one of the limits in Fanon's writing: that by using Bhabha's approach one can attempt to take the narrative beyond what the text is able to say.

It may be, as Hall suggests, that 'Fanon constantly and implicitly poses issues and raises questions in ways which cannot be adequately addressed within the conceptual framework into which he seeks often to resolve them; and that a more satisfactory and complex logic is often implicitly threaded through the interstices of his text, which he does not always follow through but which we can discover by reading him against the grain'.[65]

In Achille Mbembe's writing on Fanon, one might detect a similar proximity to Fanon that also engages with the self-imposed or unconscious limits of his analysis, one that attempts to both inhabit and intervene. Mbembe comments, 'concerning the colonial world its arrangement its geographical layout and the violence presiding at its constitution, Fanon mentions first the barracks and police station.'[66] Violence, he notes, is built into structures and institutions.

> It is implemented by persons of flesh and bone such as the soldier, the French commandant, the police officer and the native chief. A violence that insinuates itself into the economy, domestic life, language, consciousness. It does more than penetrate every space: it pursues the colonised even in sleep and dream. It produces a culture; it is a cultural praxis.[67]

For Mbembe, the violence that inhabits and terrorises the colonised and colonial societies cannot be clearly marked off from emotional sensibilities and psychic traumas. Mbembe's reading of colonial violence and its discourses, its cultural praxis, emphasises a 'tactile perception of the native' bodies in close proximity, and insists on a forceful sexualised reading of the 'spaces of terror' that constitute the colonies. Colonial discourse likewise must 'as in the act of copulation and rape, grope, lick and bite, rise and descend'.[68] For Mbembe,

> such a figuring of violence refuses the border between real and imagined, between 'actual' conquering, penetration, and the imaginary. In the colonial

world says Fanon 'the colonized's emotional sensibility is kept on the surface of his skin like an open sore which flinches from the caustic agent. It is literally in a state of erection. Retraction, relaxation, obliteration and discharge are its main components'.[69]

The distinguished Senegalese filmmaker Sembene Ousmane co-directed the film *Camp de Thiaroye* with Thierno Faty Sow in 1988, which revisits French colonial constructions and destructions of black bodies during World War II and which intersects significantly with Fanon's observations about his own experiences in black fighting units.[70] Sembene explores the relationships between the regimes of power and representation that operated over the *Tirailleurs Senegalais*. This account of the experiences of one battalion, cynically and brutally betrayed by their French commanders as they are demobilised in 1944 in a transit camp in Dakar, has at its centre the paradoxical and ambivalent narratives of colonialism that intersect with the violence and violation of colonial power. The film revisits a notorious massacre of African soldiers on African soil by the French, and can be seen as part of a broader revisiting and documenting of this repressed and hidden event in French colonial history by Senegalese historians and artists.

The film follows a battalion made up of soldiers from across French colonial Africa, waiting to be paid and allowed to return to their respective countries, who communicate together in '*petit nègre*', the derogatory term for the common language of the colonised French Africans, utilised in the *Banania* advertisement. Their Senior N. C. O. is Senegalese, who is visited while in the camp by his uncle, cousin and extended family members. They discover he has married a white woman and has a daughter in France. They find this impossible to believe as they have suffered severe brutality from French colonial forces, having their villages destroyed and family murdered, and have arrived to welcome him home to a possible marriage. However, he speaks perfect French, and finds himself compromised between his different families. He also negotiates between the white commanders and his men when a dispute about pay erupts in the camp.

The decision to exchange black soldiers' pay at half the rate of white soldiers opens up a chasm in French narratives of *egalite* and *fraternite* that the black soldiers have been fighting to defend, but find they do not qualify for. They have participated in the liberation of Europe and Paris itself. Their experiences open up the related questions of *liberté*, both personal and national, that put the camp into crisis, as the white officers anticipate an escalation of dissent that prefigures the liberation struggles of black African nations. The paradox of being black and feeling 'French' appears to extend further than Fanon's Martinique, even though as a department it is a special case. The black Senegalese sergeant major Diatta listens to jazz and reads poetry books that are later interpreted as a sign of his communist sympathies. He is French educated, but his adoption of French culture threatens to blow apart the colonial system, such that French culture is suddenly unhomed, made unfamiliar and uncanny, a threat to the stability, dominance and hegemony of the French themselves.

Two critical scenes mark out the perversities and paradoxes of colonial discourse in relation to identity and the body. The men arrive in the camp dressed in American army uniforms that have been provided for them as France has been 'liberated'. The black officer gets leave to go outside the camp and attempts to visit a bar and brothel, set aside for white officers while wearing his American uniform and a pair of sunglasses. He is initially made welcome as a US officer, despite his blackness, but clearly has little English; he reveals his true origins by ordering *un Pernod* at the bar. The manageress is called in a panic, to throw him out; '*un nègre*' has found his way inside. For him the Pernod and his excellent French aligns him with the stated French culture of *égalité, fraternité* and sophistication (he initially refuses a drink of local palm wine from his relatives). For the women, it signals his non-status, as one of the colonised there are no rewards for being a good mimic of the French, only for passing as American. Interestingly it is through speech and not the visual that the Sergeant's mimicry fails. The insertion of the colonised subject into the language of the coloniser as Bhabha notes in 'Dissemination' produces unforeseen effects. It is not the shock of a 'different' language that provokes rejection, but the use of the coloniser's words, whose meanings sharply diverge from those intended. The words will not translate, they remain opaque. 'Through the opaqueness of words, we confront the historical memory of the Western nation which is 'obliged to forget'.[71] The effects of the order for *un Pernod,* as Bhabha illustrates with an example of a Turkish *Gastarbeiter,* are to break the silence that has held the illusion, such that 'the body returns now, shrouded not in silence but eerily untranslated in the racist site of its enunciation; to say the word girl is to be a randy dog, to ask for coffee is to encounter the colour bar'.[72]

The potentially parallel oppressions of the women working in the brothel and the black African solider serving the French colonial regime resonate in this moment of 'recognition', where passing collapses into mimicry. However, this exposure of a colonised identity does not initiate a moment of revelation of common political cause between raced and gendered positions under French colonialism. Rather, recognition that the exchange of money for female bodies in the form of prostitution, or for Black African bodies as paid soldiers, shares a common role in the service of the colonial regime threatens to emasculate the black male body.

After a short time in the camp, the soldiers are required to give up their US army uniforms and put on the traditional *Tirailleurs* uniforms and the red chechia. This is performed out in the open and en masse in the central parade ground, a stripping off of a black identity that they have valued, associated with an American narrative of status, modernity and economic success, and certainly from the French perspective a returning to their previous state. This is experienced as a demoralising loss of status. As they give up their boots, the camp is deflated and despondent. Now that the French have returned their bodies to their 'proper state' they cannot be mistaken for 'men'. They are more vulnerable to exploitation and poor treatment, but at the same time have been radicalised by their experiences. However, the idealised view of American soldiers as having a better status is a local one, at least in French West Africa, where their American identity overrides their black skin, for this temporary raising of status of Black Americans shares in precisely the same ambivalent position in colonial/imperialist discourse. Sembene interrogates this when Diatta and a black G.I. meet to discuss their respective positions and recognise parallels in their experiences and oppressions, something that does not take place between Diatta and the women of the brothel.

The uprising in the camp depicted in the film re-presents the actual historical event, where the protests over pay and the temporary hostage-taking of a white French general result in a vicious and brutal reprisal, with tanks opening fire on the camp during the night and killing over forty men. However, although the material brutality of the events is unswervingly represented in the film, it is in the nature of the way the French used black troops to police other black colonies, that the soldiers firing on the camp would also have been African.

Fanon's own experiences of fighting with the *Tirailleurs Senegalais* suggest the potentially explosive paradoxes of the status of colonial troops. As David Macey comments, 'what happens when the colonized liberate their colonizers, and then realize that they themselves are still colonized?'[73] Fanon's experience in the French Army emerges as a central radicalising experience, one founded not just in the traumas of war, but in his closest-yet proximity to the war machine of colonial power and discourse, functioning inside it as one of its bodies.

Macey's account of the war marks the paradoxes of colonial involvement and national affiliations, 'When New Year parcels from America arrived for the mixed colonial and French units, a French officer decided that they should be distributed on the basis of one parcel for each Frenchman, and one parcel to be shared between three Moroccans. When an Algerian sergeant protested, he was told that he was an agitator and did not deserve the *Medaille Militaire* for which he had been recommended. The sergeant was Ahmed Ben Bella, the future first president of independent Algeria. His feelings about the war he was fighting were becoming dangerously ambiguous, "I was fighting for a just cause, and I believe that I was happy. Or at least I would have been happy, if the thought of unhappy Algeria had ever left me for a moment." '[74] Fanon, like Ben Bella, was caught by the paradoxes of this potentially explosive position that crossed and unravelled the material and ideological boundaries of colonial power and ideology. He puzzles over the problematic use of the colonised to perpetuate the colonial establishment.

> Whenever there has been any attempt at insurrection the military authorities have ordered only coloured soldiers into action. They were men of colour who nullified the liberation efforts of other men of colour, proof that there was no reason to universalise the procedure.
>
> (*BSWM* p. 103)

For Bhabha, the salient point about mimicry is demonstrated in the paradoxes of the black colonial soldier's predicament, mimicry can turn to menace. Indeed, it is coterminous with it. 'The ambivalence of colonial authority repeatedly turns from mimicry – a difference that is almost nothing but not quite – to menace – a difference that is almost total but not quite.'[75] Although this menace is quite literally enacted on the *Tirailleurs* and memorialised in Sembene's film, it is also present in the film as prefiguring a dawning of a politicised African population, radicalised in part through their experiences fighting in Europe, their bitter knowledge of colonialism and in their active interrogation of the politics of mimicry.

4   Bhabha's Postal Politics

> When the path is clear and given when a certain knowledge opens up the way in advance, the decision is already made, it might as well be said that there is none to make: irresponsibility, and in good conscience.
>
> Jacques Derrida, The Other Heading, p. 41

> How does the deconstruction of the 'sign', the emphasis on indeterminism in cultural and political judgment, transform our sense of the 'subject' of culture and the historical agent of change? If we contest the 'grand narratives', then what alternative temporalities do we create to articulate the differential (Jameson), contrapuntal (Said), interruptive (Spivak), histories of race, gender, class, nation within a growing transnational culture.
>
> Homi K. Bhabha, 'The Postcolonial and the Postmodern',
The Location of Culture, p. 173

What is the meaning of postcolonialism in an increasingly globalised world? How might one understand the proliferation of the term 'post' that appears so frequently in contemporary critical and political language? Does 'post' carry the same provenance when it occurs in postmodernism, post-structuralism, in so-called post-feminist or post-Marxist forms? How does the temporality of the 'post' relate to the contestation of 'grand narratives' as Bhabha sees it?

The 'post' seems to imply a kind of movement, through time or space that is by no means easy to arrest. It comes after something else, but also appears to inflect that thing with a new tone, to supersede or supplant that which it inflects. This is suggestively illustrated by the title of Ian Adam and Helen Tiffin's book, *Past the Last Post: Theorising Post-colonialism and Post-modernism*, suggesting images of a race, a break, or an ending or completion, as well as a kind of going beyond, venturing into uncharted territory, past 'the last outposts of empire'.[1]

It is this sense of coming after that has taken up an immense amount of discussion in postcolonial criticism. Just as it may be difficult to decide when postcolonialism began, it is also problematic to try to limit the remit of the postcolonial and ask what might come after postcolonialism.

The very interesting temporality of the postcolonial begins to reveal itself in this question of its ending. Is it possible to suggest when or how colonialism or postcolonialism might be finished? Can it be understood in a linear historical temporality? It seems on one level a disarmingly simple question, which demands a straightforward response. In terms of a linear logic of succession, the question would seem to acknowledge a perception that academic inquiry and political activism has moved through a series of distinct periods, addressing say, class, gender, sexuality and race in turn. However, it also exhibits a rather uncanny property, where the 'post' would look forward to see itself in the past. The present comprehends itself as 'future anterior' as that which will have been.

The problematic relationship of different forms of postcolonialism to questions of temporality hardly needs asserting. It might be possible to say that since its inception postcolonialism has been preoccupied with questions of what comes after it, if of course it were possible to put a date on when it might end. The 'post' in postcolonialism has exercised the minds of numerous postcolonial critics, 'that troubling question of the prefix', as Stuart Hall comments.[2] However, primarily this discussion has tended to privilege linear temporal and epistemological implications in the search for beginnings and ends, which as we have seen may prove elusive. It could be argued that much of the discomfort with the term postcolonial stems from a reluctance to confront the implications of a postal condition, instead attempting somewhat unsatisfactorily to return the term 'post' into a denotation of chronology where it is inevitably found wanting. 'Post' understood as after has been discussed at length in critical circles, in several key critical texts from Ella Shohat, Vijay Mishra and Bob Hodge, Anne McClintock, Peter Hulme and Stuart Hall, among others.

In 'The Angel of Progress: Pitfalls of the Term Post-colonialism', Anne McClintock provides one of the most overtly hostile accounts of the 'post'.[3] McClintock, though, takes postcolonial to refer to everything that has happened since the 'end' of European colonialism; hence much of her argument inevitably focuses on the many ways in which colonialism cannot be said to have ended in many parts of the world. Indeed that colonialism far from having ended has entered a new even more aggressive phase in the form of neo-colonialism.

While this forms the central objection to the 'post' in postcolonial, McClintock also has other objections which are centred around a crisis of imagining the future,

> The enthusiasm for 'post' words [...] ramifies beyond the corridors of the university. The recurrent almost ritualistic incantation of the preposition 'post' is

a symptom I believe of a global crisis in ideologies of the future particularly ideologies of progress. [...] The collapse of both capitalist and communist teleologies of progress has resulted in a doubled and overdetermined crisis in images of future time, the apocalyptic time stopped prevalence of 'post' words is only one symptom.

(p. 86)

McClintock's lament for certainty about the future is marked by the sense of an inability to locate any particular culprit to direct accusation against; the rise to prominence of the 'post' appears at once to have come from a crisis in the 'competing' ideologies of capitalism and communism, and from an obsession both within and outside the academy. However, having highlighted quite rightly a certain 'crisis in ideologies of the future', the essay expresses a frustration with what she frames as a lack of academic or political will,

> Without a renewed will to intervene in the unacceptable we face being becalmed in an historically empty space in which our sole direction is found by gazing back spellbound at the epoch behind us in a perpetual present marked only as 'post'.

(p. 89)

Bhabha's interest in postcolonialism's contramodernity prompts him to consider the ways in which, for several postcolonial cultural critics, a relationship with the past creates a kind of 'disjunctive temporality', which he suggests, is 'of the utmost importance for the politics of cultural difference'. The use of the term 'post' then surely heralds more than a descent into political impotence, and the relation of the 'post' to history and politics needs further exploration. For Mishra and Hodge, an unhyphenated postcolonialism is most effective if deemed to refer not to something after colonialism, but as an impulse already implicit in the discourses of colonialism themselves. This, they argue, would be best termed 'a "complicit postcolonialism": an always present underside within colonization itself' (p. 284). They claim that this construction would have much in common with Jean-Francois Lyotard's much quoted comment on postmodernism, that 'a work can become modern only if it is first postmodern. Thus understood, postmodernism is not modernism at its end but in a nascent state and this state is recurrent'.[4] It will be useful to return to this formulation later in the chapter.

There are several reasons for the reluctance to engage with Bhabha's avowedly post-structuralist version of the 'post' in some postcolonial circles. Elleke Boehmer's contribution to the founding issues of the postcolonial journal *Interventions* could be taken as indicative of these concerns. Her concern is precisely with the kinds of critical approaches identified with or as postcolonialism.

> Asking 'how is the postcolonial' also leads us to the question of postmodernist post-colonial theory: how is it used, how located? For, however fruitful the relationship between anti-colonial and nationalist literatures and post-structuralist theories, it is also the case that that relationship has tended to exacerbate the self-referential introversion of the Western academy mainly because the theories have at least initially borne little connection with the resistance histories out of which the literatures have emerged.[5]

Interestingly, although Boehmer's essay rightly insists that postcolonial critics need to interrogate the 'unspoken conventions' of the field, she maintains the particular orthodoxy that insists that theory, however useful, raises a problem of a 'lost or displaced context'. It is perhaps here that when the question of theory emerges in certain debates, borders between 'the West' and 'the rest' are reasserted, whereas Bhabha insists on postcolonialism as having thrived upon crossing and destabilising, chafing against both, ostentatiously *and* illicitly. It becomes necessary for him to insist that this distinction is a false one, as Robert Young does in his opening lines of *White Mythologies: Writing History and the West,*

> If so called 'so-called post-structuralism' is the product of a single historical moment then that moment is probably not May 1968 but rather the Algerian War of Independence – no doubt itself both a symptom and a product. In this respect it is significant that Sartre, Althusser, Derrida and Lyotard, among others were all either born in Algeria or personally involved in the events of the war.[6]

To this list one might also add Helene Cixous, Giles Deleuze and Emmanuel Levinas. For Young, the commonalities between post-structuralism and postcolonialism have frequently been overlooked, and thinkers such as Derrida have been too rigidly categorised as Eurocentric. Derrida's troubled relationship to Algeria as a member of its Jewish community, his critique of the founding concepts of Western philosophy and his more recent work concerning what he terms his troubled 'Franco-Maghrebian' identity suggest that his work can hardly be viewed as antithetical to postcolonial concerns.[7]

Although Bhabha draws on the work a wide variety of academics activists writers and poets, the work of these critics, and in particular Derrida, certainly contributes one of the key strands of thinking in Bhabha's work. In his essay 'The Postcolonial and the Postmodern' re-published in *The Location of Culture*, Bhabha, like Young, is fascinated by the ways that the condition of colonial and postcolonial culture might be seen to intersect with questions and predicaments explored in the theoretical debates of so-called contemporary critical theory.

For Bhabha, the relationship between postmodernism and postcolonialism can only be understood through a revisiting of the narratives of modernity itself. He suggests that narratives of modernity are marked, even if they do not know it, by what he terms a 'cut' or caesura, a temporal break. This might be understood as a kind of internal splitting, an impossibility of any narrative adding up, this cut being what he calls in places the postcolonial translation of, or intervention into, modernity. That is to say, the terms on which modernity represents itself are profoundly disturbed and radically questioned through an apprehension of the experiences of the colonised, of minorities. He comments,

> In general terms, there is a colonial contramodernity at work in the eighteenth – and nineteenth – century matrices of Western modernity that, if acknowledged, would question the historicism that analogically links, in a linear narrative, late capitalism and the fragmentary, simulacral, pastiche symptoms of postmodernity.[8]

Perhaps the distinction that is hardest to be clear about, though, is the ways in which postcolonial criticism as Bhabha practices it can be differentiated from post-structuralism. In the same essay Bhabha comments,

> My use of post-structuralist theory emerges from this postcolonial contramodernity. I attempt to represent a certain defeat, or even an impossibility, of the 'West' in its authorization of the 'idea' of colonisation. Driven by the subaltern history of the margins of modernity – rather than by the failures of logocentrism – I have tried, in some small measure, to revise the known, to rename the postmodern from the position of the postcolonial.

Here he seems to suggest that the postcolonial perspective has the ability to alter the terms of post-structuralist enquiry, substituting marginalised perspectives and experiences for a fascination with logocentrism. That is to say, the postcolonial experience is brought to bear on an existing critical framework. However, in the same essay he offers a different account, where the very nature of colonial discourse and the modes of resistance to it appear to precede any critical formulation of post-structuralist theories.

> My growing conviction has been that the encounters and negotiations of different meanings and values within 'colonial' textuality its governmental discourses and cultural practices, have anticipated, *avant la lettre*, many of

the problematics of signification and judgement that have become current
in contemporary theory – aporia, ambivalence, indeterminacy, the question
of discursive closure, the threat to agency, the status of intentionality, the
challenge to 'totalizing' concepts to name but a few.

(p. 173)

Bhabha then presents us with an interesting predicament: his model might
easily be read to imply, and indeed has been, that yet again the experience of the colonised has only belatedly been recognised and then has
been appropriated by a Western discourse – theory. The relationship might
then be easily read as a silencing one, in which a new vocabulary of minority resistance is not deemed necessary, the marginal voices silenced by
so-called Western theory. The relationship between the critic and the subject of investigation continually shifts in terms of how we are to understand
the naming of the postcolonial as *avant la lettre*, post-structuralist. In fact,
it has more to do with how the time or 'temporality' of the post(s) in post-
structuralism and postcolonialism might be understood.

Bhabha addresses this temporal 'disjunction' head-on in his essay 'The
Postcolonial and the Postmodern', by focusing on the ways in which the
language of contemporary cultural criticism locates itself in the 'peculiar
temporality of the language metaphor'.[9] In the section of his argument
devoted to 'new times', he highlights the ways in which what he terms 'a
range of transgressive and interventionary discourses around histories
of discrimination and misrepresentation' share a tendency to use post-
structuralist vocabularies, terms such as 'the arbitrariness of the sign, the
indeterminacy of writing, the splitting of the subject', in order to 'provide
a social imaginary that is based on the articulation of differential, even
disjunctive, moments of history and culture'. He is interested in the ways
in which a post-structuralist vocabulary appears to have become an enabling mode of expression, where questions of cultural difference or incommensurability are concerned. The implications of this proposal are that the
postcolonial and the postmodern share a need to understand the present in
terms of a 'disjunctive temporality'. Using Stuart Hall's discussion of ideology in *The Hard Road to Renewal*, he points to the ways in which the indeterminacy of writing is used as a metaphor for a contingent political logic
of ideology,

> The authority of customary, traditional practices – culture's relation to the his-
> toric past, is not dehistoricised, in Hall's language metaphor. Those anchor-
> ing moments are revalued as a form of anteriority – a before that has no a
> priori(ty) – whose causality is effective because it returns to displace the

present, to make it disjunctive. This kind of disjunctive temporality is of the
utmost importance for the politics of cultural difference.

(p. 177)

In a significant essay published in Bhabha's edited collection *Nation and
Narration*, 'Postal Politics and the Institution of the Nation', Geoffrey
Bennington begins his discussion with an examination of the 'post' from
both post-structuralist and postmodern positions, two approaches that
have been (contentiously) implicated in postcolonial formulations potentially from the outset.[10] This early publication, in which Bhabha published
his hugely influential essay 'DissemiNation: Time, Narrative and the Margins of the Modern Nation', had a significant impact in the field of literary
and cultural theory, suggesting as it did the ways in which post-structuralist
theories of narrative might be effectively brought to bear on questions of
cultural politics, temporal and spatial understandings of nation, and of the
writing of history. To complicate both McClintock's and Mishra and Hodge's
formulations, it may be useful to take a detour into these debates.

Bennington notes that the 'post' is of course a prefix, and whereas 'any
socio-historico-institutional analysis' of the 'post' in post-structuralism or
postmodernism would rely on an understanding of this term designating,
'what comes after, what supersedes or what sublates', the nature of the 'post'
as a prefix means that bizarrely the 'post' 'comes first, at the beginning,
at the origin'.[11] For Robert Young and Derek Attridge, the temporal and
spatial possibilities of the 'post' are a good starting point for theorising
post-structuralism, where the 'post' temporally comes after but spatially
before. Taking this claim seriously has profound effects on an understanding of the post's temporal and spatial strangeness.

They comment in their introduction to *Poststructuralism and the Question of History*, that '"far from being a matter of the absence of history",
post-structuralism involves an attentiveness to what Frederic Jameson has
called 'the crisis of historicity itself', such that it is already a simplification to
assume that post-structuralism simply comes after structuralism'.[12]

As Bennington notes, in Lyotard's account of the coming of the postmodern, there is a tension between his view that according to a chronological
view of history 'we enter the post-modern condition as we enter so-called
post-industrial society, after a modern condition and an industrial society'
and the understanding that the postmodern involves a decline or loss of
credibility of grand narratives which would include the previous account.[13]
However, by reading Lyotard's formulation in *The Postmodern Condition*
against itself Bennington suggests that, 'If the postmodern involves the

decline or the loss of credibility of grand narratives, it is difficult to describe it in terms of a grand narrative.'[14] Lyotard's own words suggest that the logic of the 'post' as Bennington and Young construct it might confound a teleological approach to postmodernism and potentially to all 'posts'. Lyotard's further claims that 'a work can become modern only if it is first postmodern'. Postmodernism thus understood is not modernism at its end, but in the nascent state, and this state is recurrent insists on a reversal of perceived order. It suggests that modernism has always been constituted or inhabited by postmodernism. The temporal paradox of this logic is termed by Lyotard as the future perfect (that which will have been), which returns us to my earlier discussion of the temporality of the 'post' in postcolonial. The postcolonial impulse might also be helpfully thought of as ceaselessly present in colonialism itself.

If we return to Mishra and Hodge's discussion, which makes the case for a version of postcolonialism that in their words, 'has much in common with Lyotard's unhyphenated postmodernism', they in fact transpire to have rather less in common with Lyotard than with Fanon's comment. Mishra and Hodge offer a dubious distinction between oppositional and complicit postcolonialism, the former referring to nationalist, pro-independence formations, the latter to 'an always present underside in colonialism itself'. Although this last definition seems promising in its refusal of a teleological postcolonialism, the authors struggle with this doubled definition in their attempts to separate and maintain a political sphere that does not keep problematically blurring with what they see as postmodernist concerns. Despite their allusion to Lyotard, they seem to wish to cleanse the most critical (post) structural aspect of postmodern inflections from postcolonialism, by holding on to a historical distinction despite a flirtation with the logic of the 'post' as Lyotard formulates it. It is also clear that McClintock's desire for a 'return' to progress also fails to address this formulation of the post. Indeed, it is hard to see how history with a capital 'H' can be appealed to when postcolonial theory has offered so many assaults on precisely this concept in colonial discourses.

Similarly, Ella Shohat's comments that the 'post' in postcolonial is different from other 'posts' in its attempts to be both epistemological and chronological seem misplaced; rather, this is precisely the condition cited by Lyotard. Mishra and Hodge's reluctant relation to Lyotard perhaps reflects an anxiety about how far deploying the logic of the 'post' as described by Bennington, Lyotard and Young is justified in a discussion of postcolonialism.

However, for Bhabha, the importance of the 'post' understood in a non-chronological sense crosses with Bennington's engagement with Derrida's work on the 'post' and postal technologies, where the actual properties of the 'post' as a postal system, a or postal network circulating signs, is central to understanding certain conditions of postcoloniality as they exist under colonialism itself.

I   Postal networks

> All the Civilizations, so good at royal arts and war
> And postal networks-
>> Les Murray, The Action, *Collected Poems*, Carcanet, 1991

Politics, Bennington argues, conforms to the logic of a postal network. Referring to Montesquieu's assertion that 'Politics, as it is today, comes from the invention of the post', he suggests, following Derrida, that politics can be seen as postal because its processes depend upon the transmission and reception of messages, promises, orders, and so on, which are disseminated but which always risk never fully arriving (being fulfilled, achieved).[15] Montesquieu distinguishes politics, as a democratic structure, from despotism, which he views through the prism of enlightenment Orientalism: 'we do not politick with the Mogul'. He assumes that a despotic system of government is not postal, because the despot imposes his will completely in a concentrated form that is (apparently) absolute, having 'the *immediate* force of law'. In this sense his words might equally be rephrased for our purposes to, 'we do not politick with the coloniser', as clearly colonialism, no matter how benignly it may represent itself, cannot conform to the logic of 'democracy'. However, against Montesquieu, we can see that despotic power does in fact depend on a postal network; he admits as much when he comments that 'in the despotic government power passes entirely into the hands of him to whom it is given. The vizar is the depot himself; and each individual officer is the vizar' (p. 125).

This leads Bennington to conclude that the despotic (and therefore potentially the colonial) model is both absolutely postal and absolutely non-postal. In other words, although in a despotic system power can be viewed as non-postal because it is seen as emanating from a single authority, it simultaneously operates through a form of delegation which retains the reliance on messages, orders, information. Even in the assertion that power resides in the individual who enacts it in the name of the despot, or assumes the role of the despot, this postal system applies, the certificate of authorisation, the uniform, the gun, the field radio. The interrogation of this distinction and the deconstruction of the opposition between democratic and despotic politics, which acknowledges them as both postal, is critical to re-situating a discussion of the 'politics of postcolonial theory' as it has been debated recently.

A central criticism of post-structuralist approaches within the field of postcolonial criticism has been a perceived focus on textuality at the expense of material conditions, whether of oppression or resistance. To illustrate Bhabha's comments on the ways in which colonial and postcolonial experience in an uncanny way prefigures post-structuralist concepts, I will focus on one of Bhabha's examples cited in the essay 'By Bread Alone'. In this, questions of the circulation of meanings during periods of revolt under colonialism are paramount, and I will read this alongside a particularly suggestive essay by Frantz Fanon, 'The Voice of Algeria', which is also concerned with the circulation of meanings and messages during the Algerian revolutionary struggle.[16] This piece resonates with Bhabha's approach and benefits from a reading focused through it. For both are texts where event and agency, and the material demands of insurrection and struggle, seem entwined with issues of iteration, indeterminacy, translation and transmission.

II   Undecidability and political panic

> From village to village, brought by one messenger and sent onward by another, passed a mysterious token in the shape of those flat cakes made from flour and water, and forming the common bread of the people, which in their language, are called chapatis. All that was known about it was that a messenger appeared, gave the cake to the head man of the village, and requested him to despatch it onward to the next; and in this way it travelled from place to place; no-one refusing, no-one doubting, few even questioning in blind obedience to a necessity felt rather than understood ... The greater number looked upon it as a signal of warning and preparation, designed to tell the people that something great and portentous was about to happen, and to prompt them to be ready for the crisis.
>
> (*History of the Indian Mutiny*, vol. 1, Sir John Kaye, cited in *TLOC*, p. 201).

In his essay 'By Bread Alone: Signs of Violence in the Mid-nineteenth Century', Bhabha considers the role of narrative in the production of states of 'emergency' through a focus on particular reports from the archives of the Indian Mutiny (1857–9) Bhabha asks, 'How is historical agency enacted in the slenderness of narrative?'[17] His careful phrasing of this question highlights the common and limited conception of 'narrative' as somehow an inadequate means of enacting agency for an oppressed or colonised group. Narrative, the argument might go, is not much good against systems of oppression that have tanks and armies at their disposal. However, in this essay he attempts to theorise a relation between the creation of panic accompanying moments of insurgency and rebellion, and more conventionally understood acts of physical mutiny and rebellion, precisely through the performance of a particularly uncanny and unsettling circulation of narratives.

His analysis is constructed through a discussion of documents relating to the Indian Mutiny of 1857. In particular, he focuses on Ranajit Guha's readings of the stories of the circulation of 'chapatis' in the rural heartlands of the mutiny and attempts to demonstrate the ways in which the circulations of meaning associated with the chapatis might be effectively read as undoing the distinction between a post-structuralist focus on signification and a materialist interest in agency.[18] Bhabha's readings of historical documents have attracted several criticisms, as well as endorsements, and this particular reading could be viewed as paradigmatic of the ways in which a post-structuralist analysis is brought to bear on historical narratives in Bhabha's work. He comments,

> Whether we take the chapatis as historical 'myth' or treat them as rumour, they represent the emergence of a form of social temporality that is iterative and indeterminate. The circulation of the chapatis constitutes an interesting problem for the agency of historical discourse. [...] The chain of communication in the rumour, its semantic content, is transformed in transmission, but despite exaggeration, hyperbole and imprecision, the messages are syntactically 'contiguous'. The indeterminacy of rumour constitutes its importance as a social discourse. Its intersubjective, communal adhesiveness lies in its enunciative aspect. Its performative power of circulation results in the contagious spreading 'an almost uncontrollable impulse to pass it on to another person'.
>
> (p. 200)

He asks what sort of agency is constituted in the circulation of the chapati, and identifies the question of time as a central force. Bhabha uses Derrida's formulation to conceive the overdetermined and contingent meanings of the circulation, 'undecidability'. He comments 'the discursive figure of rumour produces an infectious ambivalence, an "abyssal overlapping", of too much meaning and certain meaninglessness. Bhabha conceives this transformation from familiar to unfamiliar in the restructuring of time. It turns from the "customary and commonplace to the archaic, awesome and terrifying"' (*TLOC*, p. 202). Bhabha sees this transformation as a movement from symbol to sign, where 'the agency of politics is obscurely contained in the contagion of chapati flour' (p. 203). For Bhabha, the movement between symbol and sign should be understood as a temporal break, where the political is understood as a discourse of panic working through psychic affect and social fantasy, which is a particularly potent weapon and mode of agency for guerrilla warfare. If it is a temporal break it is because it opens up an 'in-between' time, suggested both by the ways in which there is a fantasy of almost timeless speed at which the circulation appears to spread, but also because it offers a temporality of 'repetition', where the same unknowable act occurs innumerable times enacted in the passing on of the chapati. Bhabha suggests that the spreading of fear was more dangerous than the spreading of anger. For instead of being contained to one side of the conflict, and producing a unified insurgency, it 'spread beyond the knowledge of ethnic or cultural binarisms, infiltrating and affecting both the British authorities, the Indian spies and the native population'. Referring to what Ranajit Guha calls the 'social psychosis' of rebel insurgency, Bhabha suggests that the transmission of fear and anxiety took place 'in a form of circulation in-between the coloniser and the colonised. This would do away with any binary notion of political antagonism. He suggests 'a contingent borderline experience opens up in-between coloniser and colonised. This is a space of cultural and interpretive undecidability produced in the "present" of the colonial moment' (*The Location of Culture*, p. 204).

Bhabha asks 'what lesson does the circulation of panic – the "time" of the chapati – have for historical agency?'(p. 204) By disavowing the politics of indeterminacy and panic, the collective agency of the insurgent peasant is given a simplistic sense of intentionality (p. 204). Bhabha suggests that historical agency is no less effective if it is understood as depending on disjunctive and displaced circulations of rumour and panic. Rather than detracting from an ability to specify political strategies or historical events, he argues that it would help to better understand certain forms of struggle. For Derrida, 'There is no decision, nor any kind of moral or political responsibility that is not haunted', that is not 'structured by [the] experience and experiment of the undecidable'.[19]

III   The future perfect

> Most effects come about in such singular ways, or depend on causes so
> imperceptible and so distant, that one can scarcely foresee them.
>
> Montesquieu, '*Mes Pensees*' *Oevres Completes*,
> ed. Daniel Oster (Paris: Seuil, 1964) p. 172.

The Algerian War will soon be entering its sixth year. No one among us in November 1954, no one in the world, suspected that after sixty months of fighting, French colonialism would still not have released its clutch and heeded the voice of the Algerian people.

Frantz Fanon, *Studies in a Dying Colonialism*, p. 23

Fanon's statement about the Algerian war anticipates the end of colonisation from a viewpoint projected back onto the past, where a future that is now the present was not foreseen or rather, not correctly foreseen. If, as Robert Young claims, post-structuralism is intimately linked to the Algerian War of Independence, it is at one level because the anti-colonial war of independence as Fanon describes it is absolutely postal. Fanon's account of the use of postal and tele-technologies during the Algerian War is found in his essay, 'The Voice of Algeria', published in *Studies in a Dying Colonialism*. Fanon's account centres around the radical changes in the way the colonised population used a range of media in their daily encounter with the coloniser, and the ways that this transformation directly interacted with the ongoing conflict.

As he describes it before the war, the exchange of signs, the postal system of Algerian politics conforms to Montesquieu's model of despotic power,

> As a system of information, as a bearer of language, hence of messages, the radio may be apprehended with the colonial situation in a special way. Radiophonic technique, the press, and in a general way the systems, messages, sign transmitters, exist in a colonial society in accordance with a well-defined statute. Algerian society, the dominated society never participates in this world of signs.

(Fanon, p. 75)

Fanon claims that the widespread avoidance of the radio as a Western product by the colonised Algerian population in the early 1950s reflected a non-organised yet pervasive refusal of acculturation, a defence of traditional familial customs and hierarchies, which listening to the radio as a family would have strained to breaking point. However, in an anti-colonial struggle, the 'politicking' taking place relies absolutely on a postal system, and the paradoxes of that postal politics are exploited for that struggle. He states that, 'The Algerian who read in the occupiers face the increasing bankruptcy of colonialism felt the compelling and vital need to be informed' (p. 75). This necessitated an interest and involvement in systems of dissemination about the war's progress, propaganda, political declarations of independence, and so on. This meant tuning in to the coloniser's system of information but creating dissident readings of the colonial text. As he describes,

'The Algerian's reaction was no longer one of pained and desperate refusal. Because it avowed to its own uneasiness, the occupier's lie became a positive aspect of the nation's new truth'(p. 76).

However, it was not just a matter of the ordinary civilian detecting ambivalence in the colonial text, which would perhaps confirm the first part of Bhabha's assertion that issues of ambivalence and indeterminacy inhabited colonialism long before they were named as such. For Fanon, the texts themselves – the local and foreign press – and colonial and anti-colonial radio broadcasts formed critical spaces of contest through which the Algerian War of Independence was pursued alongside armed combat. The engagement with postal and telecommunication systems involved an anti-colonial assault on the press and the radio, which in turn revealed the postal politics of anti-colonialism. In his article 'Frantz Fanon's Radio: Solidarity, Diaspora, and the Tactics of Listening', Ian Baucom notes that in *Black Skin White Masks*, Fanon frequently exhorts his reader to 'listen', as he 'presents a compilation of voices to which he has bent his ear'.[20] This is clearly at work in Bhabha's writing too, where he frequently exhorts us to listen, to hear, rather than only to read, the diverse and disperse voices from both past and present that people his texts.

Fanon's account of the significance of the radio broadcasts by *The Voice of Fighting Algeria* centres on his refusal of models of listening and reception, suggested by Jean-Paul Sartre and Theodore Adorno, where the agency of a subject vanishes at the moment that they enter as 'listener' into 'the public mechanism' of the radio broadcast. He comments, 'for Sartre, the listener is a destination and not, as Fanon suggests, a relay'.[21]

The fact that Fanon begins his discussion by mentioning the telephone and tele-technology underlines how a postal logic, involving the circulation of messages operated politically without reference to actual broadcasts or reports in the media, formed part of the logic of the war itself.

> In the Maghreb country, the Europeans use the term Arab telephone in speaking of the relative speed with which news travels by word of mouth in the native society. Never at any time was the expression intended to mean anything else. But in 1955 Europeans and Algerians could be heard to refer confidentially and as though revealing a state secret, to a technique of long distance communication that vaguely recalled some such system of signaling, like the tom-tom as is found in central regions of Africa. The Algerian gave the isolated European the impression of being in permanent contact with the high command.
>
> (p. 75)

The potential threat to the coloniser is characterised in terms of the immediacy with which messages relayed from high command, the so-called 'secret technique' is suggestive of a fantasised telepathy on the part of the colonised. This is perhaps because the immediacy of telepathy or something akin to it would cancel out the need for sending messages at all; it would be the fantasies/fantasy of the 'death of the postman'. Such a message system at once supersedes and bypasses the colonial infrastructure rendering its own postal structures ineffectual. Reaching the end of the post, or getting beyond the 'post' (as a system of messages), is, according to Fanon, the ambition of the colonised who follow the progress of the war through different media sources,

> In Algeria all the news is good, every bit of information is gratifying. The Fifth Column is an impossibility in Algeria. [...] These manifestations, these attitudes of total belief, this collective conviction, express the determination of the group to get as close as possible to the Revolution, to get ahead of the Revolution if possible.
>
> (p. 80)

This formulation should be familiar to us, for it surely describes the paradoxically postal logic of the desire to 'get ahead of the revolution'; to have the news before it has been made; to be *after* postcolonialism. This condition is also true of the revolutionary tactics involving the press and radio. The nationalists turn to foreign newspapers imported from France for more accurate news of the progress of the war rather than rely on the locally produced colonial propaganda. Here they expose the ambivalence at the heart of colonial discourse by appropriating the French liberal vision, which is in itself rendered impossible by the cut, the scar of the impossible doubleness of the simultaneously liberal and oppressive regime. In fact, though they do more than simply provide a good example of colonial ambivalence that can be retrospectively explored by the postcolonial critic, Fanon asserts that by seeking out the French newspaper they also involve themselves directly in the conflict.

For the Algerian to ask for *L'Express*, *L'Humanite* or *Le Monde* was tantamount to publicly confessing – as likely as not to a police informer – his allegiance to the Revolution. [...] Every time the Algerian asked for one of these newspapers, the kiosk dealer, who represented the occupier, would regard it as an expression of nationalism, equivalent to an act of war (p. 81).

Showing concern over the arrival or non-arrival of the French press was sufficient. The kiosk dealer Fanon notes, 'like the office clerk is sure to be a veteran with strong backing in ultra-colonialist circles', and hence fulfils in a catachrestic postcolonial sense the role of the vizar to the Mogul. The battle over the press, however, clearly relies on a literate part of the population. Over-emphasising this aspect of the conflict risks reaffirming a Eurocentrity to an account of the postal. Fanon too is aware of this and devotes most of his essay to a discussion of 'sound wave warfare' and the radio station the 'Voice of Fighting Algeria'. For the mass of the population who were not literate, the radio provided the means of receiving news of the revolution. To a large degree, the reliance on a postal politics meant that news of the revolution was the experience of revolution itself, for a civilian population coming increasingly to view itself as a militant, nationalist, anti-colonialist, 'having a radio meant paying one's taxes to the nation, buying the right of entry into the struggle of an assembled people' (p. 84).

Fanon argues that through listening to the 'Voice of Fighting Algeria', the civilian was transformed into a participant in the conflict. For Ian Baucom, the significance of this is multiple; listening, he argues, 'allegorises one of [Fanon's] most important writing strategies. As a practicing psychiatrist [Fanon] spent much of his life as a professional listener. As a writer he produced texts that frequently function as transcripts of his diverse acts of listening.'[22] Listening to the radio did not simply involve tuning into an authoritative pro-revolutionary voice in a straightforward propaganda war. The programmes were jammed by the French authorities, necessitating a tactical battle of wits as listeners tuned in for hours at a time on different wavelengths in the hope of hearing the jammed station broadcast. For Fanon, 'a new form of struggle has come into being', one peculiarly demonstrating a postal structure. The embattled voice was often not heard at all; any news would be fragmentary, garbled, obscured. Although such conditions make the claim to have heard 'the Voice' dubious, nonetheless Fanon describes the circulation of news of glorious successes that as a task of reconstruction that took place after each broadcast as the collected listeners 'interpreted' what had been heard. It is particularly appropriate that this process involved a kind of circulation, almost a collectively imagined broadcast,

> The voice, often absent, physically inaudible, which each one felt welling up within him found an inner perception of the Fatherland became materialised in an irrefutable way. Every Algerian, for his part broadcast and transmitted the new language.

> (p. 87)

Fanon's account of revolutionary politics, in this essay at least, needs to be understood as fundamentally postal. If those Algerians who wished to get ahead of the revolution were in a certain sense attempting to be 'post' post-colonial, they were in fact inhabiting the temporal and spatial strangeness that characterises the logic of the 'post' that Bhabha insists on.

5   Dwelling in/on the Ruins: Postcolonial Futures

I   Melancholia, and belatedness: or 'we cannot *not* want antiquity'[1]

> What has been left behind may either be mourned, or it can be used to provide a different set of lenses. Since almost by definition exile and memory go together, it is what one remembers of the past and how one remembers that determine how one sees the future.
>
> Edward Said[2]

> How can we catachrestically seize the genealogy of modernity and open it to postcolonial translation? [...] The discursive address of modernity – its structure of authority – decentres the Great Event, and speaks from that moment of 'imperceptibility', the supplementary space 'outside' or uncannily beside.
>
> Homi Bhabha, *TLOC* p. 243

In J. M. Coetzee's second volume of his memoir, *Youth* (2002), set in South Africa and London in the 1950s (following *Boyhood: Scenes from Provincial Life* (1997)), a scene occurs towards the end of the book in the British Library Reading Room where the young white South African, an aspiring poet and author, is researching a thesis on Ford Maddox Ford. Jaded and disillusioned, certain that he will 'have nothing new to say about Ford', he finds himself poring over books about South Africa.[3] Ironically they are 'books to be found only in great libraries, memoirs of visitors to the Cape like Dapper and Kolbe and Sparkman and Barrow and Burchell, published in Holland or Germany or England two centuries ago'. Coetzee depicts with clarity the dizzying predicament of postcolonial subjects who read themselves simultaneously into and out of existence in the archive.

> It gives him an eerie feeling to sit in London reading about streets – Waalstraat, Buitengracht, Buitencingel – along which he alone, of all the people around him with their heads buried in their books, has walked. But even more than by accounts of old Cape Town is he captivated by stories of ventures into the interior, reconnaissances by ox-wagon into the desert of the Great Karoo,

> where a traveller could trek for days on end without clapping eyes on a living
> soul.
>
> (p. 137)

John's experience might usefully be characterised as a melancholic
one, in the sense that his reading begins to provoke an intense desire for
authenticating histories of the nation he has left behind, one that he also
has a complicated and violent relationship to, one that is characterised by
'difference',

> Do these Englishmen around him feel the same tug at the heartstrings when
> there is mention of Rydal Mount or Baker Street in a book? He doubts it. This
> country this city, are by now wrapped in centuries of words. Englishmen do
> not find it at all strange to be walking in the footsteps of Chaucer or Tom Jones.
> South Africa is different.
>
> (p. 137)

The dizziness of the postcolonial archival moment is one where the 'reality' of South Africa emerges unsettlingly from the pages of Burchell's travels while the streets of London that he has walked along that very morning
are 'wrapped in centuries of words'. John is partly seduced by the colonial
book, which has all the trappings of 'reality', whose narrative authorises the
existence of the Karoo, but only from the self-imposed exilic space of the
British Library, whose power seems to overwhelm and seduce. We might
read this as an ironic postcolonial moment where structures of desire and
mimicry find themselves increasingly confused, in as much as he is drawn
to abandon his work on Ford Maddox Ford, which already risks marking
his interpolated status as a mimic man, weighed down by the traditions
of English literature and scholarship. Unpicking the uncertain generic
boundaries between the literary and the historical, he appears to find
himself inhabiting Bhabha's 'time-lag' – he aspires to produce a text like
Burchell's,

> Were it not for this handful of books, he could not be sure he had not dreamed
> up the Karoo yesterday. [...] What Burchell wrote really happened. Real oxen
> hauled him and his cases of botanical specimens from stopping-place to stop-
> ping-place in the Great Karoo; real stars glimmered above his head, and his
> men's, while they slept. It dizzies him even to think about it. Burchell and his
> men may be dead, and their wagons turned to dust, but they really lived, their
> travels were real travels. The proof is the book he holds in his hands, the book
> called for short, Burchell's Travels, in specific the copy lodged in the British
> Museum. He would like to do it: write a book as convincing as Burchell's and
> lodge it in this library that defines all libraries.
>
> (p. 138)

Initially, John considers the problem of producing a text that will fulfil his own fantasy of finding his work, and hence his name, among the shelves of the British Library.

> The difficult part will be to give the whole the aura that will get it on to the shelves and thus into the history of the world: the aura of truth. It is not forgery he is contemplating [...] the challenge he faces is purely a literary one: to write a book whose horizon of knowledge will be that of Burchell's time.
>
> (p. 138)

He is faced, however, with an insuperable barrier to writing the book he imagines is needed, confronted by the violence of the archive that forgets and destroys, even as it documents.

> He will have to school himself to write from within the 1820s. Before he can bring it off he will need to know less than he knows now; he will need to forget things. Yet before he can forget he will have to know what to forget; before he can know less he will have to know more. [...] Where will he find the common knowledge of a bygone world, a knowledge too humble to know it is knowledge?[4]

John's tortured response to the generic conventions of colonial historical travel narrative seeks at once to replicate the 'successes' of the colonial text. It also seeks to improve upon it, to supplement it, and return to a 'mundane knowledge' of the period that the traveller's narrative cannot reach, a 'knowledge' that does not even recognise itself as such. It is an apprehension of paradoxical and perverse 'authenticity' of the colonial archive, only acknowledged after the fact, it gestures towards a truth that can be yearned for but only produced fictitiously, with the colonial text as a kind of narrative guide that must be simultaneously overturned and in some way appealed to. As a gesture of remembering or recovering a particular moment in time, it is also marked by a need to forget what has gone on since then in order to circumvent history. However, the only way to do this is through an even more careful (but also forgetful) attention to history itself 'before he can know less he will have to know more'(p. 139).

The predicament outlined is suggestive of Sandhya Shetty and Elizabeth Bellany's discussion of the terms under which a 'postcolonial' archive might be understood: 'we should not attempt to summarise the postcolonial archive prematurely as a "desire" for antiquity. Rather, phrased more tentatively (but we hope more responsibly), the postcolonial archive means that we cannot *not* want antiquity'.[5] For Bhabha too in his essay 'Democracy De-realised', the 'new' is always marked importantly by the need for a return to history, for 'unless we recognise what is old and weary about the world – those "long histories" of slavery, colonization, diaspora, we are in no position to represent what is emergent and "new" within our contemporary global moment'.[6]

In Coetzee's text there is a postcolonial predicament, marked by belated-ness, needing to seek, through an engagement with what stands for history, the other history that is in Bhabha's analysis, uncannily beside it. The pas-sages in *Youth* relating to those fantasised, narrativised or untold histories are marked by an elegiac quality, where the ways of retrieving and valuing what has been lost are routed through fictionality and metonymy, produc-ing an 'affect' of significantly melancholic proportions.[7] For Sandhya Shetty and Elizabeth Jane Bellany, a postcolonial engagement with archives has to be understood as melancholic. The postcolonial archive is the 'impossi-ble space where a deconstructive critique of imperialism meets Orientalist scholarship, it reveals antiquity belatedly as that which must be both dis-tanced and summoned in the aftermath of colonialism'.[8]

Bhabha's observations in the opening lines of his essay 'How Newness Enters the World' also suggest the need to address the complicated haunt-ing of postcolonialism by the violence that could be said to 'found' it. In the opening section of 'How Newness Enters the World', Bhabha considers the impact of the 'long shadow' of Joseph Conrad's novel *Heart of Darkness*, which, he suggests, rightly, falls upon so many postcolonial literary and pedagogical texts. The end of the text, the important lie to 'the intended', as Bhabha puts it, the 'white lie' – where Kurtz's last words 'the Horror, the Horror!' are substituted by Marlow for his fiancée's name – marks for Bhabha, a significant moment of translation. As he retells the tragic his-tory of colonialism in a European drawing room, redrawing the boundary between the colony and the metropolis, Marlow anxiously rewrites coloni-alism as romantic tragedy. Bhabha's concern is with the psychic impacts of this re-narrating, of what he calls a split truth or a double frame, echoing Coetzee's depiction of a dizzying doubleness to the colonial travel narra-tives and histories John reads in *Youth*.

> In taking the name of a woman – the Intended– to mask the daemonic 'being' of colonialism, Marlow turns the brooding geography of political disaster – the heart of darkness – into a melancholic memorial to romantic love and historic memory. Between the silent truth of Africa and the salient lie to the metropolitan woman, Marlow returns to his initiating insight: the experience of colonialism is the problem of living in the midst of the incomprehensible.
>
>   (p. 213, Bhabha, 'How Newness Enters the World')

This substitution effacing the 'horror' confirms the postcolonial archive as 'the place where memory breaks down in the face of an archival and a so-matic/familial/institutional violence that founds postcolonialism'.[9] How-ever, this would be the place where memory and melancholia open out onto the future, 'the power of memory' Derrida notes after de Man, 'is not, first of all, that of "resuscitating"; it remains enigmatic enough to be preoccupied, so to speak, by a thinking of "the future"'.[10] In Bhabha's words, 'history's *intermediacy* poses the future, once again, as an open question'.[11]

II   Indigestible Empire: Reinventing nation, minoritising cultures

> The life of the nation has been dominated by an inability even to face, never mind actually mourn, the profound change in circumstances and moods that followed the end of Empire.
>
> Paul Gilroy, *After Empire: Melancholia or Convivial Culture?* (p. 97)

> Modernity's injunction to mourn is exemplified in the monument, as if to construct a palliative in which disposability can be located once and for all, and buried. A melancholic reading affectively resists this injunction.
>
> Ranjana Khanna,
> 'Post-Palliative: Coloniality's Affective Dissonance' (p. 13)

> Across the accumulation of the history of the West there are those people who speak the encrypted discourse of the melancholic and the migrant.
>
> Homi K. Bhabha, 'Dissemination', *TLOC*, p. 164

Bhabha's 'Manifesto for the Re-invention of Britain', conceived as a collaborative discussion forum for critics, artists and cultural practitioners with the British Council and first delivered in 1997 at a conference of the same name in the UK, set out to bring sharply into focus the ways in which the terms 'British' and 'culture' might be understood and refigured. Bhabha's concern was to propose a notion of culture that might facilitate a shift in the terms of debate around questions of multiculturalism in Britain, to shift radically definitions of British identities and the concept of 'minorities'. His stated aim in the manifesto is to 'get away from a view of culture as an evaluative activity concerned primarily with the attribution of identity'. Instead, he proposes a model of culture as always contested, always incommensurable in demands for representation, and always developing and remaking itself. This, he suggests, might help to shift the terms of discussion around race, 'minorities' and national identity, shifting perspectives from concepts of 'a core culture and its others', to an understanding of the ways in which culture is more about 'the activity of negotiating, regulating and competing often conflicting demands for collective self-representation'.[12] His account of the ways in which a changing landscape of cultural identities and a shift in the relationship between territory and tradition might be usefully harnessed for a radical shift in understanding of nation is optimistic, seeing potential in the present 'new cosmopolitanism' of British cultural production to frame new questions about nation, culture and identity.

However, it is also a position outlined in his influential essay 'Dissemi-nation: Time, Narrative and The Margins of the Modern Nation' within a decidedly more sombre section entitled 'The Foreignness of Languages', where he 'gives way' to the *vox populi* of 'the melancholic and the migrant', whose narratives he argues cannot be contained 'within the *Heim* of national culture'.

> They articulate the death-in-life of the idea of the 'imagined community' of the nation; the worn-out metaphors of the resplendent national life now circulate in another narrative of entry permits and passports and work per-mits that at once preserve and proliferate, bind and breach the human rights of the nation.[13]

Bhabha's narrative of nation, like so many that he himself unpicks, is split, ambivalent. His 'manifesto' names the possibilities of a cosmopolitan nation with an urge for a utopian vision, but his critical analysis of narra-tives of nation must pause to listen to what he terms the 'desolate silences of the wandering people'.[14] Here Bhabha discusses John Berger's account of a Turkish migrant worker in Germany attempting the break through 'the opaque disguise of words' that prevents him from translating, breaking through into the narrative of nation. Bhabha is taken with Berger's account of how the meanings of a new language learned by a migrant change as he speaks them. Bhabha composes a passage of scattered remarks in Berger's *A Seventh Man*: 'He asked for coffee. What the words signified to the bar-man was that he was asking for coffee in a bar where he should not be ask-ing for coffee. He learnt girl. What the word meant when he used it, was that he was a randy dog'.[15]

However, *After Empire: Melancholia or Convivial Culture?*, Paul Gilroy's analysis of the state of contemporary British multiculturalism written almost a decade later, would seem to be a despairing response to Bhabha's more engaged and upbeat assessment of British culture in his manifesto, much closer to his assessment of the 'failure' to translate and the estranged and melancholic position of the migrant. He adopts the psychoanalytic term 'melancholia' as a critical idea for assessing how national and cultural identity are being narrated in late twentieth and early twenty-first-century Europe. Gilroy argues for an understanding of contemporary 'post imperial melancholia', a pathological inability of the nation 'even to face, never mind actually mourn, the profound change in circumstances and moods

that followed the end of Empire and consequent loss of imperial prestige'
(p. 98). His model of melancholia is transposed from the German psycho-
analysts Alexander and Margarete Mitscherlich, whose model was applied
to the West German nation in the aftermath of World War II to account for
the social, political and psychological responses of the nation to the trauma
of the Nazi years. Gilroy suggests that this model might be appropriate in
the British case (as does Kristeva in the French case) in relation to the loss
of Empire and the sense of identity that accompanied this. In producing
this reading of certain kinds of British culture as melancholic, Gilroy shares
an approach with that of French-Bulgarian critic Julia Kristeva, whose
account of French culture published in 1998 bears many similarities. In
Contre la Depression Nationale, Kristeva diagnoses French national culture
with 'depression', not simply morose or gloomy; the French have become
melancholic.[16] When faced with their shifting influence of power on the world
stage, the loss of significance internationally of the French language and the
undigested legacies of Empire, they have become unable to mourn these perceived losses and are unable to rebuild a new national image and a future.

Gilroy's perception of melancholic Englishness is posited against the
supposedly or potentially joyful or utopian narrative of cultural diversity (or
difference) and multiculturalism. For Gilroy, contemporary British culture
and politics would be understood as displaying symptoms of 'post imperial
melancholia'.[17] Such an analysis would not be confined to Britain but, he
argues, would also be relevant to the modern histories of a range of European countries.

> These analyses would be based upon their obvious difficulties in acknowledg-
> ing the pains and the gains that were involved in imperial adventures and
> upon the problems that have arisen from their inability to disentangle the
> disruptive results supposedly produced by an immigrant presence from the
> residual but potent effects of lingering but usually unspoken colonial rela-
> tionships and imperial fantasies.
>
> (p. 109)

Gilroy's description of a neo-traditional British (and European) pathology,
morbidly fixated on 'heritage' yet unable to digest its own imperial history,
is an interesting and compelling one. It appears to answer Bhabha's arguments in his 'Manifesto for the Re-Invention of Britain' with a resounding
negative. However, the attribution of affect to different states of racist or
multiculturalist views does not produce any straightforward conclusions.
Melancholia has itself emerged as an insightful critical term for several
key critics with postcolonial concerns, who against Gilroy perceive the

postcolonial project itself, rather than a neoconservative British politics, as profoundly melancholic. Gilroy's definition of 'post imperial melancholia' attributes it the 'other side' – they (the neo-traditional white British) are melancholic but 'we' migrant or convivial multiculturalists are not, and may be at risk of reinstating the divide, 'core culture and its others' that Bhabha has suggested has brought about an impasse in critical debates. Moreover, there has been a consistent development of critical debate around the value of psychoanalytic approaches in postcolonial theory, which is clearly indebted to Bhabha's focus on stereotyping, fantasy, mimicry and identification in his own thinking.

Gilroy does not develop an extended theory of melancholia here, and offers a much less psychoanalytically inflected reading than Kristeva's, although his sense of an undigested colonial history might be partly useful. Interestingly, melancholia has emerged as a term profoundly embedded in postcolonial critical and political projects against Kristeva and Gilroy, who both erect a dialectic between a 'white' or 'conservative' melancholic attachment to Empire and a positive postcolonial 'hospitality' and conviviality.

In work by Ranjana Khanna, Seshadri-Crooks and Anne Anlin Cheng, as well as in the critical approaches of Jacques Derrida and Judith Butler, there is an act of reclamation that reverses the perceived hierarchical relationship between mourning and melancholia envisaged by Freud in his essay 'Mourning and Melancholia'. Gilroy's use of melancholia differs from this emerging postcolonially inflected one in that he, like Freud, assumes that 'once melancholia has been succeeded by mourning' a 'healthier' form of relating to loss or change, a new image of the nation can be produced that 'accommodates its colonial dimensions' (p. 115). Gilroy's discussion of melancholia seems slightly out of step with theoretical models of melancholia and mourning as they have emerged recently in postcolonial studies. However, in an American context, Anne Anlin Cheng argues for an understanding of the melancholy of race that deconstructs the opposition that appears here. She considers both dominant white identity *and* minority identities and positions in America as melancholic, as well as considering that both racist and white liberal discourses participate in the dynamics of melancholia, 'albeit out of different motivations'.[18] It would not be a question then of attributing melancholia only to those who are racist or unable to embrace multicultural cultures. Rather, she argues melancholia is a useful critical term because it accounts for guilt and denial of guilt, and further, 'those who do not see the racial problem or those who call themselves non-ideological are the most melancholic of all because in today's political climate, as Toni Morrison exclaims in *Playing in the Dark*, "it requires hard work not to see"'.[19]

Liberating melancholia from a potentially negative or derogatory term also enables Cheng to consider a specifically melancholic understanding of forms of racial suffering, how assimilation narratives and apprehensions and experiences of 'minority' identities are played out in Asian-American and African-American literary works. Cheng is very alert to the risks of re-inscribing a history of affliction through talking about 'the "melancholia" of racialised peoples', citing Werner Soller's account of the construction of 'Indian melancholy' by white American culture, and Richard Wright's dis-cussion of the naturalisation of the African-American lament in American culture, as perceptively identifying examples of this. However, she proposes that far from attempting to locate melancholia 'within' a raced subject, or culture, 'racial melancholia as I am defining it has always existed for raced subjects both as a sign of rejection and as a psychic strategy in response to that rejection'.[20]

In a British context, there is something of this understanding in Monika Ali's novel set in London's East End, *Brick Lane*. Ali addresses the complexi-ties of migration, assimilation and identification for the British-Asian com-munities in London through focusing on the life of Nazneen, a young girl who comes to Britain from Bangladesh for an arranged marriage. In the latter half of the novel, a scene occurs where Chanu, her husband, now a disillusioned father of second-generation daughters who have grown up in Britain, who longs to return to Bangladesh with his family, regales them with reasons to return. His daughters reluctantly join him as he sits reading a newspaper on the floor. He asks them to guess 'Which do you think is the happiest nation on Earth?', to which one of them, Shahana, already tired of his narratives of 'home' and guessing from his delighted expression, replies 'Bangladesh' in a monotone laden with mutinous undercurrents. Unper-turbed, Chanu reads,

> *Research led by professors at London School of Economics into links between personal spending power and perceived quality of life has found that Bangla-deshis are the happiest people in the world.* And LSE is a very respectable estab-lishment, comparable to Dhaka University or Open University.[21]

Chanu's paternal authority, which is already perilous, is further under-mined in his comparison of the London School of Economics with Dhaka and the Open universities. His reversal of the hierarchies of a highly elitist British education system confirms his own marginal position as much as he asserts his knowledge of it. He drives his point home with reference to the fact that Britain ranks thirty-second in the table. Addressing his daughters he persists, 'You see when we go there, what will you lose? Burgers and chips and [...] tight jeans and what will you gain? Happiness'. Chanu's dreams of assimilation into British society have been frustrated, persistently being passed over for promotion because of his race and origins. He sees clearly that even as an Anglophile migrant, racism has thwarted his ambitions for his professional career, which are now in tatters as he turns to taxi driving. Measuring what has been lost and gained in the process of migration, he now firmly locates happiness elsewhere, afflicted by the melancholic desire for something intangible or unspeakable that has been lost, and goes under the heading of happiness.

The moment where Chanu accepts that Nazneen and his daughters do not share his dream of return to Bangladesh is marked by a realisation of a terrible sadness. "'I can't go with you" she said. "I can't stay" said Chanu, and they clung to each other inside a sadness that went beyond words and tears, beyond that place, those causes and consequences, and became a part of them from now to wherever they went'.[22] The movement of return that Chanu decides upon to alleviate one kind of loss must inevitably initiate another as the family ties are stretched to breaking point.

In a different context, in their discussion of racial melancholia and assimilation in the USA, David L. Eng and Shinhee Han also see links between their own and Bhabha's work. Focusing on a more individualised approach to melancholia, they propose that Asian-American minority experiences of assimilation into US culture should be understood as an unattainable process. In 'Assimilation as/and Melancholia', they discuss what they see as the ambivalent predicament of Asian-Americans perceived as either/both 'eccentric to the nation or as hyper model minorities – inhumanly productive and hence pathological to the nation'.[23] They argue that as complete assimilation remains radically unattainable, they are 'suspended, conflicted, unresolved' such that 'the irresolution of this process places the concept of assimilation within a melancholic framework'.[24] They specifically link these observations to Bhabha's model of mimicry and the ambivalent logic of the stereotype; asking if it could be extended to enable an understanding of the 'model minority myth' in an Asian-American context. They suggest that mimicry, as Bhabha understands it, specifically functions as a material practice in racial melancholia, with Asian-Americans adopting an ambivalent and fraught relation to the supposedly 'positive' stereotype of 'model minority' which operates as 'a multicultural fantasy in the age of diversity management'.[25] Although Eng and Han frequently refer to case studies of individuals to outline their theoretical approach to melancholia, they resist an understanding of this purely in terms of an individualised and internalised pathology marking the subjectivity of Asian-Americans. They attempt to argue for cultural and political models, translating as Bhabha does the universalising tendencies of psychoanalytic models into localised and politicised cultural histories. They name a kind of cultural melancholia that is not necessarily a debilitating affliction but a position from which new identities and identifications might emerge. Ones that challenge the hegemonic narratives of minorities, migrants and assimilation as they both impact in different ways on a particular group or groups and simultaneously 'produce' those group identities in discourses of control or knowledge.

III Postcolonial/impossible mourning

There is a slightly different focus in Ranjana Khanna's account of a melancholic postcolonialism. She views the endemic nature of melancholia as an affect, which 'permeates all parts of the field and the political arena of post-colonialism' and might be helpfully linked to Sandhya Shetty and Elizabeth Bellany's comments on the postcolonial archive as melancholic as they both speak to Bhabha's model of postcolonial belatedness.[26] She comments that 'this melancholia initiates and in fact finds its symptoms within a constant vigilance concerning palliatives, alibis, and easy complicit and compromised gestures of sanctimonious novelty or liberalism'.[27] Clearly normative gestures, palliatives and alibis will always need to be critiqued, so that a dissatisfaction with narratives of reconciliation, of state or national apologies for historical crimes or contemporary ones, or declarations of equality or reparation, will always be necessary. A melancholic refusal to be satisfied is therefore just as much future oriented as attached to a past.

She rejects sharp divisions between ethical and political, aesthetics and politics, melancholia and utopia. In this analysis she arguably shares Bhabha's understanding of the supplementary nature of the third space, precisely because, paradoxically, melancholic responses to all histories, political gestures or narratives highlight the supplementary logic of any textual representation, in which there is always something left to say, something lost that has to be remembered, as with Derrida's 'necessary supplement' that through exclusion enables the dominant narrative to emerge.[28] She comments,

> No map, census, print or museum can be entirely successful at presenting the nation seamlessly. While the work of mourning may relegate swallowed disposable bodies to the garbage can of modern nationalism, the work of melancholia critically attesting to the fact of the lie intrinsic to modern notions of sovereignty is the only hope for the future.

(p. 15)

Derrida's logic of the supplement would confirm this problem for all narrative. The supplement is 'added' to something that is already seen as complete, to compensate for a lack that was not supposed to be there and therefore opens up onto questions of politics.

It suggests the paradox of simultaneous completion and incompletion. Khanna cites but disputes Kalpana Seshadri-Crooks' assessment of some of the dominant causes of this melancholia; an apprehension that institutionalising the critique of imperialism may render it conciliatory, the problematic position of location for many scholars, which might be qualified further, to consider how political self-legitimation may have come increasingly into crisis faced with the near collapse of a 'so-called' socialist project in the wake of the end of the Cold War.[29] This challenges the assumptions she reads in Seshadri-Crooks' analysis that such melancholia is a recent phenomenon, accompanying a shift of status for the discipline. The paradox of institutional success and the accompanying crisis of political legitimacy does not fully apprehend the peculiar 'time' of the postcolonial. Seshadri-Crooks notes the 'effective immobility' of postcolonial critics in the academy when it comes to effecting curricular change. The success of the field has, she argues, 'induced melancholia', because the critical re-readings of the canon in English, for example, have not contested sufficiently the discursive frameworks and paradigms that they now (un)comfortably inhabit.[30]

Thus melancholia emerges from colonialism, but is not necessarily in a defeatist or purely negative mode. Melancholia is understood by Freud as closely related to mourning, but differs from it in that it cannot be overcome, and unlike in mourning where a lost object is mourned and finally accommodated, what has been lost remains unknown.[31] Whereas in Freud's early work mourning is understood to be 'healthy', in that over time one comes to terms with the loss that has induced the condition, in melancholia the lost object becomes elusive and destabilises the subject, indeed it disables it. As Judith Butler observes, Freud remained undecided on the distinction between mourning and melancholia and revisited this model, in trying to establish how desires for one object or person when lost might refocus onto another.

> Freud changed his mind on this subject: he suggested that successful mourning meant being able to exchange one object for another; he later claimed that incorporation, originally associated with melancholia was essential to the task of mourning.[32]

Jacques Derrida's extensive work on mourning notes that the significant mode of figuring loss and mourning since Freud's writing has been that of

'ingestion' in some form, 'ever since psychoanalysis came to mark this discourse, the image commonly used to characterise mourning is that of an
interiorization (an idealising incorporation, introjection, consumption of
the other)'.[33] Crucially for Derrida, this model of interiorisation can never
be completed, it remains impossible. In their introduction to Derrida's
The Work of Mourning, Pascale-Anne Brault and Michael Naas comment,
mourning operates as an aporia, the law of mourning is 'success fails' and
'failure succeeds'. In other words, successful mourning would be forgetting,
hence failing to mourn, and not being able to stop mourning (melancholia)
would be a successful act of mourning.[34]

For Sam Durrant, an understanding of the critical relationship between
postcolonial narrative and mourning is imperative. In his study of work by
J. M. Coetzee, Wilson Harris and Toni Morrison, he considers the relationship between different narrative approaches to memorialising the traumatic
histories of colonialism and slavery, which he argues, following Derrida,
should be understood as haunting the present. He argues in particular
that the postcolonial work finds itself involved in impossible or inconsol-
able mourning.[35] Durrant focuses in particular on Toni Morison's novel
Beloved, in his account of the indigestible history of slavery in the USA,
which is mourned in her text, a novel that Bhabha comments on extensively in the closing section of his introduction to *The Location of Culture*.[36]
The text is overrun and afflicted with simultaneous desires to remember
and to forget, memories of serial abuse are 'rinsed out' of victim's minds, as
Sethe comments of a terribly abused woman, Ella, 'shut tight in a tobacco
tin', lodged in Paul D's chest, 'that nothing can pry open'.[37] For Durrant,
'Beloved's excessive presence, which fills 124 with indigestible memories
of "the Sixty Million and more"' to whom Morrison has dedicated the book,
'renders Sethe *incapable of digestion*', while the ghost of her child grows fat
through her insatiable appetite for stories, memories and rememberings.[38]
He comments that 'true mourning confronts an indigestible past, a past
that can never be fully remembered or forgotten.'[39] He proposes that those
critics who have read Morrison's text as straightforwardly 'reclaiming' lost
histories and memories of the trauma of slavery overlook Morrison's own
epilogue, where 'Morrison is forced to recognize the impossibility of naming and reclaiming the nameless "Disremembered and unaccounted for"'.[40]
Durrant takes Bhabha to task for failing to explore this dynamic in Morrison's text fully, commenting that he seems to view the 'ecstatic monologues'
of the three female voices at the end of the novel as an act of 'naming and
claiming' rather than as a crisis of naming and identity and a disarticulation
of personality. Certainly Bhabha addresses this moment in the text in terms

of a kind of 'interpersonal reality' that is formed through the poetic movement of the voices of Sethe, Denver and Beloved. However, he is also alert
to the ways in which a 'continual eruption of "undecipherable languages"
of slave memory' enters the domestic space of the home, the 'spiteful' 124,
rendering a relationship to the past as forever unhinged, out of joint.[41]

Like Durrant, Ranjana Khanna argues for a mourning that is 'impossible'
for postcolonial studies, precisely because the inception of postcolonial
studies is also marked by its impossibility in the sense that it cannot cat-
egorically escape from the critique of its own provenance. For Khanna, the
field of postcolonial studies has 'always been melancholic, and has always
expressed through this melancholia its profound belatedness and complicated antinomies'.[42] She argues that the postcolonial project is beset
by melancholia, 'which has always been the driving force behind it'.[43]
She comments, 'the lament, the elegiac, and the melancholic response have
always been constitutive of the field'. Thus melancholia is 'endemic to the
field of postcolonial', not a new phenomenon brought about through political or ideological compromises that have been forced upon the discipline
or by a sense of coming to a halt or 'impasse'. Precisely in the way Bhabha
understands the role of the time-lag, Khanna proposes that 'melancholia's
temporality is dragged backwards and forwards' she states, 'affect weighs
against the palliative of newness, which is often alibi for conducting politics
in a compromised vein. An incipient future oriented hope manifests itself
textually in remainders, in dissonance, and in untimeliness'.[44] Furthermore,
in her discussion of haunting and the future, in *Dark Continents: Pyschoa-
nalysis and Colonialism*, she draws directly on Bhabha's model of time-lag
and postcolonial translation, to offer a notion of affect, 'as a concept that
acknowledges the catachresis of the origin of a trauma and that leaves its
trace upon the individual'. This, she argues, allows for a reading of 'historical and political processes as instruments of violence on groups – racism,
sexism, colonialism, slavery – rather than seeking an absolute origin that
may posit, for example, ethnic violence as always rooted in the same psychological structure of lack; or on the other hand, trauma as originating in
a singular historical event that sidelines the everyday'.[45]

The emergence of a strain of postcolonial theorising of melancholia
and the development of theories of racial melancholia in the USA is at
times explicitly indebted to, and acknowledges, Bhabha, returning to
Bhabha's critical vocabulary, belatedness, untimeliness and ambivalence, as well as depending more generally on a postcolonial re-siting
and revisiting of psychoanalytic critical models that Bhabha, among
others, has initiated.

This melancholic postcolonial theorising has not been universally welcomed by those whose work is more usually understood as involved in thinking through and with Lacan in particular, as Slavoj Zizek's scathing account of its alleged rise to 'intellectual hegemony' in the essay 'Melancholy and the Act' demonstrates.

> It is [...] necessary to insist on the need to denounce the objective cynicism that such a rehabilitation of melancholy enacts. The melancholic link to the lost ethnic Object allows us to claim that we remain faithful to our ethnic roots while fully participating in the global capitalist game. One should raise the question to what degree the whole project of postcolonial studies is sustained by this logic of objective cynicism. To make things absolutely clear: what is wrong with the postcolonial nostalgia is not the utopian dream of a world they never had (such a utopia can be thoroughly liberating), but the way this dream is used to legitimize the actuality of its very opposite, of the full and unconstrained participation in global capitalism.[46]

He views the 'rehabilitation' of melancholy, inverting Freud's model, as a cynical manoeuvre that 'enables' ethnic or minority groups to participate fully in the 'global capitalist game' while claiming to remain faithful to what he terms ethnic roots. Lack, he suggests, is not the same as loss, 'the melancholic confuses loss and lack and interprets lack as loss'.[47] Lack for Zizek, following Lacan, would be understood as a critical component of any individual's accession to a subject position. Therefore it would be in no way a property peculiar to any particular historical moment or social category, nor would it be attributable to political or personal events. However Zizek's account suggests those engaging in melancholically inflected practices or criticism gain a certain comfort or pleasure involved in an essentially inauthentic act, 'a faked spectacle of the excessive, superfluous mourning for an object even before this object is lost', which I would argue does not adequately reflect the kinds of nuanced theorising being done on mourning and melancholia in this field, which is deployed in different ways by the critics we have considered so far.[48]

An understanding of the melancholic impulse in postcolonial theory would need to attend to the ways in which melancholia in the 'peculiar temporality that drags it back and forth at the same time acts towards the future.' If, as Khanna suggests, postcolonial study from its start has been a melancholic discipline, always already celebrating/lamenting its demise because of 'the failure of so many postcolonial states to bring justice to their peoples, or because of the neo-colonialism that pervades current globalisation and Empire', this melancholic predicament also paradoxically characterises the possibilities of critical and political engagement.

These readings bear some striking parallels with Bhabha's. A consideration of the ways their models interrelate in assessing the postcolonial present is revealing and helpful. Khanna, like Bhabha, is interested in the peculiar temporality of the postcolonial. What she terms dissonance and untimeliness have parallels in Bhabha's concept of the 'disjunctive present' of the postcolonial that moves restlessly back and forth. Both also address the question of 'newness' in terms of its effects in the postmodern and postcolonial political frame. For Bhabha in 'How Newness Enters the World', newness paradoxically emerges at moments of disjuncture, of both time and space, where the emergence of contemporary globalised culture and capital produces 'interstitial and disjunctive spaces and signs crucial for the emergence of new historical subjects of the trans-national phase of late capitalism', (*TLOC*, p. 217). The melancholic impulse in postcolonial cultures, moving restlessly between past and present, should be understood not as self-defeating but as always oriented towards the future, to an imagined and hoped for freedom.

In the first section of 'How Newness Enters the World', Bhabha discusses Frederick Jameson's essay 'Secondary Elaborations' the conclusion of his volume, '*Postmodernism Or, The Cultural Logic of Late Capitalism*'. He attempts to intervene in its assessment of the postmodern condition from the perspective of the postcolonial. Although Bhabha only uses the term melancholia once, in his discussion of Marlow's lie to Kurtz's fiancée, he does offer a reading of the 'long shadow' of Conrad that very much suggests a spectral and melancholy logic to the argument. He reflects on the haunted narratives of postcolonial literature, and consistently figures Jameson as 'a kind of (Marxist) Marlow' offers a reading of Jameson's own influential reading of the Bonaventure Hotel, Los Angeles, which sees Marlow's journey echoed in it, or inhabiting it.

> The mis-en-scène of the subject's relation to an unrepresentable social totality – the germ of an entire generation of scholarly essays – is to be found in the carnivalesque description of that postmodern panopticon, the Bonaventure Hotel. In a trope that echoes the disorientation of language and location that accompanies Marlow's journey up the Congo, Jameson shoots the rapids in the elevator-gondola and lands in the milling confusion of the lobby. Here, in the hotel's hyperspace, you lose your bearings entirely. This is the dramatic moment when we are faced with the incapacity of our minds to 'map the great global multinational network and decentred communicational network'.
>
> (p. 217)

This striking infestation of Jameson's paradigm with the ghost of Conrad suggestibly relocates Jameson's foray into the heart of postmodern global culture, re-siting its observations, as Bhabha mischievously suggests 'rendering' and 'editing' him to produce a 'Conradian foreboding' that 'reveals the anxiety of enjoining the global and the local' (p. 216).

Bhabha is particularly interested in what Jameson has to say about the demands upon the senses and the body that a new international and globalised culture makes, what Jameson says is 'an imperative to grow new organs or enhance perceptual capacity, such that one can have a kind of "incommensurability-vision" that "does not pull the eyes back into focus but entertains the tension of their multiple coordinates"' (p. 218).

For Bhabha, however, Jameson's attempt to map out the new 'decentred' and 'multinational network' of global postmodernity focuses on questions of space when it should be alert to questions of time, 'the non-synchronous temporality of global and national cultures opens up a cultural space – a third space – where the negotiation of incommensurable differences creates a tension peculiar to borderline existences' (*TLOC*, p. 218).

This shifting back and forth seems to echo the restless toing and froing of Khanna's depiction of the melancholic postcolonial movement/moment of the postcolonial. Here melancholia is not the inability to digest fully a lost but uncertain history or cultural identity in the Freudian sense, but an attempt to live with and between any number of incommensurable differences. Incorporation and digestion re-emerge as figures for melancholia, assimilation and the dynamics of multiculturalism where Bhabha, citing performance artist Guillermo Gomez-Peña, notes that food provides a fascinating figure for cultural identities and transformation. Where 'hybrid' or hyphenated identities are produced, 'the bankrupt notion of the melting pot has been replaced by a model that is more germane to the times, that of the *menudo chowder*. According to this model, most of the ingredients do melt, but some stubborn chunks are condemned to float'.[49]

Afterword
Politics of *Empire*, Anxiety, Migration and Difference Post-9/11

Even though some may suggest that with the end of the cold war and the advancement of globalisation we move politically from the law of the father to the regime of the brother, postcolonial *Nachträglichkeit* may well throw a spanner in the works of such reduction of the historical to the levelling of trauma and its ahistorical postmodern after-effects and affects.

Ranjana Khanna[1]

Is the work of the '80s done and finished with, as Hardt and Negri suggest, and is the politics of difference hoist by its own petard.

Homi Bhabha[2]

In Bhabha's account of the legacy of the 'culture wars' in the 1980s, for the journal *Artforum*, as well as in his essay 'On Writing Rights' and his statement for the board of *Critical Inquiry* in 2004, he revisits the same resonant moment in a poem by Adrienne Rich. The poem 'Movement' from the series 'Inscriptions' is first encountered in Bhabha's work in his introduction to a special issue of *Critical Inquiry* in 1997, 'Frontlines/Border Posts', which he edited and was later revisited in 2004. It reflects his repeated thinking around and with this poem. In this section of 'Movement', a teacher is faced with a student who fails to see the point, unimpressed by histories of political movements, 'Race, class ... all that ... but isn't all that just history? Aren't people bored with it all?'[3] Bhabha returns to this dismissive interlocutor, in a later article in 2004, where she steps out of the poem and begins a dialogue across generations and affiliations. In Bhabha's re-write, the lines from Rich's poem haunt his interaction with a student as a tutor in his own seminar, 'the way she spoke those lines suggested she knew *that* Adrienne Rich poem – you know the poem I mean'. Bhabha is lightly self-deprecating in his account of the failure to convince, 'As she got up to leave she threw

me a rather ungainly sentence that, for a tense minute, I thought I had written myself. "[Global] power has evacuated the [binary] bastion [that you
postmodernists and postcolonialists] are attacking ... in the name of difference."[4] The student is quoting from Michael Hardt and Antonio Negri's
book *Empire*, lines that might seem to spell the end of Bhabha's critical
project, but provide a springboard for Bhabha's reflections on the legacies
of the past and the possibilities for new futures.

In their expansive account of contemporary globalisation and capitalism,
Empire, Michael Hardt and Antonio Negri demonstrate an ambivalent relation to postcolonial theory, attempting perhaps their own bloodless coup
of the critical 'stranglehold' of postcolonial critical judgements on models
of 'Empire'. Broadly speaking, their argument centres on their assertion
that postcolonial critics have failed to understand the new forms of imperialism enabled through and performed by global capitalism. Furthermore,
although postcolonial and postmodernist critical models are very useful for
reading the past, they are ill equipped to speak of the present and to understand the ways in which Empire, as they define it, operates in fundamentally
different ways to the colonialist and imperialist projects of the preceding
centuries. Edward Said, they note, was only able to condemn contemporary
global power structures 'to the extent that they perpetuate cultural and ideological remnants of European colonialist rule' (Hardt and Negri, p. 197).

For the authors of *Empire*, one of the central tenets of previous forms of
imperialist power was the modelling of sovereign subjects through the process of othering, which, they argue, does not apply to the contemporary forms
of Empire. They suggest, following Deleuze and Guattari, a model of differential inclusion, rather than an 'exclusion' that produces othering, as a more
appropriate model of power relations relating to questions of difference.

> The forms and strategies of imperial racism help to highlight the contrast
> between modern and imperial sovereignty, the first pushes difference to the
> extreme and then recuperates the other as negative foundation of the self. The
> modern construction of a people is intimately involved in this operation. A
> people is defined not simply in terms of a shared past and common desires or
> potential, but primarily in dialectical relation to its other, its outside. A people
> (whether diaspora or not) is always defined in terms of a place (be it virtual or
> actual). Imperial order in contrast has nothing to do with this dialectic. Impe-
> rial racism or differential racism integrates others within its order and then
> orchestrates those differences in a system of control.
>
> (Hardt and Negri, p. 197)

They point to an increasing incorporation of 'otherness' across perceived categories of identity and difference, where difference is understood as suspended

or put to one side in order to coordinate imperial control of different labour forces. It is also, they argue, paradoxically valorised as a way of controlling a large labour force that might otherwise organise itself around shared perceptions of oppression or rights, but which has its energies dispersed into local or cultural or religious identifications. (Although identifying this as a 'new' practice would fail to see how it resonates with very similar practices of organising labour around ethnic and linguistic groups in colonial cultures across empire.) They perceive the rise of 'identity politics' in the 1980s as having unwittingly colluded with this shifting paradigm. Indeed Hardt and Negri go so far as to relegate the kind of post-structuralist informed postcolonialism of Bhabha to being primarily a symptom of the 'epochal shift' that they outline in the book, who remain fixated on attacking an old form of power and propose a strategy of liberation that could only be effective on that old terrain. They comment that,

> The utopia Bhabha points toward after binary and totalizing structures of power have been fractured and displaced is not an isolated and fragmenting existence but a new form of community, a community of the unhomely, a new internationalism, a gathering of people in the diaspora. The seeds of the alternative community he believes, arise out of close attention to the locality of culture, its hybridity, and its resistance to binary structuring of social hierarchies.[5]

Their assessment of Bhabha perceives his work to have worked towards deconstructing binary oppositions and proposing new forms of community and identification brought about through fragmentation and dispersal, but they dismiss this model as unwittingly complicit with new forms of 'Empire'. In a short article published in *Artforum* in 2003, Bhabha revisits the scene of the 1980s culture wars and the politics of difference, and specifically responds to the assessment of his work by Hardt and Negri. Bhabha comments that,

> From the perspective of *Empire*, the '80s represent a moment of transition, an opening up of quests, and questions, beyond the static sovereignties of the 'essentialist' modern 'subject' and the 'foundationalist' nation-state. Postmodernism and postcolonialism, the twin peaks of '80s theoretical thinking, were symptomatic discourses of the period, providing a critical perspective on its immanent structures while being unable to keep up with the rapid transformations of globalised capitalism. They bravely battled against the Manichaean master narratives of modern sovereignty, Hardt and Negri concede, unsettling the binary logic of 'Self and Other, white and black, inside and outside, ruler and ruled.' However, despite their fine intentions and critical intelligence, these post-masters who deployed postmodernism and poststructuralism in their critique of global capitalism failed to realize that corporate capital and the global markets operated programs of economic power that

were themselves, in most respects, 'postmodern' and had absorbed the lessons of mobility, indeterminacy, and hybridity *avant la lettre*.[6]

Bhabha takes issue with Hardt and Negri's attempts to interrogate the politics of difference that were played out in the 1980s in terms of either triumph or failure. Instead, he asks how we might now read this moment from the present. 'The 80's inaugurated a dream of difference, which is now being haunted by horror and doubt: abhorrence of the "deterritorialised flows" of global terror networks; doubts about the feasibility of global politics with the in crease in homeland security and international surveillance'.[7] For Hardt and Negri, the structures of corporate capital have 'learnt the lessons' of postmodernism, and are the cultural logic of it. With this comes a difficulty in deciding who or what should be opposed, where protest should be located and directed.

For Hardt and Negri, protest needs an 'enemy' a figure that continually defies location in *Empire*, elusive and sought everywhere but never found. The model of a decentred globalised capitalism is vital to their assertions about shifts in structures of imperialism and modes that might be used to oppose its injustices. Indeed it becomes one of their chief organising categories in the latter half of the book, where they argue that 'the first question of political philosophy today' is not if or why there will be resistance and rebellion, 'but rather how to determine the enemy against which to rebel'.[8] Their awareness of the difficulties of enacting forms of resistance where centres of power are no longer easy to locate is useful, 'often the inability to identify the enemy is what leads the will to resistance around in such paradoxical circles. The identification of the enemy however is no small task given that exploitation tends no longer to have a specific place'.[9] However, their solution to this lack of focus, in itself surely reinstated, in a nostalgia for the binary they wish to dismiss, is to propose a form of elemental opposition, a 'being against', which exists without a particular focus. As Ernesto Laclau notes incredulously in his review of the book, 'the only solution would be to be against everything, in every place'.[10]

They propose a form of desertion, in place of traditional models of opposition to power and oppression, which might be possible to see as a solution to the need to be 'against everything', and they locate this new form of desertion, particularly the creation of a new proletarian 'multitude'. Interestingly, in their characterisation of this multitude, they turn to the figure of the migrant and to patterns of global migration as examples of a new kind of class struggle centred on mobility, but reading their account of the figure of migrancy against Bhabha's highlights the problems with Hardt and Negri's model.

In a self-conscious homage to their inheritance from the work of Karl
Marx, and to Derrida, Hardt and Negri litter their text with spectres. Fas-
cinatingly, here the key spectre is that of migration itself, which suggests a
debt to postcolonial theory far greater than the text itself admits. 'A spectre
haunts the world and it is the spectre of migration. All the powers of the old
world are allied in merciless operation against it, but the movement is irre-
sistible.'[11] Hardt and Negri characterise nomadism as forms of class struggle, 'within and against' imperial postmodernity, but their revival of class
as an overarching term to characterise 'the new nomad horde' appears suspect in its homogenising gesture.[12] In Laclau's reading, one detects a certain
exasperation with this model,

> the notion of an 'anthropological exodus' is hardly more than an abusive
> metaphor. The role attributed to migration is already extremely problematic.
> It is true that the authors recognize that misery and exploitation could be
> determinant of the will of the people to move across frontiers but this element
> of negativity is immediately subordinated to an affirmative will to migrate,
> which ultimately creates the possibility of an emancipatory subject.[13]

Bhabha argues, reflecting back on the debates of the 1980s, that the politics
of difference as opposed to the politics of 'identity' was a vital concept enabling forms of cultural community and politics that were based on 'shared
affiliations' across a range of diverse positions, interests and oppressions.

> When essentialist claims to identity become the organizational grounds for
> separatist or quasi-nationalist forms of sovereignty, we enter the realm of the
> politics of identity. In contrast the politics of difference suggests that the play-
> ing field on which equality is negotiated cannot be levelled merely by equal-
> izing or universalizing differences.[14]

Hardt and Negri have no such qualms, as they produce a homogenised
multitude, seemingly without internal divisions or contesting claims of any
kind, which might be considered as kind of universal class, something that
for Marxism, as Laclau notes, heralds the end of the state,

> If the *volonté générale* is the will of a subject whose limits coincide with those
> of the community, there is no need for any relation of representation, nor
> for the continuation of politics as a relevant activity. That is why, as we men-
> tioned earlier, the emergence of a universal class heralded, for Marxism, the
> withering away of the state. But if a society is internally divided, the will of
> the community as a whole has to be politically constructed out of a primary –
> constitutive - diversity. In that case, the *volonté générale* requires representation
> as its primary terrain of emergence. In that case any 'multitude' is constituted
> through political action – which presupposes antagonism and hegemony.[15]

This homogenised condition of migrancy, a 'nomad horde', differs starkly from any account that Bhabha offers, despite criticism to the contrary. Although there has been a line of critical interrogation of Bhabha that persistently resists the rise of the figure of diaspora as over-dominant in the postcolonial critical field, Bhabha has been far less celebratory of the diasporic condition than Hardt and Negri are here. Bhabha has been careful in his own work to consider how the 'scattering that becomes a gathering' is marked by internal fissures, and differing experiences of disempowerment in an unceasing process of remaking, and unmaking of identities. In his discussion of how narratives of multiculturalism have addressed these transformations in a British context, he has been particularly careful to distinguish between the terms difference and diversity. This is because of his awareness of the ways in which programmes of 'cultural diversity' and celebrations of multiculturalism have risks attached to them in performing essentialising and homogenising gestures, as well as the potential to be appropriated and incorporated into existing power structures that seek to valorise or celebrate diversity as a manageable category. Bhabha insists that difference operates differently, in that it is in its nature to open up new ways of identifying rather than ossifying and caricaturing cultures into archaic models of identification. It cannot be appropriated unproblematically, but must continually be negotiated with and remakes itself in their negotiations. Bhabha goes further in his response to Hardt and Negri's celebratory account of the migrant, not necessarily the counter-intuitive move it might seem. While he has been taken to task for embracing the pleasures of exile too enthusiastically, he resists Hardt and Negri's insistence on flight and desertion as a central truth of the 'nomad horde' and focuses instead on the ways in which this precipitates new forms of belonging and demands, paying taxes, seeking education and housing,

> Such an emancipatory ideal -so affixed on the flowing, borderless, global world – neglects to confront the fact that migrants, refugees, and nomads don't merely circulate. They need to settle, claim asylum or nationality, demand housing and education, assert their economic and cultural rights, and come to be legally represented.[16]

He is wary of what he views as a metaphoric of appropriation of the movement involved in migrancy that overlooks the ways new identities and communities emerge at the national level, critically dependent on taxation for example in order to access welfare services that the nation provides: medical care, education and other rights, that the 'sans papiers' in France for example or the unregistered and criminalised workforces in other parts of

Europe and the US campaign for. Discussions of political and legal 'amnesties' for undocumented workers have gained increasing significance in national debates about black economies and hidden workforces, for the workers, their claims for recognition are a crucial to their accessing other rights.

Hardt and Negri's text was published before the events of 9/11 in the USA the subsequent invasions of Afghanistan and Iraq, and, as the authors themselves point out, 'well after the end of the Persian Gulf War and well before the beginning of the war in Kosovo'. So it does not reflect on what changes to the global political landscape these events might be said to have precipitated, and which also might have produced fresh assertions by the authors. Bhabha therefore responds from a different moment, and questions the assumptions in Hardt and Negri that new forms of Empire eschew binary models in order to enact power. He comments on the resurgence of such thinking in response to the attacks on US soil, the widespread use of Samuel Huntington's concept of the 'Clash of Civilizations' originally proposed in 1993, in the media, and on the rise of a model of world order and disorder, proposed by Thomas L. Friedman, where so-called rogue, unstable or failed states are pitted against the 'stable' pillars of world order.[17]

> There is no old-style polarity here of East and West or North and South; nevertheless, the presence of a networked universe and diffused technologies doesn't prevent the discourse of world power from becoming bipolar: the World of Order and the World of Disorder. Why the differences between superpowers and the super-empowered should somehow naturally assume a pattern of polarity is a question for another time.[18]

Bhabha argues that 'the spectre of binary or bipolar explanation rises to exert order and meaning when we are confronted by realities that seem partial and indeterminate, in conditions that are contingent, contradictory, and fearsome'.[19] In a short article for the *Chronicle of Higher Education* written in the days after the attacks of September 11, Bhabha comments, 'ironically the "clash of civilizations" is an aggressive discourse often used by totalitarians and terrorists to justify their worst deeds'.[20] This point is also made beautifully in Edward Said's discussion of Huntington's model, in his highly critical essay 'The Clash of Definitions'.[21] He comments,

> What is [...] troubling to me about proclaimers of the clash of civilizations is how oblivious they seem of all we now know as historians and as cultural analysts about the way definitions of these cultures themselves are so contentious. Rather than accepting the incredibly naïve and deliberately reductive notion that civilizations are identical with themselves, and that is all, we must

always ask which civilizations are intended, created and defined by whom and for what reason.[22]

Laclau too is sceptical of the provenance of their model. He rejects their statement that 'no nation state can today from the centre of an imperialist project' given the events in the world after September 11. For Bhabha, the significance of the politics of difference is precisely its resistance to such models of culture and identity or community: 'At its best, I believe, the politics of difference seeks to rethink the minority not as an "identity" but as a process of affiliation (rather than autonomy) that eschews sovereignty and sees its own selfhood and interests as partial and incipient in relation to the other's presence.'[23]

Bhabha expands on this affiliative model in 'Minority Maneuvres and Unsettled Negotiations', his editor's introductory essay to a special issue of *Critical Inquiry*, Frontlines/Border Posts. He insists on the necessity of understanding the complicated mechanisms that emerge through one's attempts to dwell in or espouse minority identities and differences. He considers what he calls the 'remarkable speculations' of Wendy Brown's argument in her book *States of Injury: Power and Freedom in Late Modernity*, on the pitfalls of identity politics based around claims for rights and recognition. She proposes that the 'subject' of emancipatory claims cannot be seen as simply an I who claims 'I want', but should be read in an identificatory mode as 'I want this for us', where 'I am' is read as 'potentially in motion', not as fixed.[24] Bhabha is engaged by this argument as it unfolds around the question of a politicised identity and what is 'wants'. Contentiously, Brown argues that 'the politicized identities of gender, race and sexuality cannot articulate what they want' because their emancipatory claims are too often frozen by 'entrenching and restating, dramatizing and inscribing their pain in politics.'[25] Bhabha sees the potential of such an argument in dislodging the political project of 'recognition and reciprocity' and enabling a shift to his own proposals of a minoritarian position of 'identification and proximity.'[26]

> The emerging formation of minorities is a moment in the identification with otherness. It constitutes an experience of being-in-difference, which may take various forms: a sudden collapse of epistemological distance; a dawning awareness of historical overdetermination; the inseparability of antagonistic elements into orderly, or disorderly opposites of progressive/regressive, tradition/modernity.[27]

Bhabha describes his model of the minoritarian position as 'the ethical need to negotiate what is incommensurable yet intolerable' and asserts that it is affected by 'the awareness of the ambivalence in our identifications – with others, object, ideas, ourselves – the agonistic choices that determine the antagonists we engage, the solidarities that we seek the values that we serve.'[28] His repeated insistence on the ambivalent forces of identification that he sees as unavoidable in the process of espousing and negotiating difference in the political sphere reinforces the sense of his model of minoritarian politics as the minoritarian 'performative'. It is one that insists on always undoing positions that might be seen to offer a stable ground from which to speak, and it seeks to create new identifications through messy, anxious and potentially antagonistic relations.

Bhabha turns again to Adrienne Rich's poetry when he outlines this view more extensively in his keynote address to the *Re-Inventing Britain* conference organised by the British Council in 2000, 'Minority Culture and Creative Anxiety'. In this address, Bhabha again turns to the question of how to negotiate a minoritarian political performance in the face of globalised and technologised forms of mass culture and communication.

> Before the celebration of global connectivity becomes vaunting, let us spin the globe to reveal another view of culture and community on our time. In counterpoint there emerges a discourse of community that provides a more modest moral measure against which transnational cultural claims and demands may be measured. What these ambiguities in the global condition produce are profound anxieties about the way in which we see ourselves as part of a 'shared' history of the past.[29]

Bhabha reads this restlessness and anxiety in Rich's poetry, citing the ever-changing and mutating identity of the speaker in Rich's series of poems 'Eastern War Time', who appears to shift insistently and uncertainly in the embodiment of contradictory and incommensurable positions, written across by historical traumas as well as reaching out to other positions and places.

> I'm a table set with room for a Stranger
> I'm a field with corners left for the landless

The poem inhabits both the 'minor' and the 'major' positions but concludes with a refusal of closure, 'I am standing here in your poem unsatisfied.'[30]

Rich's poetry occurs repeatedly in Bhabha's work, appearing at times to have the ability to access the structures of identification and affiliation that Bhabha tries to reach through critical discourse. Indeed, it is characteristic of Bhabha's writing that he yields at critical moments where the poetic has the ability to speak otherwise, or to gesture towards emergent ideas. In this poem the insistent and uncertain repetitions are, Bhabha argues, 'not representative of a postmodern soufflé', where difference is homogenised, but they remain unsatisfied and open on to the political. This resonates with

Rich's own recent critical essays, such as 'Making the Connections', where she argues for a nuanced understanding of the anti-war campaigns she is involved with in the USA,

> Links between militarization, racism, economic and gender inequity, perversion of the criminal justice system and the electoral system are made not because of laundry-list sectarian opportunism but because more and more the actual connections are being laid bare by the activities of the current administration and its corporate family.[31]

Bhabha also insists there must be a way of confronting the politics of terror that can reach out to and make 'common cause' with those living under totalitarian regimes, or living with the effects of the colonial and the post-colonial. 'To confront the politics of terror, out of a sense of democratic solidarity rather than retaliation, give us some faint hope for the future, hope that we might be able to establish a vision of a global society informed by civil liberties and human rights, that carries with it the shared obligations and responsibilities of common collaborative citizenship.'[32]

For Bhabha, Rich's poetry represents this need to make demands for 'recognition' under the auspices of different 'minority' from intercultural and interstitial locations. 'The poem opens up the space of what I called chiasmatic, diagonally crossed, lateral "side by side" solidarity where differences do not aspire to be represented in sovereign autonomy; Rich made it difficult for us to rank "class" above race, or gender above generation.'[33] This is an important shift for Bhabha because he sees it as resisting the tendency to understand demands of recognition or 'cultural respect' as made through 'whole' or 'developed' societies, groups, or identities, rather than through partial and interstitial identifications. He resists both a model of pluralism – a valuing of discrete holistic cultures or one of social constructivism, where values are located in a particular social context, commenting, 'in both cases there is a closing off of the kind of partial cultural milieux that I have proposed.'[34]

Perhaps nowhere moreso than in his 'Manifesto for the Reinvention of Britain' has Bhabha demonstrated more clearly his engaged and political agenda for issues of multiculturalism, the politics of race and representation in the nation, and working alongside activists and artists within minority communities in Britain to initiate cultural activism.

> To 'minoritise' might be a verb: a positive identification, where the affiliative decision to act in the cause of exclusion, or to participate in the emergence of new social movements, engenders a mode of public discourse articulated with strong affective and imaginative charge. We are identified within the

cause of the minority not only out of principle but from a passion, a structure of feeling.[35]

That structure of feeling might be read as a way of framing the potential for postcolonial melancholia to disrupt the national tendency to forget in the memorialising that initiates and sanctions amnesia. To register the need to live with and work through a sense of the political necessity of engaging passionately with the significance of some of Bhabha's most compelling critical observations on incommensurability, translation and difference.

Interview between Eleanor Byrne and Homi K. Bhabha, 31 July 2008 Highbury Terrace, London

EB

This book has examined the ways in which your work has enabled the formation of new vocabularies within postcolonial literary and cultural studies and the different kinds of impacts that your work has had on postcolonial theory. It traces the new directions that your work has taken in the studies of colonialism, race, identity and nation. I was interested in the ways in which terms like hybridity, the third space and ambivalence developed in your writing and how new ways of understanding these terms have evolved in critical and theoretical discourse. These are terms that have become so embedded in postcolonial critical thinking and have promoted the reframing of questions, of approaches and of postcolonial epistemologies more generally. Your work has notably allowed for new interventions into the archives of postcolonial studies through an approach that crucially thinks in-between and in interstitial ways. So I was interested in looking at how that had come about, and then attempted to read you alongside some of the critics that you are in dialogue with: Fanon, Said, Derrida and Lacan. I then looked to explain what you had done with them and to further study the critical responses to your work and the way in which this material has been taken up and worked on by others.

This book offers a survey of your published work to the present, but the interview is a space to consider the work that you are currently involved in and to indicate the fresh directions that your work is taking. Obviously you're now based in the US, and have been for some time, and this has perhaps occasioned further refinements and developments in your thinking. Have you also found different approaches to your work and the questions it raises?

HB

It is interesting to go back to the moment at which I was invited to go to the States. My earliest invitations came from feminists who were interested in race issues but also in psychoanalysis more generally, so I owe a great debt to the Pembroke Centre for Women's Studies at Brown University, and especially to Joan Scott, who was the Centre's director, as well as Elizabeth Weed. I mention them because I think they are very significant figures. They heard me somewhere, and said, well you've got to come and talk to this constituency of women who are very much interested in gender studies, questions of race, psychoanalysis and queer studies. So that's one constituency that claimed me. Then of course Judith Butler's interest in my work represented another constituency – just to show you how this *gestalt* works, how one gets constituted. I have also had a very warm reception from African American studies, and in particular, from Toni Morrison and Skip Gates. Running through these constituencies is a tradition of Marxism, but it is a Marxism inflected by questions of *difference*, infused with the thought of Russian Formalism, Adorno, Sartre and Bakhtin. There has always been a tradition of classical Marxism that has been critical of my work because of my emphasis on questions of race and the psyche, on phantasmatic political affect, on the unconscious, and on minoritization, rather than on class formation. But there is also a kind of Marxism inflected by an interest in colonial conditions, open to post-structuralism, deconstructionism and psychoanlaysis, that has been remarkably generous to my work – critics like Stuart Hall, Robert Young and Fred Jameson. As far as what others have done with my work, I'm known not to respond to critics directly in their terms. I don't engage people in great public debates; I take what I need, learn as much as I can and move on to do the next thing. Those coming to Cultural Studies through the Stuart Hall tradition in the States and in Australia, as well as in Italy and Germany and in sections of the British left and its theory, have an understanding of the different threads that hold my work together, this matrix of sources and influences.

I'm returning to inaugurate an International Centre of Cultural Studies that is being established in London. Generally I find I have been very generously received and I'm obviously grateful beyond my expectations. We might call these affiliations to feminist studies, as I do in my work on DuBois, a process of 'minoritisation', meaning 'non-sovereign adjacencies across difference', rather than a desire for autonomy and authenticity of difference as a prior condition for creating a larger set of social and cultural relations.

EB

I'm interested in the claiming by feminists, because I think whilst it's not immediately apparent, although you do address quite a lot of women's writing (for example Adrienne Rich, Toni Morrison, Nadine Gordimer), clearly psychoanalysis acts ironically, as a dividing line, between a materialist approach that finds your approach to psychoanalysis one that challenges it and then of course a feminist tradition actually embracing psychoanalytic models. I'm quite interested if, as you put it, there's been a claiming upon you, as you have contributed to the remaking of a disciplinary area that has an interest for feminism, why there's still some ambivalence there. It has been one of the most widely discussed areas in terms of your utilization of psychoanalysis. To what extent do you think the rejection of psychoanalysis as a profoundly colonizing gesture, within Eurocentric approaches has marked a schism in responses to your work? Such a rejection seems to me to fail to see the ways in which a postcolonial subject is already implicated in the foundations of psychoanalysis, a subject who might pick this material up and transform it. Might it be the case, just as 'woman' has been the 'unknown continent' of psychoanalysis, and yet gender studies has been enabled through its engagement with Freud and Lacan, as well as Klein, that the colonized subject or racialized subject might find a use for psychoanalysis?

HB

That's intricately put – it's a complex issue, you've been very subtle and nuanced. Let me be very crude and say so much for the idea that psychoanalysis isn't interesting to the colonial subject. One of the earliest chairs in psychoanalysis was established in the University of Calcutta, as Ashis Nandy tells us in *The Savage Freud*, in the chapter on Girindrasekhar Bose, founder of the Indian Psychoanalytical Society in 1922. He started translating Freud's work into Bengali and then wrote to Freud and sent him a portrait he had drawn of Freud based on his reading, saying, 'I've never seen what you look like, but this is what I think you look like,' and portrayed Freud as an Anglo-Indian gentleman, a colonial, in a solar topee, (cork colonial hat, also known as a pith helmet) dressed for the tropics, and Freud was quite horrified. Figures like Freud or Marx – I always say Marx is a Bengali – You know, people would have *died* in Calcutta to defend Marx or save his honour, so I think what people don't realize is how much of the intellectual history of the West, whether it's the whole problem of individualism, whether it's the concept of law, whether it's the issue of liberalism – how many of these 'subjects' of modernity have complex colonial or postcolonial genealogies. I think that that's really what is most interesting here – the way in which colonized subjects embrace and appropriate these subjects, these materials of modernity.

That's what I mean in the work I'm doing at the moment, what I mean by the term vernacular cosmopolitanism, a translational cosmopolitanism. Now what most people have tried to do in this regard is take the concept of the unconscious in Freud and to look for analogical notions in the philosophy or Islamic thought or in another cultural discourse. That is an interesting project but it doesn't quite get at the phenomenon that I'm suggesting, which is that there is a deep internal process of both translation and dialogue *within* concepts that are seen to be or claimed later to be the intellectual icons of Western modernity. That's an entirely different project. I think the former project, looking for analogies, is more like saying, we too have our Liberalism, we too, as in India, have our notion of tolerance. That's an argument against conceptual hegemony, and I think that's an important diversifying or pluralizing argument, showing that there are other traditions in the world where tolerance has been a major public virtue. But that's a different form of intervention than one that suggests that the these iconic thinkers of modernity, when plunged into the postcolonial field, open up in different ways and open up into very different readings, readings that cannot be defined as being Indian versus Austrian but readings that themselves are both a deep unpicking of the opennesses of those thoughts and those forms of textuality and then a reconstellation of them. Do you see what I'm saying?

EB

Absolutely. What has made your work so significant is precisely your nuanced recasting of the relation of Modernity to those histories that have been perceived to be outside of it or at the limits or border of its own reasoning. You have demonstrated the interdependency of Modernity and entities ostensibly outside it, and your resistance to that binary has led to some of your most interesting interventions, like the histories of transatlantic slavery in the Caribbean in relation to the French republic and the overturning of rights, highlighting the complexity of the erection of the modern subject as it occurs simultaneously with the erection of the colonial subject.

HB

Right, and Toussaint L'Ouverture's plea, 'I believed in the French revolution only it didn't come to Haiti, I believed in it, but somehow the good news hasn't reached me,' is not so different from Fanon asking *what is this European humanism that keeps talking about brotherhood and fraternity and alliance and equality, and yet resorts to killing and incarceration and conquest?* So for me, there is a great usefulness in saying *look there are these parallel universes of public virtues and of progressive concepts.* On the other hand, I think, in a way, what that project does, is to place various cultural traditions on the same plinth in a *musée imaginaire*: they all have equal value within their own domains, but very often the domains in which those discourses talk preserve the concept of nationality, nationhood at one level, or a certain uninterrupted notion of tradition. They display a kind of discrete equality but each domain is constituted within certain kinds of cultural, political or national closures, whereas what I'm suggesting is that the great lesson of colonization is, whether sometimes positive, or sometimes very negative, is that it shows the richness of the interpretative intervention into or within any one concept. Colonization does not set up a plural and parallel universe of concepts. Instead, these different values are in contestation within any one concept, and then it's much more difficult to say this is the Western strand, Asian strand, European strand, because the threads have become much more crossed and knotted, and we ourselves in our political interpretations or our interventions have to read in between the lines.

EB

Do you think to some extent that this combination of psychoanalysis and an attention to post-structuralism, problematizing the times and spaces of the postcolonial, is why a certain tradition of materialist thought, notwithstanding your affiliations with Adorno, Benjamin and Fred Jameson, has consistently taken issue with your work?

HB

The response to my work on Fanon could quite simply be traced to the following issue: I was very interested in the way in which Fanon's deep immersion in psychiatry and psychoanalysis informed his thinking about political agency, action and social ethics more generally. I thought that this was crucial to his understanding of revolution and in his attempt to suggest that the revolutionary cadre consisted of affiliations across classes, genders, the lumpenproletariat and the radicalized sections of the middle class. This motley crowd, I thought, was a rather innovative way of thinking about the revolutionary avante-garde. My critics had a much more Manichean view of Fanon's thinking on revolution and political agency. This is a genuine difference of interpretation and I wish the debate had generated more light than heat.

EB

One of the areas of contestation that I have focused on in the book is that around the uses and interpretations of Franz Fanon in postcolonial theory. Your most recent work in this area has been to write a new preface to *The Wretched of the Earth*. Your preface to *Black Skin, White Masks* is central to the project of re-reading Fanon in terms of contemporary concerns with race and identity, and also underpinned your theorizing of mimicry and ambivalence. It has also been a controversial piece of writing. Would you like to comment on the concerns of this new preface?

HB

The important term for me in this reading is the concept of the psycho-affective, which enables me to go beyond the question of subjectivity and take the question of psychoanalysis into the question of citizenship. I propose that Fanon's great contribution to our understanding of ethical judgment and political experience is to insistently frame his reflections on violence, decolonization, national consciousness and humanism in terms of the psycho-affective realm, which I understand as neither subjective nor objective but a place of social and psychic mediation.

EB

You comment in the preface that for Hannah Arendt, Fanon's violence leads to the death of politics whilst for Sartre it 'draws the fiery first breath of human freedom.' In what ways does the concept of the 'psychoaffective' enable you to produce a different reading?

HB

Yes, I argue that there is more to the psycho-affective realm than the sub-ject of violence that has become the *cause célébre* of the first chapter of *The Wretched of The Earth*. I propose a different reading. Fanonian violence is, in my view, part of a struggle for psycho-affective survival and a search for human agency in the midst of oppression. It does not offer a clear choice between life and death or slavery and freedom because it confronts the colonial condition of life-in-death. It (the psycho-affective imagination of violence) is a desperate act of survival on the part of the 'object man', a struggle to keep alive. The false or masked guilt complex, as I have called it, emerges when the very desire to live becomes faint and attenuated, more and more indecisive, more and more phantom-like. Fanon also argues strongly for the redistribution of wealth. By seeing the need for equitable distribution as part of a humanistic project, Fanon transforms its economic terms of reference. He places the problem of development in the context of those forceful and fragile 'psycho-affective' motivations and mutilations that drive our collective instinct for survival, nurture our ethical affiliations and ambivalences and nourish our political desire for freedom.

EB

I particularly like your assessment of the pitfalls of 'transparent' political action, where you ask 'Is the clear mirror of violence not something of a mirage in which the dispossessed see their reflections but cannot slake their thirst?' Could you comment on the related concept of the psychoaffective 'curse' that you refer to towards the end of your preface to *TWOTE*?

HB

I've long been interested in the way in which political action is a complex form of agency. It is too easily assumed that political consciousness of one stripe or another issues forth into a particular intention that is articulated into a form of action which may be individual or collective. There is an expectation that this whole process, give or take the faltering of the will, has a linear and causal logic associated with it. What is striking about Fanon's understanding of political action and political agency is the emphasis he places on the process of displacement – violence directed toward the oppressor has a strange way of violating the oppressed. At the end of my preface to *TWOTE*, I argued that a just political cause might well be experienced by the colonized as both an occasion for resistance and violence directed toward the oppressor, as well as a deeper sense of being humiliated or cursed, a sense that unleashes its own kind of double violence against the mind and body of the colonized subject.

EB

Is it your sense that to an extent your work on this later Fanon text has put an end to the perceived divide that critics have proposed between the early 'psychoanalytic' Fanon and the later 'revolutionary' one? That in a sense this writing on the first and the last text has disrupted that chronology and disrupted it, finding in the later work this important psychoanalytic process being examined in relation to the calls for violence?

HB

Yes. I think this introduction has been very well received and put an end to some of those arguments.

EB

The times and spaces of the postcolonial are something that preoccupies your writing: time-lag, belatedness, the ambivalence of modernity and the third space. The work on the third space has been taken up by a variety of theorists, and has travelled across disciplinary boundaries very effectively. The collection *Communicating in Third Space* (Routledge 2008) is an example of this, where critics from literary studies, as well as social scientists and cultural geographers, all engage with the ideas and consider their relevance in their respective fields. In their introduction Karin Ikas and Gerhard Wagner explicitly take your concept of the Third Space as their starting point for thinking through cultural and political encounters between different groups or traditions, and assert that given the popularity of the term beyond the confines of postcolonial studies, a reassessment of the term and its theoretical premises and empirical implications is needed. It has been widely employed but can be a rather slippery term, as Robert Young notes, and many find it difficult to clearly define. Young's article in the collection entitled, 'The Void of Misgiving', traces the origins of the term Third Space in your work via Emile Beveniste, and Lacan and Jameson. He argues that the Third Space can be usefully understood as your attempt to develop a counterspace of modernity in response to Jameson's theory of postmodern space. The spatial aspect of this term is somewhat problematic though. He comments, 'You will never find yourself walking by accident into the Third Space!' According to Young's definition it is best described as a moment of *anxiety* – 'The third space is above all a site of production, the production of anxiety, an untimely place of loss, of fading, appearance and disappearance.' This is characterized by an enunciative split, inherent in any act of narrative that undoes its meaning. He goes on to say, 'Bhabha's whole work could be summarized in his own phrase as 'the implication of this enunciative split for cultural analysis.' In your afterword to *Communicating in the Third Space*, you comment, 'The Third space, for me, is unthinkable outside of the locality of cultural translation.' Could you elaborate its significance in your thinking?

HB

In my afterword to *Communicating in the Third Space*, 'Third Space: In the Cave of Making', I consider such an enunciative split in Joseph Conrad's *Heart of Darkness*. If you will allow me to cite a section,

> Conrad's Marlow, the ethical and narrative protagonist of the novel, knows only too well what it means to live in conditions of moral opacity shrouded in a forest of signs that render the conditions of speech and action barely intelligible: 'We were cut off from the comprehension of our surroundings; we glided past like phantoms, wondering and secretly appalled, as sane men would be before an enthusiastic outbreak in a madhouse' (37). In the midst of this bedlam he sees a French man-of-war shelling the bush, 'firing into a continent' in pursuit of a 'camp of natives – [they] called them enemies! – hidden out of sight somewhere' (17). Conrad's theatre of asymmetric warfare is accompanied by a narrative insistence that the knowledge of identity and difference is as much a question of epistemology and history as it is a perceptual and phenomenological problem that relates to *how we see* and *from where we look*. Are natives taken to be enemies because they are hidden, 'out of sight somewhere'? Is this an existential anxiety in the face of what seems alien, or does such alienation mask the annihilatory strategy of the Imperialist? Is it self-protection or self-projection? Where should the ethical line be drawn?

To draw a line that distinguishes friend from enemy, Marlow approaches the 'other', shrinks the distance, and enters into a form of ethical proximity. When the 'natives' are observed 'within six inches', Marlow is convinced of the injustice of naming them enemies or criminals: 'these men could by no stretch of imagination be called enemies. They were called criminals and the outraged law like the bursting shells had come to them, an insoluble mystery from the sea' (19). As Conrad's narrative destroys the naming frameworks of war ('enemy') and legality ('criminal'), it moves us closer towards identifying with the native's historic situation and his human condition, rather than accepting those projected 'identities' and self-serving vocabularies that are shaped for the purposes of war and the laws of conquest: '... half-effaced within the dim light, in all the attitudes of pain, abandonment and despair. ... They were not enemies, they were not criminals, they were nothing earthly now – nothing but black shadows of disease and starvation. ... Then glancing down, I saw a face near my hand ... and the sunken eyes looked up at me, enormous and vacant. ... I found nothing else to do but to offer him one of my good Swede's ship's biscuits I had in my pocket. ... *He had tied a bit of white worsted round his neck – Why? Where did he get it? Was it a badge – an ornament – a charm – a propitiatory act?* Was there any idea at all connected with it. It looked startling around his black neck this bit of white thread from beyond the seas' (21, my emphasis).

Not enemy. Not criminal. Not even native. Having glimpsed the Levinasian face of the other, Marlow can now focus closely on the tiny bit of white worsted whose social origins and cultural significance are ambiguous and enigmatic – open to question. As the arbitrary sign shifts across the open frame of signification, it marks the distance – and the cultural difference – that lies in-between the relative familiarity of a badge and the relative unknowability of a Congolese propitiatory act. Somewhere between the two, Marlow enters a third space. He is now engaged in a translational temporality in which the 'sign' of the white worsted from beyond the seas, is an object of intention that has lost its mode of intention in the colonial space, or vice versa. The familiar origin of the worsted as a commodity of colonial trade passes through an estranging realm of untranslatability in the heart of darkness, and emerges ready to be '... *raised anew* and at other points of time'. The arbitrary signifier is no longer a linguistic rule or a semiotic process. The openness of the sign to translation – that living flux that marks the 'difference' between intention as object and as modality – shifts the balance of discourse from the language of enmity to the language of proximity: 'I saw a face near my hand ... and the sunken eyes looked up at me, enormous and vacant'. But that is not all.

If Marlow's gaze had stopped there, it could have been read as merely an act of pity and philanthropy. But beyond the duality of the silent face-to-face encounter, lies the white worsted, a mediating, material element from the object-world that talks back to Marlow as he probes its origin and function.

It is the thread as a mediating third space that designates the dialogical relation between the narrator and the native as contending and contradictory
positions within a conflictual discourse. The white thread is a text of signs and
symbols that reintroduces, to the reader and the narrator, the silent, dying
native as an agent caught in the living flux of language and action: 'He had
tied a bit of white worsted round his neck – Why? Where did he get it?' This
goes beyond any notion of respect for the other's identity or humanity as a
universal subject that has an *a priori* right to representation. It is an identification, in third space, with the thought and action of the other as having
an opacity of its own that cannot be simply 'read off' the face of things; the
thread signifies a 'thickness' of culture that is as enigmatic as the obliquity
of the signifier through which it is enunciated. Even in his prone state, 'the
moribund shape as free as air – and nearly as thin' induces an infectious
introjection that comes from outside, from an intuition of the intended act of
the other – '*Why? Where did he get it?*' – in order to drive, as if from the inside,
the narrator's decision to make up his own mind against the received wis-
dom of his wretched times. After all, it is only moments before this incident,
in the process of making his deliberate decision to undertake his Dantesque
descent into 'the gloomy circle of some Inferno', that Marlow has this to say of
himself and his life: 'You know I am not particularly tender; I've had to strike
and to fend off. I've had to resist and to attack sometimes – that's only one way
of resisting – without counting the exact cost – according to the demands of
such sort of life as I had blundered into. I've seen the devil of violence, and the
devil of greed, and the devil of hot desire ...' (19). In reaching out to the specific thought of the other and grappling with what is not entirely intelligible
within it – rather than acknowledging an 'identity' – there lies the possibility
of identifying also with the unconscious of the other, and extending oneself in
the direction of the neighbor's legible will and his unreadable desire. '*Where
did he get it? Was it a badge – an ornament – a charm – a propitiatory act?*'

EB

Do you see the worsted as enacting this enunciative split? Defying any
single attempt to interpret or read its meaning in a singular way?

HB

I think its significance is the multiple meanings and readings it produces. The
third space is a challenge to the limits of the self in the act of reaching out to
what is liminal in the historic experience, and the cultural representation, of

other peoples, times, languages, texts. And it is quite fitting that we should end with a series of questions and interpretations that attempt to decipher the acts of agency. If the white worsted tells a political story of unfair trade and slavery, it is also a figural narrative suggestive of ornamentation, charms and cultural magic. As a shibboleth of the third space, this little piece of thread raises profound questions and awakens important voices.

EB

This links to your more recent work on witnessing and trauma, in particular your discussion of the third space in the Gacaca trials in Rwanda which you also refer to as an example of the peculiar time/space of Third Space.

HB

Yes, in my work on witnessing in Rwanda I became interested in the traditional meeting place, the Gacaca, that has provided a name and a place for local practices of post-genocide adjudication in Rwanda. The Gacaca Courts could also qualify as a 'Third Space'. The Gacaca is not simply a neutral area of confusion, nor is it principally a space of confrontation and guilt. It is a place and a time that exists in between the violent and the violated, the accused and the accuser, allegation and admission. I describe it as a site of in-betweenness that becomes the ground of discussion, dispute, confession, apology and negotiation through which Tutsis and Hutus together confront the inequalities and asymmetries of societal trauma, not as 'common people' but as a people with a common *cause*. I considered the Gacaca process because it emphasizes the domain and discourse of rights and representation as ethical potential, as aspirational acts. In my recent work 'On Global Memory', I talk about the face-to-faceness of the photograph – obviously with some ironies because it is not quite face-to-face, it's a highly produced controlled object. But it's something quite interesting that emerges in the testimony of one of the accused '*génocidaires*' and I was just reading the testimonies from one of the most recent reports and it's very interesting to see what he said. He was part of one of the genocidal brigades and then he finally decides to break with them and he says what especially drove me to confront the murderers was that I'd never until then seen a man killed. So when I saw people run after a man on the hill to kill him, when I saw someone was going to be speared to death, it had a great effect on me ... it was clearly unjust ... it was as if they were making a mistake about someone in your presence ... at that point you can't help but say that it was wrong.

In the way in which photographs confront you there is something of this. We know what complex forms of representation photographs are, but they still do maintain something of the face-to-face encounter. Something about their presencing. The stillness of photography is neither passive nor fixed. What photography and memory share is a belief in the moment of time and history, a process by which the past intrudes into the present and renders it incomplete by displaying what it takes to make the transition between times and places.

EB

You attempt to enact such readings of photography that can open up new 'image worlds' in your readings of the photography of Michal Safdie, whose work on Rwanda you have written on. In your recent work this question is further developed through your exploration of the concept of 'barbaric transmission' in relation to questions of trauma, witnessing and memorialization.

HB

There has to be a way of remembering barbarism, not at the point at which it is made safe nor worked through (in the Freudian sense). There must be some affective way in which the transmission of barbarism brings with it some of the anxiety ... the terror of barbarism and its unrepresentability; otherwise, there is no way to confront it and move beyond it.

EB

In your account of barbaric transmission you state, 'There is nothing – nothing – in the ethic of ameliorative witnessing, however sincere in its pursuit of human fairness ... that prepares you today for the vacuum that such dispossessed cultural monuments create, the half-life of heritage, on the other side of which lies the death of human culture.' This would seem to call for a new theorization or thinking through of the processes of witnessing and mourning that relate to traumatic events, genocides and atrocities.

HB

Yes, I've been interested for a long time in Walter Benjamin's lines in *The Theses on the Philosophy of History*, 'There is no document of civilization which is not at the same time a document of barbarism. And just as such a document is not free of barbarism, barbarism taints also the manner in which it was transmitted from one owner to another'. And this became for me very suggestive, over the last few years, when I kept thinking what will we transmit of the barbarism in which we are involved now, how do we transmit that barbarism, what will happen, and what does Walter Benjamin mean when he talks about the manner in which it was transmitted from one owner to the other, what is this form of transmission, how do you transmit Barbarism? What does it mean to be able to transmit Barbarism without being taken over by it, when, in order to transmit it you have to reproduce it?

I found this in a particular history of the 23-year old Tutsi seamstress Jeanette Ayiukaimye from Namata, Rwanda, when reading some of the recent transcripts of the trials, who in summing up her own experience draws a hideous conclusion about the world's history

'I now know,' she says, 'that a man can become of an incredible wickedness very suddenly, I do not believe the genocides have ended, I don't believe that those who say that we have reached the depths of atrocity for the last time speak the truth. When there has been one genocide in one village there can be another one at any moment in the future, in any place, in Rwanda, or elsewhere, if the cause is still there, and we do not know what it is'.

Now that synchronizes with Jean Baptiste Munyankore's image of an ever-present day in Rwanda once and every day.

> What happened in Nyamata in the churches, in the marshes and in the hills is a supernatural action carried out by quite natural people. The headmaster of the school where I teach and the inspector of my district participated in the slaughter with spiked bludgeons. A priest, the mayor, the lieutenant governor, a magistrate, the assistant chief of police, a doctor all killed with their own hands. These well educated people were calm and they rolled up their sleeves to firmly take hold of a machete so for the man who like me has taught the humanities his whole life, these criminals are a terrible mystery.

So I was interested in considering what these testaments now bring back, and how they bring it back. What does this now mean when we said instead of those 'never again' nows? My interest in this practice, of barbaric transmission, was immensely sharpened by two perspectives on the afterlife of trauma, Martin Jay's essay 'Walter Benjamin and Remembrance in World War One' and Claude Lanzmann's 'The Obscenity of Understanding'.

It is this question of a barbarism repeated, each time made different but each time repeated precisely in the place where we thought instead of saying now we would say never again. Benjamin refused to seek some sort of new symbolic equilibrium through a process of collective mourning that would successfully work through the grieving – thus the seemingly paradoxical call in his Dostoyevsky essay for an unforgettable immortal life that is all the while without monument and without memory, rather than letting the wounds scar over. Lanzmann says talking of his film *Shoah* that 'the real problem is to transmit, although I think there is no real knowledge before transmission it is difficult to say, it is difficult to explain, it is difficult to understand. I did not try to add new things to the knowledge or the documentation that we now have but in spite of this what was really important to me, what was at stake was precisely this transmission.'

What is so interesting is not the newness of the knowledge, not the proposition of what happened. When in Rwanda people say we can't describe it, we don't know what happened, it's not that it is in the unconscious inarticulacy of trauma. Although that too exists, what is interesting is the conscious production of a form of speech which at one level knows exactly the history and its causes and explanations but at another level almost cannot articulate them ... the space of enunciation resists making such statements.

Notes

Prelims

1. See Salman Rushdie, *The Satanic Verses*, Continuum, p. 5.
2. Homi K. Bhabha, 'Preface to the Routledge Classics Edition' *The Location of Culture*, 2004, viii.
3. Bhabha, 'Preface', *TLOC*, x.
4. Homi K. Bhabha, 'Preface to the Routledge Classics Edition', *The Location of Culture* (Routledge, 2004), xi.
5. Ibid., xi.
6. Ibid., xvii.
7. Ibid., xvii.
8. Mahmoud Darwish, *Memory for Forgetfulness: August, Beirut, 1982*, trans. Ibrahim Muhawi, University of California Press, 1995, p. 105. Original Arabic edition, *Al Karmel* (*Journal of the General Union of Palestinian Writers and Journalists*), Nicosia, Cyprus, nos. 21–2 (1986), 4–96.
9. Ibid., pp. 140–1.
10. Ibid., p. 139.

Introduction   'The Missing Person': Re-/Locating Homi K. Bhabha

1. Adil Jussawalla, *Missing Person* (Bombay: Clearing House, 1977).
2. 'And now a few words on behalf of the worst writer in Chicago', Steve Rhodes, *Chicago Magazine*, http://.chicagomag.com/chicagomag/text/people/features/bhabha/0999a.htm, September 1999. Steve Rhodes comments in this article that, '*Philosophy and Literature* is an obscure journal that seems to be known – at least among American scholars – only for its bad writing awards. And the winners are consistently among the most influential in the academy.'
3. Bart Moore-Gilbert, *Postcolonial Theory* (London: Verso, 1994), p. 115.
4. Homi K. Bhabha, 'The Commitment to Theory', *The Location of Culture* (London & New York: Routledge), p. 20.
5. Ibid., p. 20.
6. Homi K. Bhabha, 'Indo-Anglian Attitudes', *Times Literary Supplement*, April 21, 1978, p. 445.
7. Macaulay identified the need to create a class of educated and anglicised Indians as a kind of go-between class between the British colonial authorities and the mass of the population in India. Bhabha crucially sees this minute as inaugurating and formalising a kind of colonial mimicry that was sought out by the British but which became an uncomfortable

form of imitation, menacing rather than supporting the British sense of themselves and their superiority.

8. Homi K. Bhabha, *The Location of Culture* (London & New York: Routledge), p. 226.

9. Salman Rushdie & West (eds), *The Vintage Book of Indian Writing: 1947–1997* (London: Vintage, 1997), xv.

10. David Bennett & Terry Collits, 'The Postcolonial Critic: Homi Bhabha Interviewed', Postcolonialism, *Arena*, 96 (Spring 1992), 47–63.

11. Ibid., p. 48.

12. *Artforum*, vol. 33, no. 7 (March 1995): 80–4, p. 80.

13. Rohinton Mistry, *A Fine Balance* (London: Faber, 1996); *Family Matters*(London: Faber, 2002).

14. Tabish Khair, *Babu Fictions: Alienation in Contemporary Indian English Novels* (New Delhi: Oxford University Press, 2001).

15. Tabish Khair, *Babu Fictions*, p. 45.

16. Bhabha, *Artforum*, vol, 33, no. 7, March 1995: 80–4, p. 80

17. 'Between Identities: Homi Bhabha interviewed by Paul Thompson', *Migration and Identity*, International Yearbook of Oral History and Life Stories, vol. III, eds, Rina Benmayor & Andor Skotnes (Oxford: Oxford University Press, 1994), p. 184.

18. Homi K. Bhabha, 'The Postcolonial and the Postmodern', *The Location of Culture*, p. 172.

19. Ibid., p. 179.

20. Aijaz Ahmad, *In Theory*, 'Literary Theory and Third World Literature' (London & New York: Verso, 1992).

21. Rohinton Mistry, *Family Matters* (London: Faber, 2002), p. 472.

22. *Family Matters*, p. 478.

23. Homi K. Bhabha, *Nation and Narration* (London & New York: Routledge, 1991), p. 4.

24. Homi K. Bhabha, 'Interrogating Identity', *The Location of Culture* , p. 45.

25. Bhabha, 'On the Irremovable Strangeness of Being Different', *Four Views on Ethnicity*, p. 36

26. Ibid., p. 37.

27. Ibid., p. 37.

28. Ibid., p. 37.

29. Ibid., p. 36.

30. Ibid., p. 37.

31. Jhumpa Lahiri, 'My Two Lives', *Newsweek*, March 6, 2006.

32. Jhumpa Lahiri, *Interpreter of Maladies* (Flamingo, 1999), p. 25.

33. Ibid., p. 31.

34. Jacques Derrida, *Spectres of Marx: The State of Debt, the Work of Mourning and the New International*, trans. Peggy Kamuf (New York: Routledge, 1994).

35. Edward Said, 'Reflections on Exile', in *Reflections on Exile and Other Literary and Cultural Essays* (London: Granta, 2000), p. 176.

1 Migrant Visions

1. Edward Said, 'Reflections on Exile', in *Reflections on Exile and other literary and cultural essays* (London: Granta, 2000), p. 184.

2. Ibid., p. 173.

3. Ibid., p. 183.

4. Ibid., p. 175.

5. Ibid., p. 177.

6. Homi Bhabha, 'DissemiNation', *The Location of Culture* (London & New York: Routledge, 1994), p. 139.

7. Said, 'Reflections on Exile', p. 176.

8. Ibid., p. 176.

9. Ibid., p. 186.

10. Ibid., p. 186.

11. Homi K. Bhabha, 'DissemiNation', *Nation and Narration*, p. 294.

12. Ibid., p. 302.

13. Meera Syal, *Anita and Me* (London: Flamingo, 1997), p. 165.

14. Geoff Bennington, 'Postal Politics and the Institution of the Nation', *Nation and Narration*, ed. Homi K. Bhabha, p. 130.

15. Hanif Kureishi, 'The Rainbow Sign', *My Beautiful Laundrette and Other Writings* (London: Faber and Faber, 1996), p. 81.

16. Salman Rushdie, *Shame* (Picador: London, 1983), p. 87.

17. Aijaz Ahmad, 'Salman Rushdie's Shame: Postmodern Migrancy and the Representation of Women', *In Theory: Classes, Nations, Literatures* (London & New York: Verso, 1994), pp. 123–158.

18. *Midnight's Children* won the Booker Prize in 1982. In a poll of all winners on the twenty-fifth anniversary of the prize in 1994, it won the prize for best Booker winner, the 'Booker of Bookers'.

19. Aijaz Ahmad, *In Theory*, p. 332.

20. Geoffrey Bennington, 'Postal Politics and the Institution of the Nation', *Nation and Narration*, p. 121.

21. Shahid Javed Burki, *Pakistan Under Bhutto, 1971–1977* (London: Macmillan, 1980), p. 11.

22. Salman Rushdie, *Shame*, p. 64.

23. Homi Bhabha, 'DissemiNation', *Nation and Narration*, p. 294.

24. Samir Dayal, 'The Liminalities of Nation and Gender: Salman Rushdie's *Shame*', *The Journal of the Midwest Modern Language Association*, vol. 31, no. 2. (Winter, 1998) p. 39.

25. Urvashi Butalia, 'Community, State and Gender: Some Reflections on the Partition of India,' in *The Oxford Literary Review (OLR), On India: Writing History, Culture, Post-Coloniality*, eds, Ania Loomba & Suvir Kaul (vol. 16, 1994), p. 44.

26. For a full discussion see Urvashi Butalia, 'Community, State and Gender'. The agreement was known as the Inter Dominion Treaty. Its terms were to recover by force if necessary, women on both sides of the border and restore them to their families. Clause 2 (quoted below), as Butalia points out, is of particular interest here because it demonstrates the ideological importance of women for the nation as taking precedence over any individual wish on the part of a particular women:

'2. Conversions by persons abducted after March 1947 will not be recognised and all such persons MUST be restored to their respective Dominions. The wishes of the persons concerned are irrelevant and consequently no statements of such persons should be recorded before Magistrates.'

See *OLR*, (vol. 16, 1994), p. 44.

27. Salman Rushdie, *Shame* (London: Picador, 1984), p. 81.

28. Homi Bhabha, *Nation and Narration*, p. 3.

29. Salman Rushdie, *Shame* (London: Picador, 1984), p. 87.
30. Jacques Derrida, *Specters of Marx, The State of the Debt, the Work of Mourning and the New International* (trans. Peggy Kamuf) (London & New York: Routledge, 1994,) p. 82.
31. Homi Bhabha, 'Interrogating Identity', *Identity: The Real Me*, ICA Documents 6 (London: ICA, 1987), p. 10.
32. Salman Rushdie, *Shame*, p. 24.
33. Iain Chambers, *Migrancy, Culture, Identity*, p. 72.
34. Homi K. Bhabha, 'Dissemination', *The Location of Culture* (London & New York: Routledge, 1994), p. 170.
35. Homi. K. Bhabha, 'The Third Space', *Identity: Community, Culture, Difference*, ed. Jonathan Rutherford (London: Lawrence and Wishart, 1990), p. 209.
36. Ibid., p. 209.
37. Ibid., p. 209.
38. Ibid., p. 209.
39. Homi Bhabha, 'Interrogating Identity', *Identity: The Real Me, Post-Modernism and the Question of Identity*, p. 9. This was reprinted in a different version in *The Location of Culture* (Routledge, 1994), in which the previously explicit references to Derrida are not made.
40. Iain Chambers, *Migrancy, Culture Identity*, p. 32.
41. Salman Rushdie, *Shame*, p. 235.
42. Jacques Derrida, *Specters of Marx*, p. 1.
43. Ibid., p. 108.
44. Gayatri Spivak, 'Reading *The Satanic Verses*', *The Spivak Reader* (London and New York: Routledge, 1994), p. 219. First published, *Public Culture: Bulletin of the Center for Transnational Cultural Studies* (Fall 1989), 2 (1), p. 77–99.
45. Timothy Brennan, 'The Cultural Politics of Rushdie Criticism: All or Nothing', *Critical Essays on Salman Rushdie*, ed. M. Keith Booker, 1999.
46. Sabina Sawhney & Simona Sawhney, 'Reading Rushdie after September 11th 2001' ,Introduction, *Twentieth Century Literature*, Winter 2001.
47. Aamir Mufti, 'Reading the Rushdie Affair: An Essay on Islam and Politics', *Social Text*, Duke University Press, 1991, p. 96.
48. Ibid., p. 99.
49. Homi K. Bhabha, *The Location of Culture*, p. 225.
50. Homi K. Bhabha, *New Statesman*, 3 March 1989, cited in Appignanesi, L. & Maitland, S., *The Rushdie File*, ICA, 1989, p. 140.
51. Rajeswari Sunder Rajan, 'The Third World Academic in Other Places, Or, the Postcolonial Intellectual Revisited', *Critical Inquiry*, vol. 23, no. 3, Front Lines/Border Posts, (Spring 1997), p. 600.
52. Salman Rushdie, *The Satanic Verses* (Consortium, 1992), p. 70.
53. Ibid., p. 5.
54. Gayatri Chakravorty Spivak, 'Post-structuralism, Marginality, Postcoloniality and Value', *Literary Theory Today*, (eds), P. Collier & H. Geyer-Ryan, (Oxford: Polity Press, 1990), p. 225.
55. Homi Bhabha, 'Interrogating Identity', ICA Documents 6, p. 5.
56. Salman Rushdie, *The Satanic Verses*, p. 5.
57. Homi K Bhabha, 'How Newness Enters the World', *The Location of Culture*, p. 225.
58. Sara Suleri, 'Review: Whither Rushdie?' *Transition*, no. 51 (1991), p. 203.
59. Gayatri Chakravorty Spivak, 'Post-structuralism, Marginality, Postcoloniality and Value', *Literary Theory Today*, eds, P. Collier & H.Geyer-Ryan (Oxford: Polity, 1990), p. 225.

60. Salman Rushdie, *The Satanic Verses* (Consortium: 1992), p. 159.
61. Homi. K. Bhabha, 'Dissemination', *The Location Of Culture* (London & New York: Routledge, 1994), p. 165.
62. Salman Rushdie, *The Satanic Verses* (Consortium: 1994), p. 287.
63. Pnina Werbner, 'Allegories of Sacred Imperfection: Magic, Hermeneutics and Passion in *The Satanic Verses*', *Current Anthropology*, 37, Supplement, 1996, p. 59.
64. Gayatri Spivak, 'Reading *The Satanic Verses*', *The Spivak Reader* (London & New York: Routledge, 1994), p. 222.

2 Unpacking Homi Bhabha's Library: Bhabha, Said and the Postcolonial Archive

1. Jacques Derrida, *Archive Fever*, p. 1.
2. Homi K. Bhabha, 'Unpacking My Library Again' in Iain Chambers & Lidia Curti, *The Postcolonial Question: Common Skies, Divided Horizons* (London: Routledge, 1996).
3. Walter Benjamin, 'Unpacking My Library', *Illuminations*, (London: Fontana, 1973).
4. Bart Moore-Gilbert, *Postcolonial Theory: An Introduction*, 'The Bhabalian Performance', (London: Verso, 1994), p. 114.
5. Robert Young, *White Mythologies*, p. 146.
6. Anish Kapoor, Homi K. Bhabha & Pier Luigi Tazzi, *Anish Kapoor* (Berkeley, Los Angeles & London: University of California Press with the Hayward Gallery, 30th April–14th June 1998).
7. Homi K. Bhabha, 'Unpacking my Library Again', in Iain Chambers & Lidia Curti, *The Postcolonial Question: Common Skies Divided Horizons* (London: Routledge, 1996), p. 199.
8. Homi K. Bhabha, 'Unpacking My Library Again', p. 199. Bhabha is referring to Foucault here, *The Order of Things*, trans. A Sheridan, New York: Pantheon Books, 1970.
9. Walter Benjamin, *Illuminations*, Unpacking My Library (London, Fontana, 1973).
10. Walter Benjamin, 'Theses on the Philosophy of History', *Illuminations* (London: Fontana 1973).
11. Jacques Derrida, *Archive Fever*, trans. Eric Prenowitz (University of Chicago Press), 1996, p. 2.
12. Homi K. Bhabha, 'Race, Time and the Revision of Modernity', *The Location of Culture* (London & New York: Routledge), p. 240.
13. Michel Foucault, *The Archaeology of Knowledge*, p. 102.
14. Homi K. Bhabha, *The Location of Culture*, p. 253.
15. 'The Postcolonial Critic: Homi Bhabha Interviewed by David Bennett and Terry Collits', 'Postcolonialism', *Arena*, 96 (Spring 1992), 47–63.
16. Edward W. Said, *Orientalism*, p. 4.
17. Bart Moore-Gilbert, Gareth Stanton & Willy Maley, *Postcolonial Criticism* (Longman, 1997), p. 1.
18. Ania Loomba, *Colonialism/postcolonialism* (London & New York: Routledge), p. 7.
19. 'By this term I do not mean the sum of all texts that a culture has kept upon its person as documents attesting to its own past; or as evidence of a continuing identity [...] The archive is the first law of what can be said, the system that governs the appearance of statements as unique events [...] The archive is not that which, despite its immediate escape, safeguards the event of the statement, and preserves, for future memories its status as an escapee, [...] nor is it that which collects the dust of statements that have become inert once more,

and which may make possible the miracle of their resurrection; it is that which defines the mode of occurrence of the statement-thing; it is the system of its functioning'. Michel Foucault, *The Archaeology of Knowledge*, p. 129.

20. Said, *Orientalism*, p. 25.

21. Homi K. Bhabha, 'Opening the Floodgates', *Poetics Today*, vol. 8, no. 1 (1987), pp. 181-7.

22. Ibid., p. 182.

23. Lola Young, Teaching Black History, *The Guardian*, December 14th 2001, p. 7.

24. Henry Louis Gates Jr, Black Literature and Literary Theory, New York & London, Methuen, 1984, cited in Bhabha, 'Opening the Floodgates', p. 182.

25. 'Opening the Floodgates', p. 182.

26. Sarah Salih, Introduction & ed., Mary Seacole, *Wonderful Adventures of Mrs Seacole in Many Lands* (Penguin, 2005), xx.

27. Edward Said, *Orientalism* (Harmondsworth: Penguin), 1991, p. 25.

28. Said, *Orientalism*, p. 25.

29. Aijaz Ahmad, *In Theory*, p. 162.

30. Ibid., p. 173.

31. Homi. K. Bhabha, The postcolonial critic, Interviewed by David Bennett and Terry Collits, *Arena*, 96 (Spring 1991), 47-63.

32. Edward Said, *Orientalism*, p. 25.

33. Edward Said, 'Cairo Recalled: Growing Up in the Cross Currents of 1940s Egypt', *Reflections on Exile, and Other Literary and Cultural Essays* (London: Granta, 2000), p. 270.

34. 'Cairo Recalled', p. 272.

35. Homi Bhabha, 'Adagio', *Edward Said: Continuing the Conversation*, eds, Homi K. Bhabha & W. J. T. Mitchell (The University of Chicago Press, 2005), p. 14.

36. Homi Bhabha, 'Adagio', *Edward Said: Continuing the Conversation*, p. 15.

37. Sigmund Freud, 'A Disturbance of Memory on the Acropolis', 1936, *Standard Edition of the Complete Psychological Works*. p. 241.

38. Ranjana Khanna, *Dark Continents: Psychoanalysis and Colonialism*, 'Psychoanalysis and Archaeology' (Durham, NC, & London: Duke, 2003), p. 63.

39. Sigmund Freud, 'The Uncanny', in *The Standard Edition of the Complete Psychological Works of Sigmund Freud*, ed. & trans. James Strachey, vol. XVII (London: Hogarth, 1953), pp. 219-52.

3 Fanon, Bhabha and the 'Return of the Oppressed'

1. Neil Lazarus, 'Mythemes of Fanon and the Burden of the Present', *New Formations, After Fanon*, volume 47, Summer 2002, p. 11.

2. Homi K. Bhabha, 'Remembering Fanon, Self, Psyche and the Colonial Condition', Foreword, *Black Skin White Masks*, p. ix (London: Pluto, 1986).

3. Lazarus, p. 11.

4. Gautam Premnath, 'The Afterlife of National Liberation: Fanon Today', *New Formations, After Fanon*. p. 43.

5. Frantz Fanon, *Black Skin White Masks*, p. i.

6. Fanon's original French version of this might be more accurately translated as 'the lived experience of the black man'.

7. Stuart Hall, The Fact of Blackness, p. 17.

8. Nigel C. Gibson, *Fanon: The Postcolonial Imagination* (Polity, 2003), p. 16.

9. Henry Louis Gates Jr, 'Critical Fanonism', *Critical Inquiry*, Spring 1991, p. 458.

10. A good example of this kind of revival of critical and artistic interest in Fanon is the collection *The Fact of Blackness, Frantz Fanon and Visual Representation*, ed. Alan Read (Seattle: Bay Press, 1996), containing work by leading critics in postcolonial and critical theory, and black cultural studies, including Stuart Hall, Françoise Vergès, bell hooks, Lola Young, Kobena Mercer, Isaac Julien and Homi Bhabha.

11. Henry Louis gates, Jr, 'Critical Fanonism', *Critical Inquiry*, Spring 1991, p. 457–70.

12. Henry Louis Gates, p. 457.

13. Françoise Vergès 'Creole Skin, Black Mask: Fanon and Disavowal', *Critical Inquiry* p. 578, 23 Spring 1997.

14. Stuart Hall, 'The Fact of Blackness' *The Fact of Blackness: Franz Fanon and Visual Interpretation*, ed. Alan Read (London: ICA; Institute of International Visual Arts; Seattle: Bay Press), 1996, p. 17.

15. Stuart Hall, 'The Fact of Blackness', p. 15.

16. Ibid., p. 17.

17. Diana Fuss, *Identification Papers*, 'Interior Colonies; Frantz Fanon and the politics of identification', (Routledge), 1995, p. 164.

18. Stuart Hall, *The Fact of Blackness: Frantz Fanon and Visual Interpretation*, ed. Alan Read (ICA, Bay Press 1996), p. 14.

19. Homi K. Bhabha, Introduction, *Black Skin White Masks*, Pluto, viii.

20. Frantz Fanon, *Black Skin White Masks*, p. 112.

21. Homi K. Bhabha, p. 116.

22. Hall, *The Fact of Blackness*, p. 18. Fanon, *BSWM*, p. 112. NB: I have restored Fanon's original comment in French here, as the translation into English has Americanised the racist stereotype that Fanon was originally referencing. Although it is interesting to note that both France and the USA produced a similar grotesque caricature of benign blackness associated with eating and black vernacular speech recommending a product, the specificity of Fanon's original reference to the *Tirailleur Senegalaise* who has been used to advertise the drink *Banania* is important for my subsequent readings.

23. Said, *Orientalism*, pp. 58–9.

24. Bhabha, *The Location of Culture*, p. 75.

25. Ibid., p. 73.

26. Ibid., p. 73.

27. Ibid., p. 74.

28. Ibid., p. 74.

29. Ibid., p. 76.

30. Ibid., p. 72.

31. Ibid., p. 75.

32. Ibid., p. 74.

33. Ibid., p. 79.

34. Ibid., p. 79.

35. Ibid., p. 80.

36. Ibid., p. 80.

37. Stuart Hall, 'The After-Life of Frantz Fanon: Why Fanon? Why Now? Why Black Skin, White Masks?', *The Fact of Blackness*, ed. Alan Read (ICA, Bay Press, 1996), p. 24.

38. Hall, 'The After-Life of Frantz Fanon', *The Fact of Blackness*, p. 30.

39. Ibid., pp. 29–30.
40. Bhabha, *The Location of Culture*, p. 80.
41. Hall, p. 30.
42. Ibid., p. 30.
43. Ibid., p. 30.
44. Ibid., p. 30.
45. David Macey, *Frantz Fanon: A Life*, p. 194.
46. Françoise Vergès, 'Creole Skin, Black Mask: Fanon and Disavowal', *Critical Inquiry*, Spring 1997, p. 579.
47. Ibid., p. 580.
48. Ibid., p. 581.
49. Bhabha, *The Location of Culture*, p. 76.
50. Vergès, 'Creole Skin, Black Mask', *Critical Inquiry*, p. 587.
51. Macey, *Frantz Fanon: A Life*, p. 62.
52. Bhabha, *TLOC*, p. 67.
53. David Macey, 'Fanon, Phenomenology, Race', *Radical Philosophy*, May/June 1999.
54. Fanon, *BSWM*, pp. 49–50, cites Bernard Wolfe, *Les Temps Modernes*, May 1949, p. 888.
55. David Macey, 'Fanon, Phenomenonlogy, Race', *Radical Philosophy*, May/June 1999.
56. Ibid. p. 1.
57. Ibid., p. 2.
58. Fanon, *BSWM*, p. 26.
59. Ibid., p. 38.
60. Bhabha, *TLOC*, p. 86.
61. Ibid., p. 86.
62. Ibid., p. 75.
63. Fanon, *BSWM*, p. 106.
64. Stuart Hall, 'The After-Life of Frantz Fanon: Why Fanon? Why Now? Why Black Skin, White Masks?' *The Fact of Blackness: Frantz Fanon and Visual Representation*, p. 28.
65. Ibid.
66. Achille Mbembe, 'Out of the World', *On the Postcolony* (California: University of California Press, 2000), p. 174.
67. Mbembe, p. 174.
68. Ibid., p. 178.
69. Ibid., p. 182.
70. Sembene Ousmane & Thierno Faty Sow, *Camp de Thiaroye*, Senegal, 1987.
71. Homi K. Bhabha, Dissemination, *The Location of Culture*, p. 165.
72. Ibid., p. 166.
73. Macey, *Frantz Fanon: A Life*, p. 99.
74. Ibid., p. 99.
75. Bhabha, *TLOC*, p. 91.

4   Bhabha's Postal Politics

1. Ian Adam & Helen Tiffin, *Past the Last Post; Theorising Postcolonialism and Postmodernism* (Calgary: University of Calgary Press, 1990). For another discussion of the 'post' see, Vijay Mishra & Bob Hodge, What is Post (-) Colonialism? *Textual Practice*, 5 (1991), 399–414.

2. Stuart Hall, 'On Postmodernism and articulation: an interview with Stuart Hall', *Journal of Communication Inquiry*, vol. 10, no. 2 (1986), p. 58.

3. Anne McClintock, 'The Angel of Progress: Pitfalls of the Term "Postcolonialsim" ', *Social Text*, No. 31/32, Third World and Postcolonial issues, 1992, pp. 84–98.

4. Vijay Mishra & Bob Hodge, 'What is post (-) colonialism?'.

5. Elleke Boehmer, 'Questions of Neo-Orientalism', *Interventions: International Journal of Postcolonial Studies*, vol. 1, no. 1, 1998, pp. 18–21.

6. Robert Young, *White Mythologies: Writing History and the West*, p. 1.

7. Jacques Derrida, *Monolingualism of the Other or The Prothsesis of Origin*, trans. Patrick Mensah, Stanford University Press, Stanford, California, 1998, originally published in French, *Le monolinguisime de l'autre: ou la prothese d'origine*, 1996, Editions Galilée.

8. Bhabha, 'The Postcolonial and the Postmodern', *TLOC*, p. 175.

9. Ibid., p. 176.

10. Geoffrey Bennington, 'Postal Politics and the Institution of the Nation', in *Nation and Narration*, ed. Homi K. Bhabha (London & New York: Routledge, 1990), pp. 121-37.

11. Ibid., p. 123.

12. Derek Attridge & Robert Young, eds, Introduction, *Post-structuralism and the Question of History*, (Cambridge: Cambridge University Press, 1989), p. 8.

13. Geoffrey Bennington, 'Postal Politics and the Institution of the Nation', in *Nation and Narration* ed. Homi K. Bhabha (London & New York: Routledge, 1990), p. 123.

14. Ibid., p. 123.

15. Ibid,, p. 125.

16. Frantz Fanon, 'The Voice of Algeria', *Studies in a Dying Colonialism*, (London: Earthscan, 1989, originally published in France, under the title *L' An Cinq de la Révolution Algerienne*, François Maspero).

17. Bhabha, 'By Bread Alone', *TLOC*, pp. 198–211.

18. Ranajit Guha, *Elementary Aspects of Peasant Insurgency* (Delhi: Oxford University Press, 1983), ch. 6, pp. 239–46, cited in Bhabha, *TLOC*, p. 200.

19. Jacques Desrida, 'Afterword: Toward an Ethic of Discussion', in *Limited Inc*, trans. Samuel Weber (Evanston, Illinois: Northwestern University Press, 1988), p. 116.

20. Ian Baucom, 'Frantz Fanon's Radio: Solidarity, Diaspora and the tactics of Listening', *Contemporary Literature*, vol. 42, no 1 (Spring, 2001), p. 15.

21. Ibid., pp. 15–49.

22. Ibid., p. 15.

5   Dwelling in/on the Ruins: Postcolonial Futures

1. Sandhya Shetty & Elizabeth Jane Bellamy, 'Postcolonialism's Archive Fever', *Diacritics*, Spring 2000, 30, 1, p. 44.

2. Edward Said, Introduction, *Reflections on Exile and Other Literary and Cultural Essays* (London: Granta, 2000), xxxv.

3. J. M. Coetzee, *Youth* (London: Vintage, 2003), p. 137.

4. Ibid., pp. 137-9.

5. Sandhya Shetty & Elizabeth Bellany, 'Postcolonialism's Archive Fever', *Diacritics*, Spring 2000, 30, 1, p. 44.

6. Homi K. Bhabha, 'Democracy De-Realised', *Diogenes* (Sage), March 2003, 50, 27–35.

7. Affect would be understood as the process by which an emotion initiated by a traumatic event is detached from it and attaches in a different form in the psyche. For Freud, this could happen in one of three ways: transformation (hysteria), displacement (obsessions) or exchange (anxiety, neurosis and melancholia).

8. Sandhya Shetty & Elizabeth Jane Bellany, p. 44.

9. Ibid., p. 47.

10. Jacques Derrida, *Memoires for Paul de Man*, ed. Eduardo Cadava, trans. Cecile Lindsay, Jonathan Culler & Eduardo Cadava (New York: Columbia University Press), p. 3.

11. Bhabha, How Newness Enters the World', *The Location of Culture*, p. 235.

12. *Wasafiri*: The magazine of International Contemporary Writing, Manifesto, vol. 29 (1999), pp. 38–39.

13. Homi K. Bhabha, 'Dissemination: Time, Narrative and the Margins of the Modern Nation' *The Location of Culture* (London & New York: Routledge, 1994), p. 164.

14. Ibid., p. 165.

15. John Berger, *A Seventh Man* (Harmondsworth: Penguin, 1975).

16. Julia Kristeva, *Contre La Depression Nationale: Entretien avec Phillippe Petit* (Paris: Textuel, 1998).

17. Paul Gilroy, *After Empire* (London and New York: Routlege, 2004) p. 109.

18. Anne Anlin Cheng, *The Melancholy of Race: Psychoanalysis, Assimilation and Hidden Grief* (London: Oxford University Press, 2003), p. 11.

19. Ibid., p. 11.

20. Ibid., p. 20.

21. Monika Ali, *Brick Lane* (London: Black Swan, 2004), p. 350.

22. Ibid., p. 478.

23. David L. Eng & Shinhee Han, 'A Dialogue on Racial Melancholia' in eds, David L. Eng & David Kazanjian, *Loss: The Politics of Mourning* (University of California Press, Berkeley, Los Angeles & London, 2003), p. 345.

24. Ibid., p. 345.

25. Ibid., p. 366.

26. Ranjana Khanna, 'Post-Palliative: Coloniality's Affective Dissonance, Postcolonial Text, vol. 2, no. 1, (2006).

27. Ibid.

28. Jacques Derrida, *Of Grammatology*, trans. Gayatri Chakravorty Spivak (Baltimore: Johns Hopkins University Press, 1976), p. 144.

29. Kalpana Seshadri-Crooks, 'At the margins of Postcolonial Studies: Part 1', *The Pre-occupation of Postcolonial Studies*, eds, Fawzia Afzal-Khan & Kalpana Seshadri-Crooks (Durham: Duke UP, 2000), pp. 3–4.

30. Ibid.

31. Sigmund Freud, 'Mourning and Melancholia', 1917 *The Standard Edition of the Complete Psychological Works of Sigmund Freud*, trans. & ed. James Strachey, vol. xiv, London: The Hogarth Press and the Institute of Psychoanalysis, 1953–74, pp. 237–60.

32. Judith Butler, *Precarious Life: The Powers of Mourning and Violence* (London & New York: Verso, 2004), p. 20.

33. Pascale-Anne Brault & Michael Naas, 'To Reckon with the Dead: Jacques Derrida's Politics of Mourning' in *The Work of Mourning*, Jacques Derrida (Chicago: University of Chicago Press, 2001), p. 4.

34. Ibid., p. 4.

35. Jacques Derrida, *Memoires for Paul de Man*, trans. Eduardo Cadava, Jonathan Culler & Cecile Lindsay, ed. Cadava and Avital Ronell (New York, Columbia University Press, 1986), p. 6.

36. Sam Durrant, *Postcolonial Narrative and the Work of Mourning: J. M. Coetzee, Wilson Harris, and Toni Morrison* (Albany: State University of New York Press, 2004), p. 91.

37. Bhabha, *The Location of Culture*, Introduction, pp. 15-18.

38. Toni Morrison, *Beloved* (Picador, 1987), p. 113.

39. Sam Durrant, p. 31.

40. Ibid., p. 91.

41. Homi K. Bhabha, *The Location of Culture*, p. 15.

42. Ranjana Khanna, 'Post-Palliative: Coloniality's Affective Dissonance,' *Postcolonial Text*, vol. 2, no. 1. (2006).

43. Ibid.

44. Ibid., p. 13.

45. Ranjana Khanna, *Dark Continents: Psychoanalysis and Colonialism* (Durham & London: Duke University Press, 2003), p. 220.

46. Slavoj Zizek, 'Melancholy and the Act', *Critical Inquiry*, vol. 26, no. 4 (Summer 2000), pp. 657-681.

47. Ibid.

48. Ibid.

49. Guillermo Gomez-Pena, 'The new world (b)order', *Third Text*, vol. 21, Winter, 1992-3), p. 74, in Bhabha, 'How Newness Enters the World', *TLOC*, p. 218.

Afterword   Politics of *Empire*, Anxiety, Migration and Difference Post-9/11

1. Ranjana Khanna, 'The ethical ambiguities of transnational feminism', *Dark Continents* (Durham & London: Duke University Press, 2003), p. 220.

2. Homi K. Bhabha, 'Making Difference: The Legacy of the Culture Wars', *Artforum*, April 2003.

3. Adrienne Rich, *Dark Fields of the Republic: Poems 1991-1995* (New York and London: Norton , 1995), pp. 61-2.

4. Homi K. Bhabha, 'Statement for the Board, The Future of Criticism – A Critical Inquiry Symposium', *Critical Inquiry*, 2004, 30 (2), pp. 342-9.

5. Michael Hardt & Antonio Negri, *Empire* (Harvard University Press, 2001), p. 145.

6. Homi K. Bhabha, 'Writing the 1980s', *Artforum*, p. 1.

7. Ibid., p. 2.

8. Hardt & Negri, p. 211.

9. Ibid.

10. Ernesto Laclau, 'Can Immanence explain social struggles?' *Diacritics*, Winter, 2001, 31: 4, p. 5.

11. Hardt & Negri, p. 213.

12. Ibid.

13. Laclau, p. 5.

14. Bhabha, 'Writing the 1980s', *Artforum*, p. 2.

15. Laclau, p. 5.

16. Bhabha, 'Writing the 1980s', *Artforum*, p. 5.

17. Samuel Huntington first published the article 'The Clash of Civilizations' in *Foreign Affairs*, vol. 72, no. 3, summer 1993, pp. 22–49. This was followed in 1996 by the book *The Clash of Civilizations and the Remaking of World Order*, New York: Simon and Schuster.

18. Bhabha, Writing the 1980s, *Artforum*, p. 4.

19. Ibid., p. 4.

20. Bhabha, 'A Narrative of Divided Civilizations', *The Chronicle of Higher Education*, 28 September 2001.

21. Edward Said, 'The Clash of Definitions', *Reflections on Exile and Other Literary and Cultural Essays* (London: Granta, 2000), pp. 569–90.

22. Ibid., p. 586.

23. Bhabha, 'Writing the 1980s', *Artforum*, p. 5.

24. Wendy Brown, *States of Injury: Power and Freedom in Late Modernity* (New Jersey: Princeton University Press, 1995), p. 52.

25. Ibid., p. 74.

26. Bhabha, 'Editor's Introduction: Minority Manoeuvres and Unsettled Negotiations', *Critical Inquiry*, vol. 23, no. 3 (Spring 1997), p. 452.

27. Ibid., p. 437.

28. Ibid., p. 452.

29. Bhabha, Re-Inventing Britain: 'Minority Culture and Creative Anxiety', A Manifesto, Part I, *Wasafiri: Journal of Caribbean, African and Associated Literatures and Film*, Spring 1999, vol. 29, p. 39.

30. Adrienne Rich, 'Eastern War Time', *An Atlas of the Difficult World: Poems 1988–1991* (New York and London: Norton, 1991).

31. Adrienne Rich, 'Making the Connections', *The Nation*, 13 December 2002.

32. Homi Bhabha, 'A Narrative of Divided Civilizations', *The Chronicle of Higher Education*, 28 September 2001.

33. Homi K. Bhabha, 'On Writing Rights', *Globalising Rights*, Oxford Amnesty Lectures, 1999, ed. Matthew J. Gibney, Oxford University Press: Oxford, 2003, p. 182.

34. Ibid., p. 183.

35. Bhabha, Homi K. 'Re-Inventing Britain: 'Minority Culture and Creative Anxiety', A Manifesto' Part 1 *Wasafiri: Journal of Caribbean, African and Associated Literature and Film*, Spring, 1999, vol. 29, p. 39.

Bibliography

Adam, Ian & Helen Tiffin, *Past the Last Post: Theorising Postcolonialism and Postmodernism* (Calgary: University of Calgary Press, 1990).

Afzal-Khan, Fawzia & Kalpana Seshadri-Crooks, eds, *The Pre-occupation of Postcolonial Studies* (Durham: Duke UP, 2000).

Ahmad, Aijaz, *In Theory: Classes, Nations, Literatures* (London & New York: Verso, 1992).

Ali, Monika, *Brick Lane* (London: Black Swan, 2004).

Appignanesi, Lisa & Sara Maitland, eds, *The Rushdie File* (London: ICA, 1989).

Attridge, Derek, Geoffrey Bennington & Robert Young, eds, *Post-structuralism and the Question of History* (Cambridge University Press, 1989).

Baucom, Ian, 'Frantz Fanon's Radio: Solidarity, Diaspora and the tactics of Listening', *Contemporary Literature*, Vol. 42, No. 1 (Spring, 2001), pp. 15–49.

Bellamy, Elizabeth Jane, & Sandhya Shetty, 'Postcolonialism's Archive Fever', *Diacritics* (Spring 2000, 30, 1).

Benjamin, Walter, *Illuminations* (London: Fontana, 1973).

Benmayor, Rina, & Andor Skotnes, eds, 'Between Identities: Homi Bhabha interviewed by Paul Thompson', *Migration and Identity*, International Yearbook of Oral History and Life Stories, Vol. III (Oxford: Oxford University Press, 1994).

Bennett, David, & Terry Collits, 'The Postcolonial Critic: Homi Bhabha Interviewed', *Arena 96* (Spring 1992), pp. 47–63.

Bennington, Geoffrey, 'Postal Politics and the Institution of the Nation', *Nation and Narration*, ed. Homi K. Bhabha (London and New York: Routledge, 1990), pp. 121–37.

Berger, John, *A Seventh Man* (Harmondsworth: Penguin, 1975).

Bhabha, Homi K., 'Indo-Anglian Attitudes', *Times Literary Supplement*, April 21, 1978.

Bhabha, Homi K., 'Remembering Fanon, Self, Psyche and the colonial condition' Foreword to Frantz Fanon, *Black Skin White Masks* (Pluto, 1986).

Bhabha, Homi K., 'Opening the Floodgates', *Poetics Today*, Vol. 8, No 1 (1987) pp. 181–7.

Bhabha, Homi K., 'The Third Space', *Identity: Community, Culture, Difference*, ed. Jonathan Rutherford (Lawrence and Wishart: London, 1990).

Bhabha, Homi K., *Nation and Narration* (Routledge: London & New York, 1991).

Bhabha, Homi K., *The Location of Culture* (Routledge: London & New York, 1994).

Bhabha, Homi K., 'Writing the 1980s – Making Difference: The Legacy of the Culture Wars', *Artforum* (April 2003), XLI, No. 8.

Bhabha, Homi K., 'The White Stuff', *Artforum*, Vol. 36, n. 9 (May, 1988, 21–3).

Bhabha, Homi K., 'Minority Culture and Creative Anxiety', Re-Inventing Britain: A Manifesto, Part I, *Wasafiri: Journal of Caribbean, African and Associated Literatures and Film*, Spring 1999.

Bhabha, Homi K., 'On the Irremovable Strangeness of being Different', Four Views on Ethnicity, Linda Hutcheon, Homi K. Bhabha, Daniel Boyarin and Sabine I. Gölz, *PMLA*, Vol. 113, No. 1, Special Topic: Ethnicity (MLA, January, 1998), pp. 28–51.

Bhabha, Homi K., 'Unpacking My Library Again', in Iain Chambers and Lidia Curti, *The Postcolonial Question: Common Skies, Divided Horizons* (London: Routledge, 1996).

Bhabha, Homi K., Anish Kapoor, and Pier Luigi Tazzi, *Anish Kapoor* (Berkley, Los Angeles, London: University of California Press with the Hayward Gallery, June 1998).

Bhabha, Homi K., 'A Narrative of Divided Civilizations', *The Chronicle of Higher Education*, 28 September 2001.

Bhabha, Homi K., 'Democracy De-Realised', *Diogenes* (Sage) March 2003, 50: pp. 27–35.

Bhabha, Homi K., 'Adagio', *Edward Said: Continuing the Conversation*, eds, Homi K. Bhabha & W. J. T. Mitchell (The University of Chicago Press, 2005).

Bhabha, Homi K., Statement for the Board, The Future of Criticism – A Critical Inquiry Symposium, *Critical Inquiry*, 2004: 30 (2) pp. 342–9.

Bhabha, Homi K., 'Editor's Introduction: Minority Manoeuvres and Unsettled Negotiations' *Critical Inquiry* (University of Chicago Press, 1997).

Bhabha, Homi K.,'On Writing Rights', *Globalising Rights*, Oxford Amnesty Lectures, 1999, ed. Matthew J. Gibney (Oxford: Oxford University Press, 2003).

Boehmer, Elleke, 'Questions of Neo-Orientalism', *Interventions: International Journal of Postcolonial Studies*, Vol. 1, Issue 1, 1998.

Brennan, Timothy, 'The Cultural Politics of Rushdie Criticism: All or Nothing', in *Critical Essays on Salman Rushdie*, ed. M. Keith Booker (New York: G. K. Hall & Co, 1999).

Brown, Wendy, *States of Injury: Power and Freedom in Late Modernity* (Princeton University Press, 1995).

Burki, Shahid Javed, *Pakistan Under Bhutto, 1971–1977* (London: Macmillan, 1980).

Butalia, Urvashi, 'Community, State and Gender: Some Reflections on the Partition of India,' in *The Oxford Literary Review, On India: Writing History, Culture, Post-Coloniality*, eds, Ania Loomba & Suvir Kaul (Vol. 16, 1994).

Butler, Judith, *Precarious Life: The Powers of Mourning and Violence* (London & New York: Verso, 2004).

Chambers, Iain, *Migrancy, Culture, Identity* (London & New York: Routledge, 1994).

Cheng, Anne Anlin, *The Melancholy of Race: Psychoanalysis, Assimilation and Hidden Grief* (Oxford University Press, 2001).

Coetzee, J. M., *Youth* (London: Vintage, 2003).

Dayal, Samir, 'The Liminalities of Nation and Gender: Salman Rushdie's *Shame*', *The Journal of the Midwest Modern Language Association*, Vol. 31, no. 2. (Winter, 1998).

Derrida, Jacques, *Spectres of Marx: The State of Debt, the Work of Mourning and the New International*, trans. Peggy Kamuf (London & New York: Routledge, 1994).

Derrida, Jacques, *Archive Fever*, trans Eric Prenowitz (Chicago: University of Chicago Press, 1996).

Derrida, Jacques, *Monolingualism of the Other or The Prothsesis of Origin*, trans. Patrick Mensah, Stanford University Press, Stanford California, 1998. Originally published in French, *Le monolinguisime de l'autre: ou la prothese d'origine*, 1996, Editions Galilée.

Derrida, Jacques, *Memoires for Paul de Man*, eds, Avital Ronell and Eduardo Cadava, trans. Cecile Lindsay, Jonathan Culler and Eduardo Cadava (New York: Columbia University Press). *Of Grammatology*, p. 144.

Durrant, Sam, *Postcolonial Narrative and the Work of Mourning: J. M. Coetzee, Wilson Harris, and Toni Morrison* (Albany: SUNY Press, 2004).

Eng, David, L., & David Kazanjian, eds, *Loss: The Politics of Mourning* (Berkeley, Los Angeles, London: University of California Press, 2003).

Fanon, Frantz, *Black Skin White Masks*, trans. Charles Lam Markmann (New York: Grove Press, 1967).

Fanon, Frantz, *Studies in a Dying Colonialism*, Sociologie d'une revolution (*L'An Cinq de la Révolution Algérienne*) (Paris: Francois Maspero, 1959 and 1968). Studies in a Dying Colonialism, trans. Haakon Chevalier (London: Earthscan Publications, 1989).

Fanon, Frantz, *The Wretched of the Earth*, trans. Constance Farrington (New York: Grove Press, 1963).

Foucault, Michel, *The Archaeology of Knowledge* (London & New York: Routledge, 1972).

Foucault, Michel, *The Order of Things*, trans. A Sheridan, New York: Pantheon Books, 1970.

Freud, Sigmund, 'Mourning and Melancholia', *The Standard Edition of the Complete Psychological Works of Sigmund Freud*, Trans and ed. James Strachey, Vol. XIV, (London: The Hogarth Press and the Institute of Psychoanalysis, 1953-74) (1917), pp. 237-60.

Freud, Sigmund, 'A Disturbance of Memory on the Acropolis', 1936, *The Standard Edition of the Complete Works*, 22: 237-48.

Freud, Sigmund, 'The Uncanny', (1919) *in The Standard Edition of the Complete Psychological Works of Sigmund Freud*, ed. & trans. James Strachey, Vol. XVII (London: Hogarth, 1953-74) pp. 219-52.

Fuss, Diana, *Identification Papers*, Interior Colonies; Frantz Fanon and the politics of identification (London & New York: Routledge, 1995).

Gates, Henry Louis, Jr., *Black Literature and Literary Theory* (New York and London: Methuen, 1984).

Gates, Henry Louis, Jr., 'Critical Fanonism', *Critical Inquiry* (Spring 1991) pp. 457-70.

Gibson, Nigel, C., *Fanon: The Postcolonial Imagination* (Polity, 2003).

Gilroy, Paul, *After Empire: Melancholia or Convivial Culture* (London & New York, 2004).

Gomez-Pena, Guillermo, 'The new world (b)order', *Third Text*, Vol. 21, Winter, 1992-3.

Guha, Ranajit, *Elementary Aspects of Peasant Insurgency* (Delhi: Oxford University Press, 1983).

Hall, Stuart, 'The Fact of Blackness', in *The Fact of Blackness: Franz Fanon and Visual Interpretation*, ed, Alan Read (ICA, Bay Press) 1996.

Hall, Stuart, 'The After-Life of Frantz fanon: Why Fanon? Why Now? Why Black Skin, White masks?' *The Fact of Blackness*, ed. Alan Read (ICA and Bay Press, 1996).

Hardt, Michael and Antonio Negri, *Empire* (Harvard University Press, 2001).

Huntington, Samuel, 'The Clash of Civilizations', in *Foreign Affairs*, Vol. 72, no. 3, Summer 1993, pp. 22-49.

Huntington, *The Clash of Civilizations and the Remaking of World Order* (New York: Simon and Schuster, 1996).

Jussawalla, Adil, *Missing Person* (Clearing House: Bombay, 1977).

Khair, Tabish, *Babu Fictions: Alienation in Contemporary Indian English Novels* (New Delhi: Oxford University Press, 2001).

Khanna, Ranjana, 'Post-Palliative: Coloniality's Affective Dissonance', *Postcolonial Text* (Vol. 2, No 1. 2006).

Khanna, Ranjana, *Dark Continents: Psychoanalysis and Colonialism* (Durham and London: Duke, 2003).

Kristeva, Julia, *Contre La Depression Nationale: Entretien avec Phillippe Petit* (Paris: Textuel, 1998).

Kureishi, Hanif, *My Beautiful Laundrette and Other Writings* (London: Faber and Faber, 1996).

Laclau, Ernesto, 'Can Immanence explain social struggles?' *Diacritics*, Winter, 2001, 31: 4.

Lahiri, Jhumpa, 'My Two Lives', *Newsweek*, March 6, 2006.

Lahiri, Jhumpa, *Interpreter of Maladies* (Flamingo, 1999).

Lazarus, Neil, 'Mythemes of Fanon and the burden of the present: After Fanon', *New Formations* 47, Summer 2002.

Loomba, Ania, *Colonialism/postcolonialism* (London & New York: Routledge, 1998).

McClintock, Anne, 'The Angel of Progress: Pitfalls of the Term "Postcolonialism", *Social Text*, No. 31/32, Third World and Postcolonial issues (1992), pp. 84–98.

Macey, David, *Frantz Fanon: A Life* (London: Granta, 2000).

Mishra, Vijay, & Bob Hodge, 'What is Post (-) Colonialism?' *Textual Practice*, 5 (1991) pp. 399–414.

Mistry, Rohinton, *A Fine Balance* (London: Faber, 1996).

Mistry, Rohinton, *Family Matters* (London: Faber, 2002)

Mitchell, Warren, J. T., Translator Translated: Interview with Homi Bhabha, *Artforum*, v. 33, n. 7 (March 1995), pp. 80–4.

Moore-Gilbert, Bart, *Postcolonial Theory: An Introduction* (London: Verso, 1994).

Morrison, Toni, *Beloved* (London: Picador, 1988).

Mufti, Aamir, 'Reading the Rushdie Affair: An Essay on Islam and Politics', *Social Text*, Duke University Press, 1991.

Premnath, Gautam, 'The Afterlife of National Liberation: Fanon Today' *New Formations, 'After Fanon'*.

Read, Alan, ed., *The Fact of Blackness, Frantz Fanon and Visual Representation* (Bay Press, 1996).

Rajan, Rajeswari Sunder, 'The Third World Academic in Other Places, Or, the Postcolonial Intellectual Revisited', *Critical Inquiry*, vol. 23, no.3, Front Lines/Border Posts, ed. Homi K. Bhabha (Spring 1997).

Rhodes, Steve, 'And now a few words on behalf of the worst writer in Chicago', ChicagoMagazine, http://.chicagomag.com/chicagomag/text/people/featrues/bhabha/0999a.htm, September 1999.

Rich, Adrienne, *Dark Fields of the Republic: Poems 1991–1995* (Norton, 1995).

Rich, Adrienne, *An Atlas of the Difficult World: Poems 1988–1991* (Norton, 1991).

Rich, Adrienne, 'Making the Connections', *The Nation*, December 13, 2002.

Rushdie, Salman, & West eds, *The Vintage Book of Indian Writing: 1947–1997* (London: Vintage, 1997).

Rushdie, Salman, *Shame* (Picador: London, 1983).

Rushdie, Salman, *The Satanic Verses* (The Consortium, 1992).

Said, Edward, W., *Orientalism* (New York: Pantheon Books; London: Routledge & Keegan Paul; Toronto: Random House), 1978.

Said, Edward, W., *After the Last Sky: Palestinian Lives* [photographs by Jean Mohr] (New York: Pantheon; London: Faber, 1986).

Said, Edward, W., *Out of Place: A Memoir* (New York: Knopf, 1999).

Said, Edward, W., *Reflections on Exile and Other Literary and Cultural Essays* (London: Granta, 2000).

Sawhney, Sabina & Simona Sawhney, 'Reading Rushdie after September 11th 2001', Introduction, *Twentieth Century Literature*, Winter 2001.

Seacole, Mary, *Wonderful Adventures of Mrs Seacole in Many Lands,* Ed. & introduction, Sarah Salih (Penguin, 2005).

Spivak, Gayatri Chakravorty, 'Reading The Satanic Verses', *The Spivak Reader* (London & New York: Routledge, 1994), p. 219. First published, *Public Culture: Bulletin of the Center for Transnational Cultural Studies* (Fall 1989), 2 (1): pp. 77–99.

Spivak, Gayatri Chakravorty, 'Post-structuralism, Marginality, Postcoloniality and Value', in (eds), P. Collier & H. Geyer-Ryan, *Literary Theory Today* (Oxford: Polity Press, 1990).

Sara Suleri, 'Review: Whither Rushdie?', *Transition*, No.51, (1991).

Syal, Meera, *Anita and Me* (London: Flamingo, 1997).

Vergès, Françoise 'Creole Skin, Black Mask: Fanon and Disavowal', *Critical Inquiry* p. 578. 23 Spring, 1997.

Werbner, Pnina 'Allegories of Sacred Imperfection: Magic, hermeneutics and passion in *The Satanic Verses*, *Current Anthropology*, 37, Supplement, 1996.

Young, Lola, 'Teaching Black History', *The Guardian*, December 14, 2001, p. 7.

Young, Robert, *White Mythologies: Writing History and the West* (London & New York: Routledge, 1990).

Zizek, Slavoj, 'Melancholy and the Act', *Critical Inquiry*, vol. 26, no.4 (Summer, 2000), pp. 657–81.

Index